Fodor's

KT-519-943

Toronto
by Allan Gould

PRAISE FOR FODOR'S GUIDES

"Fodor's guides . . . are an admirable blend of the cultural and the practical."
—The Washington Post

"Researched by people chosen because they live or have lived in the country, well-written, and with good historical sections . . . Obligatory reading for millions of tourists."
—The Independent, *London*

"Usable, sophisticated restaurant coverage, with an emphasis on good value."
—*Andy Birsh*, Gourmet restaurant columnist, *quoted by Gannett News Service*

"Packed with dependable information."
—Atlanta Journal Constitution

"Fodor's always delivers high quality . . . thoughtfully presented . . . thorough."
—Houston Post

"Valuable because of their comprehensiveness."
—Minneapolis Star-Tribune

Fodor's Travel Publications, Inc.
New York • Toronto • London • Sydney • Auckland

Tenth Edition

ISBN 0–679–02766–1

Fodor's Toronto

Editor: David Low
Contributors: Robert Blake, Janet Foley, Echo Garrett, Bevin McLaughlin, Mary Ellen Schultz, Nancy van Itallie, Sarah Waxman
Creative Director: Fabrizio La Rocca
Cartographer: David Lindroth
Illustrator: Karl Tanner
Cover Photograph: Bob Krist
Design: Vignelli Associates

About the Author

Allan Gould has written 20 books, including an earlier guide to his chosen city, *The Toronto Book,* as well as biographies of Canadian businesspeople *(The New Entrepreneurs: 75 Canadian Success Stories), The Great Big Book of Canadian Humour,* and an award-winning study of the Stratford Festival, coauthored with its founder, Tom Patterson *(First Stage: The Making of the Stratford Festival).* Gould writes for many Canadian magazines and has both written and performed political satire and biographical sketches for radio and TV. He has lived in Toronto with his wife, son, and daughter since 1968.

Special Sales

MANUFACTURED IN THE UNITED STATES OF AMERICA
10 9 8 7 6 5 4 3 2 1

Contents

Maps

Foreword

The publisher thanks Steve Johnson of the Metropolitan Toronto Convention and Visitors Association for all his help in gathering information for this book. The author thanks Andrew Sun of *Now* magazine for his generous help with nightclubs, bars, jazz, and other nightlife entries; Larry Leblanc for his radio insights; Annette Poizner for her work on the Nightlife chapter; Sandra Bernstein for hers on the Shopping chapter; the author's wife, Merle, for all her help and patience; and his children, Judah and Elisheva, for enjoying Toronto with him.

While every care has been taken to ensure the accuracy of the information in this guide, the passage of time will always bring change, and consequently, the publisher cannot accept responsibility for errors that may occur.

All prices and opening times quoted here are based on information supplied to us at press time. Hours and admission fees may change, however, and the prudent traveler will avoid inconvenience by calling ahead.

Fodor's wants to hear about your travel experiences, both pleasant and unpleasant. When a hotel or restaurant fails to live up to its billing, let us know and we will investigate the complaint and revise our entries where the facts warrant it.

Send your letter to the editors of Fodor's Travel Publications, 201 East 50th Street, New York, NY 10022.

Highlights and Fodor's Choice

Highlights

The economic recession of the early 1990s hit Toronto with a near knockout blow. This city continues to be Canada's version of New York City's Manhattan, in terms of wealth, poverty (and extremes of both), costly housing, horrendous traffic jams (try to avoid driving between 7 and 9 each morning and 4 to 6:30 each afternoon, please!), sports, communications, industry, theater, and filmmaking.

One of the more interesting things that happened to Toronto recently had to do with its burgeoning growth: In late 1993, 1.6 million phone customers who lived around, but outside of, the municipality of metropolitan Toronto, woke up to discover that their area code was no longer 416, but had been changed to 905. (This change included such nearby cities as Thornhill to the north and Mississauga [the airport] to the west, all the way down to Niagara-on-the-Lake, where the popular Shaw Festival takes place, and Niagara Falls.) Now if you have to phone a friend or business associate in the downtown area from the airport, right after you land, you must dial 416 before the number. This call is **not** long distance, and you will not have to deposit anything more than your original 25¢.

Toronto can now truly be called "Broadway North"—for better or for worse. Many critics and theater lovers wonder if this country will ever be able to create its own, indigenous culture, as long as its theaters are filled with huge, costly musicals from London and New York City.

At press time, the $45-million **North York Performing Arts Centre,** which opened in late 1993, still has *Show Boat* ensconced within its glamorous walls. It's a fine production of a classic musical (and you'll pay about $80 for a decent seat), with many of its original star players moved down to Broadway in October of 1994—but what does it say to and about Canadians? Still, the Performing Arts Centre is a fabulous complex, with its main 1,850-seat theater, a 1,025-seat recital hall, a 250-seat studio theater, and a two-story, 5,000-square-foot art gallery. It is located in the suburban city of North York, just a 20-minute drive up Yonge Street from midtown Toronto. The genius behind the arts complex is Garth Drabinsky, the entrepreneur who created and later lost the Cineplex movie-house empire, and now runs the **Pantages Theatre,** where *The Phantom of the Opera* may run forever.

The wonderful Ed Mirvish and his son David, owners/operators of the lovely **Royal Alexandra Theatre,** just built a stunning 2,000-seat theater down the block from the Alexandra—**The Princess of Wales.** It was constructed especially for *Miss Saigon* (a dime-store version of *Madame Butterfly,* true, but vastly better than the original Broadway production); this musical, too, will probably run into the next century, even if tickets cost as high as $90. Note: The always-decent Mirvishes have dropped their prices precipitously for Wednesday matinees (all seats $25–$50), and hundreds of seats are now available Tuesday–Thursday for $25–$50.

At press time, the same Mirvishes (who also own the charming discount store called Honest Ed's, at the southwest corner of Bathurst and Bloor, with the world's largest neon sign) planned to bring The Who's rock opera *Tommy* (Broadway version) to the **Elgin Theater** in downtown Toronto in January 1995. Meanwhile, *Crazy for You*, a witty and irresistible musical with Gershwin songs, played at the **Royal Alexandra Theatre** through 1994, and may still be running in 1995.

Terminal 3 at the overworked **Pearson International Airport** continues to relieve Terminals 1 and 2 of their overwhelming volume, primarily handling Canadian Airlines International and American Airlines, now a part-owner of the former. Terminal 2, the home of Air Canada, is no longer overcrowded, after its two-year, $50-million-plus face-lift, but the whole airport could use some renovation.

Welcome additions to Toronto's skyline are the two towers of **BCE Place**—one at Bay and Front streets, the other next door on Wellington Street. Canada's five largest banks and two biggest trust companies (Canada Trust and Royal Trust) all do business at BCE Place. The beautiful 1885 **Bank of Montreal**, standing majestically at the northwest corner of Front and Yonge streets, is now fully restored and incorporated into one of the towers. BCE Place also serves as the new home of the **Hockey Hall of Fame.**

The handsome $380-million Toronto headquarters for the always financially-beleaguered **Canadian Broadcasting Corporation** is still in the works. The $1-billion complex on a 9.3-acre gravel parking lot, just southwest of Roy Thomson Hall (and just north of SkyDome), will eventually include two office towers, a hotel, a retail plaza, and condominiums.

Visitors should bear in mind the much-debated, much-hated **Goods and Services Tax** (alias "the GST," or Grab and Soak Tax). Even though it replaced quite a few other, previously hidden, federal taxes (e.g., Canadian car prices actually dropped a bit), the impact on tourism to Canada has been brutal. Furthermore, the GST not only applies to various services, such as barbers and lawyers, for the first time, but it also hits books, which has been devastating to the always-struggling publishing industry of the country. Hundreds of firms went under, over the first few years of this decade, with many more teetering on the edge. Still, tourists need not be irritated too much by this tax (or by the all-time-high 8% Ontario sales tax); just be sure to inquire about rebates on hotel bills and any major purchases. You *could* save quite a bit of money.

For over a century, Sunday was an enforced day of rest for large Toronto stores, with exceptions made for movie houses (and those only since the '60s), and, more recently, a number of tour-

ist areas such as Harbourfront, Mirvish Village, and Chinatown. But finally the socialist New Democratic Party (NDP)
gave in to endless pressure from tourist officials and store owners (the latter had been losing millions of bucks to cross-border
shoppers) and agreed to allow all stores in Ontario to open on
Sunday. So now even the Eaton Centre, the city's biggest attraction, is open seven days a week, along with large department stores, suburban malls, and pretty much everything else.
Tourists need no longer squish all their shopping into six days,
or fear that, by arriving in the city on a Sunday, they are
doomed to visit the Metro Toronto Zoo and Ontario Science Centre, but little else.

In sports, the city continues to rejoice over the **Toronto Blue
Jays,** its beloved professional American League baseball team,
which took the World Series in 1992 and 1993; and the **Toronto
Maple Leafs,** its long-laughable, but now impressive National
Hockey League team. In 1994, the city landed a professional
N.B.A. basketball team—the **Toronto Raptors,** which plays its
first season in 1995 at SkyDome, but hopes to have its own,
knockout stadium, next door to the Eaton Centre, for the 1996
season.

Fodor's Choice

No two people will agree on what makes a perfect vacation, but it's fun and helpful to know what others think. We hope you'll have a chance to experience some of Fodor's Choices yourself while visiting Toronto. For detailed information about each entry, refer to the appropriate chapters within this guidebook.

Sights Worth at Least a Quick Look

Casa Loma
CN Tower
Metro Toronto Library
New City Hall
Roy Thomson Hall
Royal Bank Tower
SkyDome

Sights Worth Two Hours or More

Black Creek Pioneer Village
Eaton Centre
Harbourfront Centre
Metro Toronto Zoo
Ontario Place
Ontario Science Centre
Royal Ontario Museum

Sights Worth a Two-Hour Drive

African Lion Safari
Algonquin Park
Marineland and Niagara Falls

Parks

Bluffers Park and Cathedral Bluffs Park, Scarborough
High Park (including the zoo)
Leslie Street Spit
Riverdale Farm
Toronto Islands and Centreville

Shopping Areas

Eaton Centre
Hazelton Lanes and Yorkville
Kensington Market/Chinatown
Mirvish (or Markham) Village
Queen's Quay Terminal on Lake Ontario
Queen Street West

Theaters and Cultural Events

Canadian Opera Company at the O'Keefe
Concerts and symphonies at Roy Thomson Hall
Miss Saigon at the Princess of Wales
National Ballet of Canada at the O'Keefe
The Phantom of the Opera at the Pantages Theatre
Shaw Festival (Niagara-on-the-Lake)
Show Boat at the North York Performing Arts Centre
Stratford Festival
Theater at the Royal Alexandra Theatre
Theater at the St. Lawrence Centre

Seasonal Events

Caravan (June)
Caribana (July)
Canadian National Exhibition (August/September)
The Toronto International Film Festival (September)
Harbourfront Reading Series (late October–November)
Royal Agricultural Winter Fair (November)

Drives

Cabbagetown
Forest Hill
Rosedale
Toronto Islands (by bike; cars not allowed!)

Hotels

The Four Seasons Toronto, *$$$$*
The Harbour Castle Westin, *$$$$*
King Edward Hotel, *$$$$*
Sutton Place Hotel, *$$$$*
Royal York, *$$$*
Sheraton Centre, *$$$*
Novotel Toronto Centre, *$$*
Journey's End Suites, *$*

Restaurants

Centro, *$$$$*
Joso's, *$$$$*
North 44, *$$$$*
Pronto, *$$$*
Grano, *$$*
KitKat Bar and Grill, *$$*
Le Bistingo, *$$*
Studio Cafe, *$$*
Giovanna Trattoria, *$*
Il Fornello, *$*
Masquerade, *$*
Wah Sing, *$*

Toronto Area Orientation

Georgian Bay

Bruce Peninsula

O   N

Lake Huron

Owen Sound

Port Elgin

26

Collingwood

21

10

Kincardine

6

Durham

Shelburne

4

Wingham

9

Arthur

Listowel

6

Goderich

86

24

Clinton

23

Guelph

8

Waterloo

Kitchener

Stratford

MICHIGAN

Dundas

Lucan

Woodstock

Brantford

69

Sarnia

Watford

2

Port Huron

London

3

94

St. Thomas

Thames River

Detroit

Lake St. Clair

Chatham

75

Windsor

Lake Erie

Erie

Leamington

79

90

Cleveland

80 90

OHIO

80

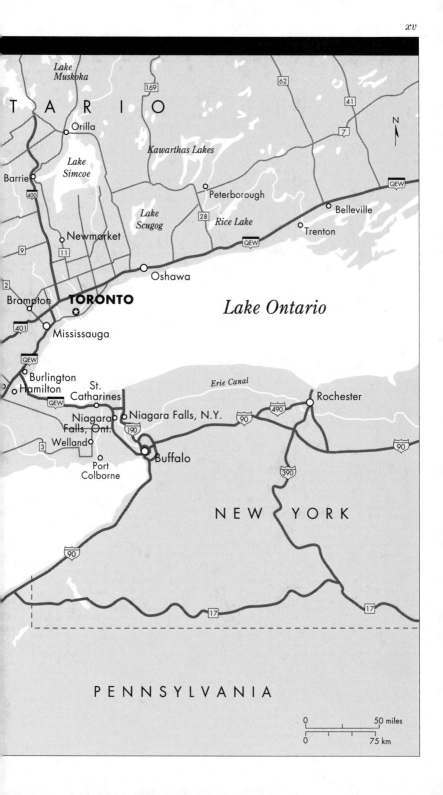

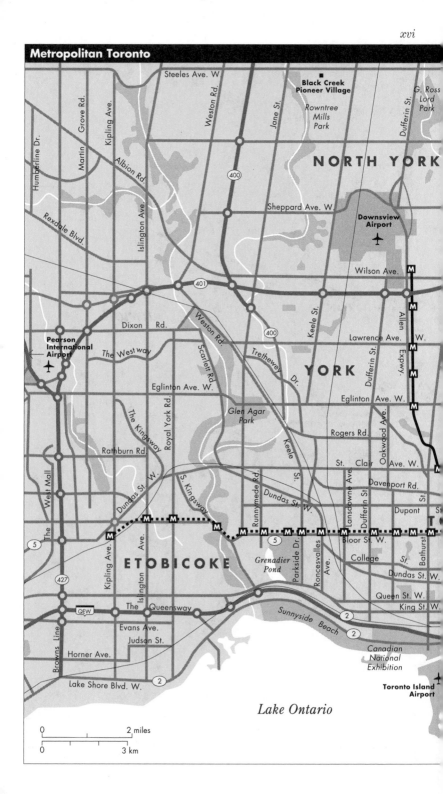

World Time Zones

Numbers below vertical bands relate each zone to Greenwich Mean Time (0 hrs.).
Local times frequently differ from these general indications,
as indicated by light-face numbers on map.

Algiers, **29**

Anchorage, **3**

Athens, **41**

Auckland, **1**

Baghdad, **46**

Bangkok, **50**

Beijing, **54**

Berlin, **34**

Bogotá, **19**

Budapest, **37**

Buenos Aires, **24**

Caracas, **22**

Chicago, **9**

Copenhagen, **33**

Dallas, **10**

Delhi, **48**

Denver, **8**

Djakarta, **53**

Dublin, **26**

Edmonton, **7**

Hong Kong, **56**

Honolulu, **2**

Istanbul, **40**

Jerusalem, **42**

Johannesburg, **44**

Lima, **20**

Lisbon, **28**

London (Greenwich), **27**

Los Angeles, **6**

Madrid, **38**

Manila, **57**

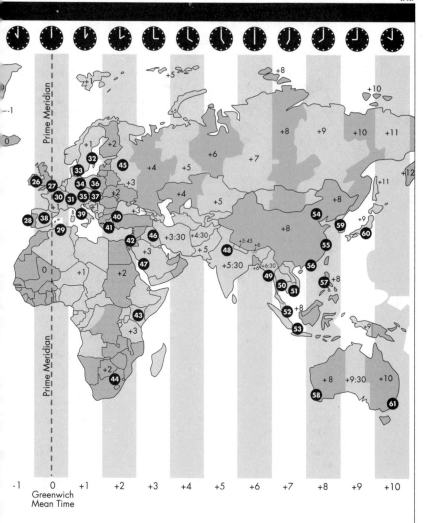

Introduction

A joke popular in the neighboring province of Quebec between the wars went "First prize, one week in Toronto. Second prize, two weeks in Toronto. Third prize, three weeks in Toronto." And who could blame them for laughing? Toronto was a deadly city right into the 1950s, at which time its half-million citizens used to rush off to Detroit (a four-hour drive to the southwest) and Buffalo (90 minutes to the south, around Lake Ontario) for a good time. Today, of course, the rush is in the opposite direction, for hundreds of reasons that are sprinkled through this volume.

Yet, is not Toronto the city that American novelist John Dos Passos called "a beastly place" in his letter to a friend in 1907? And the city that the great British poet Rupert Brooke, during a visit in 1913, gave halfhearted, one-handed applause to, by writing that "the only depressing thing is that it will always be what it is, only larger"? The city that Ernest Hemingway, while honing his writing craft at *The Toronto Star* in the 1920s, could not wait to escape from, for fear of going mad with boredom?

Even as late as 1960, the witty Irish dramatist Brendan Behan was letting the city have it: "Toronto will be a fine town when it is finished." And in the words of Leopold Infeld, the Polish-born mathematical physicist who worked with Einstein: "It must be good to die in Toronto. The transition between life and death would be continuous, painless and scarcely noticeable in this silent town. I dreaded the Sundays and prayed to God that if he chose for me to die in Toronto he would let it be on a Saturday afternoon to save me from one more Toronto Sunday."

What on earth could have happened in so short a period? And why was no one surprised (in Toronto, at least) when various participants at the 1982 International Conference on Urban Design, in Toronto, ran around spouting such superlatives as "This is the most livable city in North America" and "It is an example of how a city could grow"?

Much of Toronto's excitement is explained by its ethnic diversity. Nearly two-thirds of the 3.8 million people who now live in the metropolitan Toronto area were born and raised somewhere else. And that somewhere else was often very far away.

Nearly 500,000 Italians make metropolitan Toronto one of the largest Italian communities outside of Italy. It is also the home of the largest Chinese community in Canada and the largest Portuguese community in North America. Close to 150,000 Jews. Nearly as many Muslims. Tens of thousands of Germans. Greeks. Hungarians. East Indians. West Indians. Vietnamese. Maltese. South Americans. Ukrainians. More than 70 ethnic groups in all, speaking over 100 different languages. Certainly, a city worthy of inviting the United Nations to consider moving here from Manhattan.

What this has meant to Toronto is the rather rapid creation of a vibrant mix of cultures that has echoes of turn-of-the-century New York City—but without the slums, crowding, disease, and tensions. Toronto undoubtedly would have had this, too, had Canada been decent and wise enough to open its gates wide back then, as the Yanks had. (This fact the city continues to bemoan and tried to atone for by accepting more "boat people" in the 1970s than any other country in the world. Yet, there are still tensions over large immigration to this very day.)

Still, to give to its burgeoning ethnic population all, or even most, of the credit for Toronto's becoming a cosmopolitan, world-class city in just a few decades would be a kind of reverse racism, and not totally correct, either. Much of the thanks must be given to the so-called dour Scots who set up the banks, built the churches, and created the kind of solid base for commerce, culture, and community that would come to such a healthy fruition in the three decades following World War II. Now a minority in the city they helped make, the much-maligned white Anglo-Saxon Protestants had their noses tweaked mercilessly in an issue of *Toronto*, a now-folded monthly magazine which used to come with the *Globe and Mail*. In the March 1988 edition, a writer noted that the city was about to hold its first St. Patrick's Day parade ever: "But Toronto—Toronto was for generations known as the Belfast of the North, a city so firmly in the grip of Protestants, Loyalists, and Royalists that a Roman Catholic celebration would have been unthinkable. Well, it's not anymore." In a subsequent issue of *Toronto*, historian William Kilbourn added, "Once, Toronto the Good was embodied by the masters of the Orange Order: defenders of abstinence, Protestantism, and the British race." His closing words are striking: "My own childhood was pure British colonial . . . But I know I couldn't stand living in that kind of Toronto now. Instead, I think of my two Italian grandsons and my Chilean granddaughter, and of this city as a welcoming and exciting place for them, and I celebrate my non-WASP home."

The letters to the editor in the next issue of the magazine were scathing, with many of the WASPs who had built the city screaming (perhaps justifiably), "Racist!" And one might fairly ask, would Toronto be the decent place it is today had it not been for those harshly criticized white Protestants? Who opened the gates to foreigners, if not those same, now-outnumbered, supposedly boring sons and daughters of what was once the British Empire?

The city that once united Canadians from the Atlantic to the Pacific in a shared hatred of Toronto's sanctimoniousness and industriousness now tends to draw their collective envy at how well the place works. Other critics insist that Toronto remains too smug (well, yes); too regulated (would they prefer chaos?); too provincial (actually, it's municipal; Ontario is provincial); too prim and proper (would they rather be mugged?); too young (as a major city, perhaps, but it was hardly born yesterday).

We have to laugh with the Montrealers—a wildly different culture of primarily French-speaking Catholics—who joke that "Toronto is a city where people go around saying 'Thank God it's Monday.'" To this day, indeed, Torontonians seem to actually enjoy working, and they appear to lack the ability to enjoy themselves doing anything else. But with the prices of houses, who can afford not to work? And as for "having a good time," there have never been more fine restaurants, theaters, movie houses, concerts, and bars to enjoy oneself in—even on Sunday!

The city officially became Toronto on March 6, 1834, more than 150 years ago, but its roots go back to 1615. A Frenchman named Etienne Brûlé was sent into the not-yet-Canadian wilderness in 1610 by explorer Samuel de Champlain to see what he could discover. And he discovered plenty: the river and portage routes from the St. Lawrence to Lake Huron, possibly Lakes Superior and Michigan, and, eventually, Lake Ontario.

His discoveries surprised the local Indians, who had known about all these places for centuries and had long since named the area between the Humber and Don rivers Toronto, which is believed to mean "a place of meetings." (How prescient!) It was later a busy Indian village named Teiaiagon, a French trading post, a British town named York (if the British hadn't won the Seven Years' War in the late 1700s, you would be reading this in translation from the French), and finally the city we know today, once again bearing the original Indian name of Toronto.

The city had the usual history of colonial towns of the last century: It was invaded by the Americans in 1812; there were many Great Fires; there was a rebellion in 1837; and there was a slow but steady growth of (you guessed it) white Anglo-Saxon Protestants, from about 9,000 in the 1830s to nearly 500,000 before World War II, at which time they outnumbered the non-WASPs by five to two.

And now, as we've noted, it has somehow metamorphosed into a great world city. There are countless reasons why this has happened, and we have touched on but a few. Toronto is clearly this country's center of culture, commerce, and communications— "New York run by the Swiss," according to Peter Ustinov's marvelously witty description of the place—and this is partly by chance. For example, Mikhail Baryshnikov chose to defect from the Bolshoi in Toronto in 1974 and has returned frequently to work with its ballet corps.

But far more of Toronto's success can be credited to thoughtful and sensitive government actions, such as the limits that the city council set in the 1970s on the number and size of new buildings, and the decision by the Ontario government to put a stop to a major (Spadina) expressway, which would have slashed like a knife through many precious, long-standing neighborhoods. Toronto is a collection of little neighborhoods united by an enlightened metropolitan form of city government.

With occasional lapses, metropolitan Toronto has encouraged urban renewal, and many of the city's building projects have mixed low-rent housing with luxury condos, restaurants, offices, and businesses. Somehow, Toronto has managed to avoid the situation in many North American cities, where the middle class has fled to the suburbs, taking their taxes and children with them. On the contrary, one can see tens of thousands of young couples eagerly moving back to the same areas in the heart of the city where they grew up, and where they know that they will have fine schools for their kids and a healthy community to live in.

There are a growing number of problems, to be sure. In late 1988, there were 303 vacant apartments available to rent in Toronto, out of a total of 234,568—in other words, a vacancy rate of .1%. And in a single month in late 1988, the average house price shot up $30,000, making the average resale cost of a home in the metropolitan Toronto area a towering $250,000 and more. In other words, one has to be upper class anywhere else to live even lower middle class in Toronto. As of late 1993, the vacancy rate was up to around 2% in the metropolitan Toronto area, and house prices had fallen by up to a third, even more, since the late '80s, but there's still no question that the city remains a very expensive place to live.

Toronto has gained the nickname "Hollywood North" because literally dozens of major films have been made in this city, from *The Black Stallion* to *Three Men and a Baby;* from *Naked Lunch* to *Searching for Bobby Fisher;* from *Moonstruck* to *Cocktail;* and don't forget such popular television series as *The Kids in the Hall* and *Road to Avonlea.* Over $600 million was spent by film and television companies in metropolitan Toronto in 1992 and 1993 alone, with a total of 67 movies and television shows using the city as its location in the latter year. Indeed, it is hard to walk about the city nowadays without tripping over a movie crew and a number of famous people. A story is still told about one particular film made in the downtown area in 1987. Since it was a crime movie set in New York City, street signs had to be put up and several tons of garbage trucked in and spread around the city street. After filming all morning, the cast took a lunch break. When they returned barely an hour later, all the garbage had been cleaned up!

That's Toronto, in a nutshell: Clean. Safe. Orderly. Yet somehow dynamic and exciting. Groucho Marx sang an old vaudeville tune back in 1967 that went "It's better to run to Toronta/Than to stay in a place you don't wanta." And he was right. But nearly three decades later, we can honestly change the words to "It's best that you run to Toronta/There's no better place that you'd wanta."

1 Essential Information

Before You Go

Government Information Offices

The best source of specific information on travel to Toronto is the **Metropolitan Toronto Convention and Visitors Association** (Queen's Quay Terminal, 207 Queen's Quay W, Suite 509, Box 126, Toronto, Ontario M5J 1A7, tel. 416/203–2500 or 800/363–1900, fax 416/867–3995).

American and Canadian visitors can also contact the **Ministry of Ontario Tourism/Ontario Travel** (Queen's Park, Toronto, Ontario M7A 2E5, tel. 800/668–2746).

British travelers can visit or write to the **Ontario Ministry of Tourism and Recreation** (21 Knightsbridge, London SW1X 7LY, no phone).

Another excellent source of free information on Toronto and all aspects of travel to Canada is the **Canadian Consulate General** offices (ask for the tourism department):

United States 1 CNN Center, Suite 400, South Tower, Atlanta, GA 30303, tel. 404/577–6810, fax 404/524–5046; 3 Copley Pl., Suite 400, Boston, MA 02116, tel. 617/262–3760, fax 617/262–3415; 2 Prudential Plaza, 180 N. Stetson Ave., Suite 2400, Chicago, IL 60601, tel. 312/616–1860, fax 312/616–1878; St. Paul Tower, 17th Floor, 750 N. St. Paul St., Dallas, TX 75201, tel. and fax 214/922–9815; 600 Renaissance Center, Suite 1100, Detroit, MI 48243, tel. 313/567–2340, fax 313/567–2164; 300 S. Grand Ave., Suite 1000, Los Angeles, CA 90071, tel. 213/687–7432, fax 213/620–8827; 701 4th Ave. S, Minneapolis, MN 55415, tel. 612/333–4641, fax 612/332–4061; Exxon Bldg., 16th Floor, 1251 Ave. of the Americas, New York, NY 10020, tel. 212/596–2400, fax 212/596–1793; 412 Plaza 600, 6th and Stewart, Seattle, WA 98191, tel. 206/443–1777, fax 206/443–1782; 501 Pennsylvania Ave. NW, Washington, DC 20001, tel. 202/682–1740 or 800/668–2746, fax 202/682–7721.

United Kingdom **Canada House,** Trafalgar Sq., London SW1Y 5BJ, tel. 0171/629–9492 or **The Canadian High Commission (Tourism Program),** MacDonald House, 1 Grosvenor Sq., London W1X 0AB, tel. 0171/258–6595.

U.S. Government Travel Briefings The U.S. Department of State's **Overseas Citizens Emergency Center** (Room 4811, Washington, DC 20520; enclose S.A.S.E.) issues Consular Information Sheets, which cover crime, security, political climate, and health risks as well as embassy locations, entry requirements, currency regulations, and other routine matters. For the latest information, stop in at any U.S. passport office, consulate, or embassy; call the interactive hot line (tel. 202/647–5225, fax 202/647–3000); or, with your PC's modem, tap into the Bureau of Consular Affairs' computer bulletin board (tel. 202/647–9225).

Tours and Packages

When considering an escorted tour, be sure to find out (1) exactly what expenses are included (particularly tips, taxes, side trips, additional meals, and entertainment); (2) ratings of all hotels on the itinerary and the facilities they offer; (3) cancellation policies both for you and for the tour operator; and (4) what the single supplement is, should you be traveling alone. Most tour operators request that bookings be made through a travel agent—there is no additional charge for this.

Fully Escorted Tours   **Talmage Tours** (1223 Walnut St., Philadelphia, PA 19107, tel. 215/923–7100) has a five-day Niagara Falls–Toronto package. **Maupintour** (Box 807, Lawrence, KS 66044, tel. 913/843–1211 or 800/255–4266) offers a week-long Toronto–Montreal tour. **Collette Tours** (162 Middle St., Pawtucket, RI 02860, tel. 401/728–3805 or 800/832–4656) offers a five-day jaunt including Ottawa and Niagara Falls. **Globus** (5301 S. Federal Circle, Littleton, CO 80123, tel. 303/797–2800 or 800/221–0090) offers a two-week tour of Niagara Falls, Toronto, Ottawa, Montreal, Quebec City, Bar Harbour, Boston, and Newport. **Domenico Tours** (751 Broadway, Bayonne, NJ 07002, tel. 201/823–8687 or 800/554–8687) has a four-day tour of Toronto and Niagara Falls, as well as longer trips that take in more Canadian sights and cities. **Bixler Tours** (Box 37, Hiram, OH 44234, tel. 216/569–3222 or 800/325–5087) gives you eight days of touring in Toronto, Montreal, Ottawa, and Quebec City. **Mayflower Tours** (1225 Warren Ave., Box 490, Downers Grove, IL 60515, tel. 708/960–3430 or 800/323–7604), and **Parker Tours** (218-14 Northern Blvd., Bayside, NY 11361, tel. 718/428–7800 or 800/833–9600) provide several tours that include time in Toronto. **Tauck Tours** (11 Wilton Rd., Westport, CT 06881, tel. 203/226–6911 or 800/468–2825) travels from Montreal to Niagara Falls, stopping in Toronto along the way. **Trieloff Tours** (24301 El Toro Rd., Suite 140, Laguna Hills, CA 92653, tel. 800/248–6877 or 800/432–7125 in CA) has escorted, multicity tours throughout the region. **Gadabout Tours** (700 E. Tahquitz Way, Palm Springs, CA 92262, tel. 619/325–5556 or 800/952–5068) puts together an 18-day fall-foliage tour that begins with two nights in Toronto and includes stops in Montreal and Quebec City. **Brennan Tours** (1402 3rd Ave., Suite 717, Seattle, WA 98101–2118, tel. 206/622–9155 or 800/237–7249) takes in the sights of Ontario and Quebec on a nine-day deluxe tour.

Independent Packages   **Air Canada** (tel. 800/776–3000) has two-night packages with a choice of hotels. The cost depends on the hotel rating. **SuperCities** (139 Main St., Cambridge, MA 02142, tel. 617/621–9988 or 800/333–1234) offers two-, three-, and four-night packages. **GoGo Tours** (69 Spring St., Ramsey, NJ 07446, tel. 201/934–3500) has three-night city packages, which include a "Taste of Toronto Dine-A-Round" sightseeing tour and rental car. Also check with **American Fly AAway Vacations** (tel. 800/321–2121) and **United Airlines** (tel. 800/328–6877) for packages.

When to Go

The weather can often fall below freezing from late November into March and can be brutal in January and February (although the snowfalls are almost never heavy). That simple fact alone could repel some visitors while attracting ski and skating enthusiasts. Some of the best theater, ballet, opera, and concerts take place between September and May; both the Stratford and Shaw festivals, in venues each about a 90-minute drive from Toronto, are in full swing from May to October, with the latter recently beginning as early as mid-April. But remember that Toronto has recently become Broadway North, with year-round engagements of major productions of *The Phantom of the Opera, Miss Saigon, Show Boat, Crazy for You,* and more. In other words, summers are hardly dead in the city, and limited only to the Stratford and Shaw festivals!

There is no single time when the city is unbearably crowded, or disappointingly empty, in the way that Paris, say, can be. But it cannot be denied that Toronto is most pleasant to walk around, and simply enjoy, from late spring through early fall, when there are outdoor concerts and open-air dining—and the entire city seems to come to life. On the other hand, many hotels drop their prices up to 50% in the off-season, particularly in December and January.

Climate Jokes about Canadian polar bears and igloos notwithstanding, Toronto's climate is really not that harsh, except in December, January, and February. Okay, and March as well. (And sometimes in late November.) Indeed, a look at a map of North America will prove that the city is farther south than about a dozen states and that Toronto is not in the so-called Snow Belt, in which heavy and often savage storms paralyze cities such as Detroit, Buffalo, Syracuse, and Rochester. Surprising as it may seem—and as heartbreaking as it is to our ski-lift operators—prolonged snowfalls rarely come to the northern shores of Lake Ontario, and many a December and January snowfall soon melts away.

Furthermore, should you arrive during those often-bleak winter months, you will be pleased to discover that the city does not come to a frozen halt with the first sign of a snowflake—or even a snowstorm. Underground shopping concourses allow one to walk through much of the downtown area and avoid the cold.

Spring can be brief, and a (hot) summer can last through much of June, July, and August, even September. And then come the gorgeous autumn colors—seen best just north of the city and throughout our myriad parks—along with more moderate and pleasant fall temperatures, before the much-cursed winter months come blasting and howling in again.

Lake Ontario often cools the city air in the summer and warms it in the winter. The airport, therefore, being some distance from the lake, will be warmer in the summer than downtown, and colder in the winter.

The following are average daily maximum and minimum temperatures for Toronto.

Jan.	30F	– 1C	**May**	63F	17C	**Sept.**	69F	21C
	16	– 9		44	7		51	11
Feb.	30F	– 1C	**June**	73F	23C	**Oct.**	56F	13C
	15	– 9		54	12		40	4
Mar.	37F	3C	**July**	79F	26C	**Nov.**	43F	6C
	23	– 5		59	15		31	– 1
Apr.	50F	10C	**Aug.**	77F	25C	**Dec.**	33F	1C
	34	1		58	14		21	– 6

Information Sources For current weather conditions and forecasts for cities in the United States and abroad, plus the local time and helpful travel tips, call the **Weather Channel Connection** (tel. 900/932–8437; 95¢ per minute) from a touch-tone phone.

Public Holidays

Though banks, schools, and government offices close for national holidays, many stores remain open. As in the United States, the move has been to observe certain holidays on the Monday nearest to the actual date, making for a long weekend.

New Year's Day (January 1); Good Friday; Easter Monday; Victoria Day; Canada Day (July 1); Labor Day; Thanksgiving; Remembrance Day (November 11); Christmas (December 25); and Boxing Day (December 26).

Festivals and Seasonal Events

Top seasonal events in Toronto include the International Boat Show in January, the Toronto Sportsman's Show in March, Caravan celebrations in June, Caribana in July, the Toronto International Film Festival in September, and the city's New Year's Eve Party. For further details, contact the Metropolitan Toronto Convention and Visitors Association (*see* Government Information Offices, *above*).

Mid-Jan.: Toronto International Boat Show is held annually at Exhibition Place.

Late Jan.: Molson Export Ice Canoe Race and Barrel Jumping Contests take place at Harbourfront.

Late Feb.: C.D.F.A. Championship Dog Shows are at Exhibition Place.

Mid-Mar.: Toronto Sportsmen's Show is set up at Exhibition Place.

Late Mar.: Annual Springtime Craft Show and Sale is held at Exhibition Place.

Mid-Apr.: Shaw Festival begins.

Apr.–Oct.: African Lion Safari is open.

Mid-May: Stratford Festival Season opens in Stratford.

Apr.–Oct.: Toronto Blue Jays season at the SkyDome.

Mid-June: Metro Toronto International Caravan takes place throughout Toronto. This is a unique celebration of the city's ethnic communities.

Late-June: du Maurier Jazz Festival is in its tenth year. Previous years have attracted such jazz greats as Sarah Vaughan, Miles Davis, Dizzy Gillespie, and Branford Marsalis.

Early July: The **Mariposa Festival** takes place in Molson Park, about an hour drive north of Toronto. Bob Dylan and Gordon Lightfoot have appeared in past years.

Mid-July: Toronto Outdoor Art Exhibition is held in Nathan Phillips Square by the New City Hall.

July: Caribana is a Mardi Gras–like festival held by the West Indian communities, with over 500,000 visitors and a striking parade of some 5,000 brightly dressed revelers.

Mid-Aug.–early Sept.: Canadian National Exhibition is held at the Canadian National Exhibition Grounds by Lake Ontario and Ontario Place.

Early–mid-Sept.: The **Toronto International Film Festival** is a film event that attracts cinematographers and stars from many countries.

Late October: The **International Festival of Authors** at Harbourfront brings in major writers from around the world, on the level of Saul Bellow, Jay McInerney, Jan Morris, and, yes, Salman Rushdie (in 1988). This is truly one of Toronto's major cultural experiences and should not be missed.

Mid-Nov.: Santa Claus Parade travels downtown Toronto.

Dec. 31: City of Toronto's New Year's Eve Party is thrown in Nathan Phillips Square. And, since the last day of 1991, wildly successful and popular "no-booze" celebrations known as **First Night** (fit for the entire family and very low-priced) take place in many theaters and other locations across downtown.

What to Pack

Clothing Pack light because porters and baggage trolleys are scarce and luggage restrictions are tight. What you pack depends more on the time of year than on any specific dress code. Toronto has extremely cold winters; hot, steamy summers; and lots of rain in between. Winter can extend from November through April. For winter, you'll need your warmest clothes, in many layers, and waterproof boots. Salt will destroy leather shoes and boots; winter visitors will be wise to bring a cheap pair. In the summer, loose-fitting, casual clothing will see you through both day and evening events. Women should pack a sweater or shawl for summer evenings, which can get cool, and for restaurants that run their air conditioners full blast. Men will need a jacket and tie for the better restaurants and many of the night spots. Jeans are as popular in Toronto as they are elsewhere and are perfectly acceptable for sightseeing and informal dining. Toronto has an extremely low crime rate and is a wonderful place for wandering on foot, so bring comfortable walking shoes. Consider packing a bathing suit for your hotel pool.

Miscellaneous Bring an extra pair of eyeglasses or contact lenses in your carry-on luggage. If you have a health problem that requires a prescription drug, pack enough to last the duration of the trip or have your doctor write a prescription using the drug's generic name, because brand names vary from country to country. Always carry prescription drugs in their original packaging to avoid problems with customs officials. Don't pack them in luggage that you plan to check in case your bags go astray. Pack a list of the offices that supply refunds for lost or stolen traveler's checks.

The electrical current is the same as in the United States: 110 volts, 60 cycles.

Luggage Regulations Free airline baggage allowances depend on the airline, the route, and the class of your ticket; ask in advance. In general, on domestic flights and on international flights between the United States and foreign destinations, you are entitled to check two bags—neither exceeding 62 inches, or 158 centimeters (length + width + height), or weighing more than 70 pounds (32 kilograms). A third piece may be brought aboard; its total dimensions are generally limited to less than 45 inches (114 centimeters), so it will fit easily under the seat in front of you or in the overhead compartment. In the United States the Federal Aviation Administration gives airlines broad latitude to limit carry-on allowances and tailor them to different aircraft and operational conditions. Charges for excess, oversize, or overweight pieces vary.

If you are flying between two foreign destinations, note that baggage allowances may be determined not by piece but by weight— generally 88 pounds (40 kilograms) of luggage in first class, 66 pounds (30 kilograms) in business class, and 44 pounds (20 kilograms) in economy. If your flight between two cities abroad *connects* with your transatlantic or transpacific flight, the piece method still applies.

Safeguarding Your Luggage Before leaving home, itemize your bags' contents and their worth in case they go astray. To minimize that risk, tag them inside and out with your name, address, and phone number. (If you use your home address, cover it so that potential thieves can't see it.) Put a copy of your itinerary inside each bag, so that you can easily be tracked. At check-in, make sure that the tag attached by baggage handlers bears the correct three-letter code for your destination. If your bags do not arrive with you, or if you detect damage, immediately file a written report with the airline before you leave the airport.

Taking Money Abroad

Traveler's checks and major U.S. credit cards are accepted in Toronto. You'll need cash for some of the small restaurants and shops. Many establishments accept U.S. dollars.

Traveler's Checks Traveler's checks are preferable in metropolitan centers, although you'll need cash in rural areas and small towns. The most widely recognized are **American Express, Citicorp, Diners Club, Thomas Cook,** and **Visa,** which are sold by major commercial banks. Both American Express and Thomas Cook issue checks that can be countersigned and used by you or your traveling companion. Typically the issuing company or the bank at which you make your purchase charges 1% to 3% of the checks' face value as a fee. Some foreign banks charge as much as 20% of the face value as the fee for cashing traveler's checks in a foreign currency. Buy a few checks in small denominations to cash toward the end of your trip, so you won't be left with excess foreign currency. Record the numbers of checks as you spend them, and keep this list separate from the checks.

Currency Exchange Banks offer the most favorable exchange rates. If you use currency exchange booths at airports, rail and bus stations, hotels, stores, and privately run exchange firms, you'll typically get less favorable rates, but you may find the hours more convenient.

You can get good rates and avoid long lines at airport currency-exchange booths by getting a small amount of currency at **Thomas Cook Currency Services** (630 5th Ave., New York, NY 10111, tel. 212/757–6915 or 800/223–7373 for locations in major metropolitan areas throughout the U.S.) or **Ruesch International** (tel. 800/424–2923 for locations) before you depart. Check with your travel agent to be sure that the currency of the country you will be visiting can be imported.

There are more bank branches in this country than there are pubs, which tells you something, does it not? But the banks have rather abbreviated hours—usually Monday to Thursday from 10 to 3, and Friday 10 to 6. **Thomas Cook Currency Services** (10 King St. E, near Yonge St., tel. 416/863–1611; in the Manulife Centre, 55 Bloor St. W, at Bay St., tel. 416/961–9822; 60 Bloor St. W, tel. 416/923–6549; the Sheraton Centre hotel lobby, 123 Queen St. W, across from the New City Hall, tel. 416/363–4867; Yorkdale Pl., tel. 416/789–1827; and the Skyline Hotel lobby, 655 Dixon Rd., near the airport, tel. 416/247–4600) has longer hours.

Getting Money from Home

Cash Machines Many automated-teller machines (ATMs) are tied to international networks such as **Cirrus** and **Plus.** You can use your bank card at ATMs to withdraw money from an account and get cash advances on a credit-card account if your card has been programmed with a personal identification number, or PIN. Check in advance on limits on withdrawals and cash advances within specified periods. Ask whether your bank-card or credit-card PIN will need to be reprogrammed for use in the area you'll be visiting. Four digits are commonly used abroad. Note that Discover is accepted only in the United States. On cash advances you are charged interest from the day you receive the money from ATMs as well as from tellers. Although transaction fees for ATM withdrawals abroad may be higher than fees for withdrawals at home, Cirrus and Plus exchange rates are excellent, because they are based on wholesale rates only offered by major banks. They also may be referred to abroad as "a withdrawal from a credit account."

For specific Cirrus locations in the United States and Canada, call 800/424–7787. For U.S. Plus locations, call 800/843–7587 and press the area code and first three digits of the number you're calling from (or of the calling area where you want an ATM).

Bank Transfers Just have your bank send money to another bank in Toronto. It's easiest to transfer money between like branches; otherwise, the process takes a couple of days longer and costs more.

Wiring Money You don't have to be a cardholder to send or receive a **MoneyGram from American Express** for up to $10,000. Go to a MoneyGram agent in retail and convenience stores and American Express travel offices, pay up to $1,000 with a credit card and anything over that in cash. You are allowed a free long-distance call to give the transaction code to your intended recipient, who needs only present identification and the reference number to the nearest MoneyGram agent to pick up the cash. MoneyGram agents are in more than 70 countries (call 800/926–9400 for locations). Fees range from 3% to 10%, depending on the amount and how you pay.

You can also use **Western Union.** To wire money, take either cash or a cashier's check to the nearest agent or call and use MasterCard or Visa. Money sent from the United States or Canada will be available for pickup at agent locations in 100 countries within minutes. Once the money is in the system it can be picked up at any one of 25,000 locations (call 800/325–6000 for the one nearest you; 800/321–2923 in Canada). Fees range from 4% to 10%, depending on the amount you send.

Canadian Currency

The units of currency in Canada are the Canadian dollar (C$) and the cent, in the same denominations as U.S. currency. At press time, the exchange rate was fluctuating at around C$1.25 to U.S. $1 and C$2.50 to £1. Since 1987, the $1 bill has slowly been phased out in Canada and replaced with a funny-looking coin that has been nicknamed "the Loonie," after the illustration of a Canadian loon on one side. But these bills (as well as the far more useful $5, $10, and $20 bills—and, yes, the always welcome $2 Canadian denomination) should remain in circulation into the 1990s.

U.S. currency is eagerly accepted at most good-size stores and restaurants, and with good reason: Owners are always happy to give far less exchange than the daily rate. So it is financially wise for all visitors to go to a Canadian bank or exchange firm within a few hours of arrival. The sooner you exchange your money for the worth-less (if not yet worthless) Canadian dollar, the more money you'll save. When you use your credit cards, you can be assured that your expenditures will automatically go through as Canadian funds, and you will get the proper exchange rate.

What It Will Cost

Note: Throughout this guide, unless otherwise stated, prices are quoted in Canadian dollars.

It's true that the U.S. dollar is worth some 25%–30% more than the Canadian dollar, but this translates into upwards of a 15% savings only when goods in both countries are sold at the same price. The fact is that goods and services are priced slightly higher in Canada than in the United States, so the actual savings is closer to 10%. In Toronto, a can of Coke costs about 75¢; a taxi, as soon as the meter is turned on, $2.20; a movie, $8; and a glass of beer in a bar, more than $3.

A shocking amount of taxes are added to the price of your airline ticket to Toronto, but this varies, depending upon your country of departure.

If you're flying to Toronto from the United States, the U.S. airport departure tax is 10% of the fare. You'll also be charged an additional Canadian Goods and Services Tax (GST), which is 7% of the fare, plus C$6, to a maximum of C$50 (Canadian). Also, you're expected to pay a U.S. user fee of US$6 and a customs fee of US$6.50.

If you are flying to Toronto from somewhere else in Canada, you'll pay the Goods and Services Tax, which is an additional 7% of the fare, plus C$6, to a maximum of C$50.

Those travelers flying from the United Kingdom pay an additional C$50 in taxes.

You will rarely be made aware of additional taxes; they will be written into the total ticket cost at the time of purchase.

Long-Distance Calling

AT&T, MCI, and Sprint have several services that make calling home or the office more affordable and convenient when you're on the road. Use one of them to avoid pricey hotel surcharges. **AT&T** Calling Card (tel. 800/225–5288) and the AT&T Universal Card (tel. 800/662–7759) give you access to the service. With AT&T's USA Direct (tel. 800/874–4000 for codes in the countries you'll be visiting) you can reach an AT&T operator with a local or toll-free call. **MCI**'s Call USA (MCI Customer Service, tel. 800/444–4444) allows that service from 85 countries or from country to country via MCI WorldReach. From MCI ExpressInfo in the United States you can get 24-hour weather, news, and stock quotations. MCI PhoneCash (tel. 800/925–0029) is available through American Express and through several convenience stores and retailers nationwide. **Sprint** Express (tel. 800/793–1153) has a toll-free number travelers abroad can dial using the WorldTraveler Foncard to reach a Sprint operator in the United States. The Sprint operator can offer international directory assistance to 224 countries in the world. All three companies offer message delivery services to international travelers and have added debit cards so that you don't have to fiddle with change.

Passports and Visas

If your passport is lost or stolen abroad, report the loss immediately to the nearest embassy or consulate and to the local police. If you can provide the consular officer with the information contained in the passport, he or she will usually be able to issue you a new passport promptly. For this reason, keep a photocopy of the data page of your passport separate from your money and traveler's checks. Also leave a photocopy with a relative or friend at home.

Because there is so much border traffic between Canada and the United States (for example, many people live in Windsor [Ontario] and work in Detroit), entry requirements are fairly simple. Citizens and legal residents of the United States do not require a passport or a visa to enter Canada, but proof of citizenship (a birth certificate, valid passport, voter registration card, draft card, selective service card, or naturalization certificate) may be requested. If you return to the United States by air, possession of a passport can save a long wait on line. Resident aliens should be in possession of their U.S. Alien Registration or "green" card. U.S. citizens interested in visiting Canada for more than 90 days may apply for a visa that allows them to stay for six months. For more information, contact the Canadian Embassy, 501 Pennsylvania Ave. NW, Washington, DC 20001, tel. 202/682–1740.

British citizens should consult Tips for British Travelers, below.

Customs and Duties

On Arrival Clothing and personal items may be brought in without charge or restriction. American and British visitors may bring in the following items duty-free: 200 cigarettes, 50 cigars, and two pounds of tobacco; personal cars (for less than six months); boats or canoes; rifles and shotguns (but no handguns or automatic weapons); 200 rounds of ammunition; cameras, radios, sports equipment, and typewriters. A deposit is sometimes required for trailers and household equipment (refunded upon return). If you are driving a rented car, be sure to keep the contract with you. Cats may enter freely, but dogs must have proof of a veterinary inspection to ensure that they are free of communicable diseases. Plant material must be declared and inspected.

Returning Home Passengers flying from Toronto to the United States will have to go through U.S. Customs in Toronto, so allow extra time before your flight. If you have brought any foreign-made equipment from home, such as cameras, it's wise to carry the original receipt with you or to register it with U.S. Customs before you leave home (Form 4457). Otherwise, you may end up having to pay duty on your return.

U.S. Customs If you've been out of the country for at least 48 hours and haven't already used the exemption, or any part of it, in the past 30 days, you may bring home $400 worth of foreign goods duty-free. So can each member of your family, regardless of age; and your exemptions may be pooled, so one of you can bring in more if another brings in less. A flat 10% duty applies to the next $1,000 worth of goods; above $1,400, the rate varies with the merchandise. (If the 48-hour or 30-day limits apply, your duty-free allowance drops to $25, which may not be pooled.) Please note that these are the *general* rules, applicable to most countries, including Canada.

Travelers 21 or older may bring back 1 liter of alcohol duty-free, provided the beverage laws of the state through which they reenter the United States allow it. In addition, 100 non-Cuban cigars and 200 cigarettes are allowed, regardless of your age. Antiques and works of art more than 100 years old are duty-free.

Gifts valued at less than $50 may be mailed to the United States duty-free, with a limit of one package per day per addressee, and do not count as part of your exemption (do not send alcohol or tobacco products or perfume valued at more than $5); mark the package "Unsolicited Gift" and write the nature of the gift and its retail value on the outside. Most reputable stores will handle the mailing for you.

For a copy of "Know Before You Go," a free brochure detailing what you may and may not bring back to the United States, rates of duty, and other pointers, contact the **U.S. Customs Service** (Box 7407, Washington, DC 20044, tel. 202/927–6724).

Since the passage of the so-called Free Trade Agreement between the United States and Canada in late 1988, many people have come to think that all duties were being dropped overnight. *Au contraire, mon frère:* On the vast majority of goods, these duties are being eliminated gradually. It is recommended that you pick up the brochure, "Free Trade and the Traveller," published by the government, outlining how the FTA will affect goods brought into Canada from the United States. It's available at Customs offices, airport departure lounges, and border crossing points.

Tips for British Travelers

Passports and Visas Citizens of the United Kingdom need a valid passport to enter Canada for stays of up to six months; all visitors must have a return ticket out of Canada. Applications for new and renewal passports are available from main post offices as well as at the six passport offices, located in Belfast, Glasgow, Liverpool, London, Newport, and Peterborough. You may apply in person at all passport offices, or by mail to all except the London office. Children under 16 may travel on an accompanying parent's passport. All passports are valid for 10 years. Allow a month for processing.

Customs From countries outside the European Union (EU) such as Canada, you may import duty-free 200 cigarettes, 100 cigarillos, 50 cigars, or 250 grams of tobacco; 1 liter of spirits or 2 liters of fortified or sparkling wine; 2 liters of still table wine; 60 milliliters of perfume; 250 milliliters of toilet water; plus £136 worth of other goods, including gifts and souvenirs.

For further information or a copy of "A Guide for Travellers," which details standard customs procedures as well as what you may bring into the United Kingdom from abroad, contact **HM Customs and Excise** (Dorset House, Stamford St., London SE1 9PY, tel. 0171/928–3344).

Insurance Most tour operators, travel agents, and insurance agents sell policies covering accident, medical expenses, personal liability, trip cancellation, and loss or theft of personal property.

For advice by phone or a free booklet, "Holiday Insurance," that sets out what to expect from a holiday-insurance policy and gives price guidelines, contact the **Association of British Insurers** (51 Gresham St., London EC2V 7HQ, tel. 0171/600–3333; 30 Gordon St., Glasgow G1 3PU, tel. 0141/226–3905; Scottish Providence Bldg., Donegall Sq. W, Belfast BT1 6JE, tel. 01232/249176; call for other locations).

Tour Operators **Kuoni Travel** (Kuoni House, Dorking, Surrey RH5 4AZ, tel. 01306/742222) offers holiday packages in Toronto hotels and features the city in several multicenter escorted tours. It also can arrange self-drive itineraries and motor-home holidays.

Premier Holidays (Premier Travel Center, Westbrook, Milton Rd., Cambridge CB4 1YQ, tel. 01223/355977) offers city stays in Toronto, plus self-drive and escorted tours.

National Holidays Ltd. (Clarendon House, Clarendon Rd., Eccles M30 9AA, tel. 0161/707–4404) will put together a complete package to Canada, including airfare or a week's car rental. Similar plans are offered by **North American Vacations** (Acorn House, 172/174 Albert Rd., Jarrow, Tyne & Wear NE32 5JA, tel. 0191/483–6226) and **Alba-**

ny Travel (Royal London House, 196 Deansgate, Manchester M3
3NF, tel. 0161/833–0202).

Airfares Major airlines serving Toronto are **Air Canada** (tel. 0181/759–2636),
British Airways (tel. 0181/897–4000), and **Northwest Airlines** (tel.
01345/747800). If you can afford to be flexible about when you travel,
look for last-minute flight bargains, which are advertised in the Sunday newspapers.

Traveling with Cameras, Camcorders, and Laptops

Film and If your camera is new or if you haven't used it in a while, shoot and
Cameras develop a few test rolls of film before you leave. Store film in a cool,
dry place—never in the car's glove compartment or on the shelf under the rear window.

Airport security X-rays generally aren't harmful to film with ISO
below 400. To protect your film, carry it with you in a clear plastic
bag and ask for a hand inspection. Such requests are honored at U.S.
airports, up to the inspector abroad. Don't depend on a lead-lined
bag to protect film in checked luggage—the airline may increase the
radiation to see what's inside. Call the **Kodak Information Center**
(tel. 800/242–2424) for details.

Camcorders Before your trip, put camcorders through their paces, invest in a
and Videotape skylight filter to protect the lens, and check all the batteries. Most
newer camcorders are equipped with batteries that can be re-
charged with a universal or worldwide AC adapter charger (or
multivoltage converter) usable whether the voltage is 110 or 220. All
that's needed is the appropriate plug.

Videotape is not damaged by X-rays, but it may be harmed by the
magnetic field of a walk-through metal detector, so ask for a hand-
check. Airport security personnel may ask you to turn on the
camcorder to prove that it's what it appears to be, so make sure the
battery is charged.

Laptops Security X-rays do not harm hard-disk or floppy-disk storage, but
you may request a hand-check, at which point you may be asked to
turn on the computer to prove that it is what it appears to be. (Check
your battery before departure.) Most airlines allow you to use your
laptop aloft except during takeoff and landing (so as not to interfere
with navigation equipment). For international travel, register your
foreign-made laptop with U.S. Customs as you leave the country. If
your laptop is U.S.-made, call the consulate of the country you'll be
visiting to find out whether it should be registered with customs
upon arrival. Before departure, find out about repair facilities at
your destination.

Language

It amuses Canadians to see how many visitors assume (in fear) that
"everyone will speak French to me." Canada is, indeed, a bilingual
country, in that it has two official languages, French and English.
And visitors are charmed, even fascinated, to see the cereal boxes
and road signs in both languages. But Toronto is the Anglophone
center of Canada, which means that 99% of the people living here
will speak to you in English.

Insurance

For U.S. Residents Most tour operators, travel agents, and insurance agents sell specialized health-and-accident, flight, trip-cancellation, and luggage insurance as well as comprehensive policies with some or all of these features. Before you make any purchase, review your existing health and homeowner policies to find out whether they cover expenses incurred while traveling.

Health-and-Accident Insurance Specific policy provisions of supplemental health-and-accident insurance for travelers include reimbursement for $1,000 to $150,000 worth of medical and/or dental expenses caused by an accident or illness during a trip. The personal-accident, or death-and-dismemberment, provision pays a lump sum to your beneficiaries if you die or to you if you lose one or more limbs or your eyesight; the lump sum awarded can range from $15,000 to $500,000. The medical-assistance provision may reimburse you for the cost of referrals, evacuation, or repatriation and other services, or it may automatically enroll you as a member of a particular medical-assistance company.

Flight Insurance Often bought as a last-minute impulse at the airport, flight insurance pays a lump sum when a plane crashes either to a beneficiary if the insured dies or sometimes to a surviving passenger who loses eyesight or a limb. Like most impulse buys, flight insurance is expensive and basically unnecessary. It supplements the airlines' coverage described in the limits-of-liability paragraphs on your ticket. Charging an airline ticket to a major credit card often automatically entitles you to coverage and may also embrace travel by bus, train, and ship.

Baggage Insurance In the event of loss, damage, or theft on international flights, airlines' liability is $20 per kilogram for checked baggage (roughly about $640 per 70-pound bag) and $400 per passenger for unchecked baggage. On domestic flights, the ceiling is $1,250 per passenger. Excess-valuation insurance can be bought directly from the airline at check-in for about $10 per $1,000 worth of coverage. However, you cannot buy it at any price for the rather extensive list of excluded items shown on your airline ticket.

Trip Insurance **Trip-cancellation-and-interruption insurance** protects you in the event you are unable to undertake or finish your trip, especially if your airline ticket, cruise, or package tour does not allow changes or cancellations. The amount of coverage you purchase should equal the cost of your trip should you, a traveling companion, or a family member fall ill, forcing you to stay home, plus the nondiscounted one-way airline ticket you would need to buy if you had to return home early. Read the fine print carefully, especially sections defining "family member" and "preexisting medical conditions." **Default** or **bankruptcy insurance** protects you against a supplier's failure to deliver. Such policies often do not cover default by a travel agency, tour operator, airline, or cruise line if you bought your tour and the coverage directly from the firm in question. Tours packaged by one of the 33 members of the **United States Tour Operators Association** (USTOA, 211 E. 51st St., Suite 12B, New York, NY 10022; tel. 212/750–7371), which requires members to maintain $1 million each in an account to reimburse clients in case of default, are likely to present the fewest difficulties.

Comprehensive Policies Companies supplying comprehensive policies with some or all of the above features include **Access America, Inc.** (Box 90315, Richmond, VA 23230, tel. 800/284–8300), **Carefree Travel Insurance** (Box 310, 120 Mineola Blvd., Mineola, NY 11501, tel. 516/294–0220 or 800/

323–3149), **Tele-Trip** (Mutual of Omaha Plaza, Box 31762, Omaha, NE 68131, tel. 800/228–9792), **The Travelers Companies** (1 Tower Sq., Hartford, CT 06183, tel. 203/277–0111 or 800/243–3174), **Travel Guard International** (1145 Clark St., Stevens Point, WI 54481, tel. 715/345–0505 or 800/826–1300), and **Wallach and Company, Inc.** (107 W. Federal St., Box 480, Middleburg, VA 22117, tel. 703/687–3166 or 800/237–6615).

Car Rentals

If you're flying into Toronto and planning to spend some time there before exploring the rest of Ontario, save money by arranging to pick up your car in the city and then head off into the province. You'll have to weigh the added expense of renting a car from a major company with an airport office against the savings on a car from a budget company with offices in town.

Most major car-rental companies are represented in Toronto, including **Avis** (tel. 800/331–1212, 800/879–2847 in Canada), **Budget** (tel. 800/527–0700), **Hertz** (tel. 800/654–3131, 800/263–0600 in Canada), and **National** (tel. 800/227–7368). Unlimited-mileage rates range from $32 per day for an economy car to $47 for a large car; weekly unlimited-mileage rates range from $193 to $330. This does not include tax, which in Canada is 15% on car rentals.

Driver's licenses issued in the United States are valid in Canada. Although you can legally drive a car at age 18 in Toronto, in most cases you must be at least 25 to rent a car.

Requirements Your own driver's license is acceptable. An International Driver's Permit, available from the American or Canadian Automobile Association, is a good idea.

Extra Charges Picking up the car in one city and leaving it in another may entail substantial drop-off charges or one-way service fees. The cost of a collision or loss-damage waiver (*see below*) can be high, also. Some rental agencies will charge you extra if you return the car *before* the time specified on your contract. Ask before making unscheduled drop-offs. Be sure the rental agent agrees *in writing* to any changes in drop-off location or other items of your rental contract. Fill the tank when you turn in the vehicle to avoid being charged for refueling at what you'll swear is the most expensive pump in town.

Cutting Costs More economical rentals may come as part of fly/drive or other packages, even bare-bones deals that only combine the rental and an airline ticket (*see* Tours and Packages, *above*).

Insurance and Collision Damage Waiver Until recently standard rental contracts included liability coverage (for damage to public property, injury to pedestrians, and so on) and coverage for the car against fire, theft, and collision damage with a deductible. Due to law changes in some states and rising liability costs, several car rental agencies have reduced the type of coverage they offer. Before you rent a car, find out exactly what coverage, if any, is provided by your personal auto insurer. Don't assume that you are covered. If you do want insurance from the rental company, secondary coverage may be the only type offered. You may already have secondary coverage if you charge the rental to a credit card. Only **Diners Club** (tel. 800/234–6377) provides primary coverage in the United States and worldwide.

In general if you have an accident, you are responsible for the automobile. Car rental companies may offer a collision damage waiver (CDW), which ranges in cost from $4 to $14 a day. You should decline the CDW only if you are certain you are covered through your personal insurer or credit-card company.

Student and Youth Travel

Travel Agencies Council Travel Services (CTS), a subsidiary of the nonprofit Council on International Educational Exchange (CIEE), specializes in low-cost travel arrangements abroad for students and is the exclusive U.S. agent for several discount cards. Also newly available from CTS are domestic air passes for bargain travel within the United States. CIEE's twice-yearly *Student Travels* magazine is available at the CTS office at CIEE headquarters (205 E. 42nd St., 16th Floor, New York, NY 10017, tel. 212/661–1450) and in Boston (tel. 617/266–1926), Miami (tel. 305/670–9261), Los Angeles (tel. 310/208–3551), and at 43 branches in college towns nationwide (free in person, $1 by mail). Campus Connections (1100 E. Marlton Pike, Cherry Hill, NJ 08034, tel. 800/428–3235) specializes in discounted accommodations and airfares for students. The Educational Travel Centre (438 N. Frances St., Madison, WI 53703, tel. 608/256–5551) offers low-cost domestic and international airline tickets, mostly for flights departing from Chicago, and rail passes. Other travel agencies catering to students include TMI Student Travel (1146 Pleasant St., Watertown, MA 02172, tel. 617/661–8187 or 800/245–3672), and Travel Cuts (187 College St., Toronto, Ontario M5T 1P7, tel. 416/979–2406).

Discount Cards For discounts on transportation and on museum and attractions admissions, buy the International Student Identity Card (ISIC) if you're a bona fide student or the International Youth Card (IYC) if you're under 26. In the United States the ISIC and IYC cards cost $16 each and include basic travel accident and illness coverage and a toll-free travel assistance hot line. Apply to CIEE (*see* address *above*, tel. 212/661–1414; the application is in *Student Travels*). In Canada, the cards are available for $15 each from Travel Cuts (*see above*). In the United Kingdom, they cost £5 and £4 respectively at student unions and student travel companies, including Council Travel's London office (28A Poland St., London W1V 3DB, tel. 0171/437–7767).

Hostelling A Hostelling International (HI) membership card is the key to more than 5,000 hostels in 70 countries; the sex-segregated, dormitory-style sleeping quarters, including some for families, go for $7 to $20 a night per person. Membership is available in the United States through Hostelling International-American Youth Hostels (HI-AYH, 733 15th St. NW, Suite 840, Washington, DC 20005, tel. 202/783–6161), the U.S. link in the worldwide chain, and costs $25 for adults 18 to 54, $10 for those under 18, $15 for those 55 and over, and $35 for families. Volume 1 of the *AYH Guide to Budget Accommodation* lists hostels in Europe and the Mediterranean ($13.95, including postage). HI membership is available in Canada through Hostelling International-Canada (205 Catherine St., Suite 400, Ottawa, Ontario K2P 1C3, tel. 613/748–5638) for $26.75, and in the United Kingdom through the Youth Hostel Association of England and Wales (Trevelyan House, 8 St. Stephen's Hill, St. Albans, Hertshire AL1 2DY, tel. 01727/855215) for £9.

Tour Operators Contiki (300 Plaza Alicante #900, Garden Grove, CA 92640, tel. 714/740–0808 or 800/266–8454) specializes in package tours for travelers 18 to 35.

Traveling with Children

Publications
Local Guides

Toronto Loves Kids, by M. Weisman (The Can-Do Publishing Co., Inc., Toronto; $6.95), is filled with activities, sights, resources. Another resource is *Kid-Bits: Dini Petty's Guide to Toronto for Children*, by Merike Weiler and Dini Petty (Methuen; $9.95). *City Parent* (Metroland Printing, 1091 Brevik Pl., Mississauga, Ontario L4W 3R7, tel. 905/815–0045) is a superior monthly newspaper for parents, with complete listings of activities, resources, etc. It's free at libraries, bookstores, supermarkets, nursery schools, and even at many McDonald's restaurants.

Newsletter

Family Travel Times, published 10 times a year by **Travel With Your Children** (TWYCH, 45 W. 18th St., New York, NY 10011, tel. 212/206–0688; annual subscription $55), covers destinations, types of vacations, and modes of travel. TWYCH also publishes *Cruising with Children* ($22) and *Skiing with Children* ($29).

Books

Traveling with Children—And Enjoying It, by Arlene K. Butler ($11.95 plus $3 shipping per book; Globe Pequot Press, Box 833, 6 Business Park Rd., Old Saybrook, CT 06475, tel. 800/243–0495, 800/962–0973 in CT) helps plan your trip with children, from toddlers to teens. From the same publisher are *Recommended Family Resorts in the United States, Canada, and the Caribbean*, by Jane Wilford with Janet Tice ($12.95), and *Recommended Family Inns of America* ($12.95).

Getting There
Airfares

On international flights, the fare for infants under age two not occupying a seat is generally either free or 10% of the accompanying adult's fare; children ages two to 11 usually pay half to two-thirds of the adult fare. On domestic flights, children under two not occupying a seat travel free, and older children currently travel on the "lowest applicable" adult fare.

Baggage

In general, infants paying 10% of the adult fare are allowed one carry-on bag, not to exceed 70 pounds/32 kilograms or 45 inches/114 centimeters (length + width + height) and a collapsible stroller; check with the airline before departure, because you may be allowed less if the flight is full. The adult baggage allowance applies for children paying half or more of the adult fare.

Safety Seats

The FAA recommends the use of safety seats aloft and details approved models in the free leaflet "Child/Infant Safety Seats Recommended for Use in Aircraft" (available from the Federal Aviation Administration, APA–200, 800 Independence Ave. SW, Washington, DC 20591, tel. 202/267–3479; Information Hotline, tel. 800/322–7873). Airline policy varies. U.S. carriers allow FAA-approved models bearing a sticker declaring their FAA approval. Because these seats are strapped into regular passenger seats, airlines may require that a ticket be bought for an infant who would otherwise ride free. Foreign carriers may not allow infant seats, may charge the child's rather than the infant's fare for their use, or may require you to hold your baby during takeoff and landing, thus defeating the seat's purpose.

Facilities Aloft

Some airlines provide other services for children, such as children's meals and freestanding bassinets (only to those with seats at the bulkhead, where there's enough legroom). Make your request when reserving. Every other year, the February issue of *Family Travel Times* details children's services on three dozen airlines ($12; *see above*). "Kids and Teens in Flight" (free from the U.S. Department of Transportation's Office of Consumer Affairs (R-25, Washington, DC 20590, tel. 202/366–2220) offers tips for children flying alone.

Lodging **The Delta Chelsea Inn** (33 Gerrard St., Toronto, Ontario M5G 1Z4, tel. 800/268–1133) maintains a supervised Children's Creative Center and allows children under 18 to stay free with their parents. **The Inn on the Park** (1100 Eglinton Ave. E, North York, Ontario M3C 1H8, tel. 416/444–2561), a Four Seasons hotel, has a supervised children's program. The friendly **Town Inn Hotel** (620 Church St., Toronto, Ontario M4Y 262, tel. 416/964–3311) offers reliable baby-sitting services.

Baby-Sitting **Active Home Services** (110 St. Clair Ave. W, tel. 416/785–4818) has
Services been around for a quarter-century, providing sitters as far west as Jane Street, a few miles east of the airport. There's a five-hour minimum by day and a four-hour minimum at night.

Christopher Robin Services (5 Whitecap Blvd., Scarborough, tel. 416/289–4430) covers all of metropolitan Toronto. Service is also based on a five-hour daily and a four-hour nightly minimum.

Also check *City Parent* (*see* Publications, *above*) for local agencies, or make child-care arrangements through your hotel concierge (*see* Lodging, *above*).

Hints for Travelers with Disabilities

Services The **Toronto Transit Commission** (TTC) offers a bus service, called Wheel-Trans, for people with disabilities who are unable to use regular public vehicles. For advance reservations, phone 416/393–4222; for same-day requests, 416/393–4333; TTD number 416/393–4555.

Transportation to and from Pearson International Airport is available for travelers with disabilities through Wheel-Trans (tel. 416/393–4111). Three limousine companies—**Aaroport, MacIntosh** (tel. 416/741–5466 for both) and **Airline Limousine** (tel. 416/ 676–3210)—operate, wheelchair-accessible vans. By prearrangement, people with disabilities can be picked up or dropped off at points in all three of the airport's terminals.

For information on governmental services for the hearing impaired, the TTY-TDD numbers are 416/392–8069 and 416/392–7354. For general information about transportation and buildings that are accessible to visitors with disabilities, call the accessibility planner, weekdays 8–5, tel. 416/392–7339.

The **Advocacy Resource Centre for the Handicapped** (tel. 416/482–8255 or TTY number 416/482–1254) is a responsible and responsive legal center that defends the rights of the those with mental and physical disabilities.

The **Community Information Centre** (tel. 416/392–0505) provides information on various facilities, as well as social and health services for those with disabilities.

Freedom in Traveling (tel. 416/234–8511) is a liaison between people with disabilities and the travel industry, providing accessibility information. Many travel agents across North America are affiliated with it.

Greyhound/Trailways (tel. 800/752–4841) will carry a person with a disability along with one companion for the price of a single fare. **Amtrak** (tel. 800/872–7245) requests 24-hour notice to provide Redcap service and special seats. Passengers with disabilities are entitled to a 15% discount on the lowest available coach fare.

Organizations Several U.S. organizations provide travel information for people
In the United with disabilities, usually for a membership fee, and some publish
States newsletters and bulletins. Among them are the **Information Center
for Individuals with Disabilities** (Fort Point Pl., 27–43 Wormwood
St., Boston, MA 02210, tel. 617/727–5540 or 800/462–5015 in MA between 11 AM and 4 PM, or leave message; TTY 617/345–9743); **Mobility
International USA** (Box 10767, Eugene, OR 97440, tel. and TTY 503/
343–1284; fax 503/343–6812), the U.S. branch of an international
organization based in Britain (*see below*) that has affiliates in 30
countries; **MossRehab Hospital Travel Information Service** (tel. 215/
456–9603, TTY 215/456–9602); the **Travel Industry and Disabled Exchange** (TIDE, 5435 Donna Ave., Tarzana, CA 91356, tel. 818/344–
3640, fax 818/344–0078); and **Travelin' Talk** (Box 3534, Clarksville,
TN 37043, tel. 615/552–6670, fax 615/552–1182).

In the United Important information sources include the **Royal Association for
Kingdom Disability and Rehabilitation** (RADAR, 12 City Forum, 250 City
Rd., London EC1V 8AF, tel. 0171/250–3222), which publishes travel information for people with disabilities in Britain; and **Mobility
International** (228 Borough High St., London SE1 1JX, tel. 0171/
403–5688), an international clearinghouse of travel information for
people with disabilities.

Travel **Flying Wheels Travel** (143 W. Bridge St., Box 382, Owatonna, MN
Agencies and 55060, tel. 507/451–5005 or 800/535–6790) is a travel agency specia-
Tour lizing in domestic and worldwide cruises, tours, and independent
Operators travel itineraries for people with mobility problems. Adventurers
should contact **Wilderness Inquiry** (1313 5th St. SE, Minneapolis,
MN 55414, tel. and TTY 612/379–3858 or 800/728–0719), which or-
chestrates action-packed trips like white-water rafting, sea
kayaking, and dog sledding, to bring together people who have disabilities with those who don't.

Publications *Guide to Ontario Government Programs & Services for Disabled
Persons* is a superb new—and free—72-page booklet available from
the Office for Disabled Persons, 3rd Floor, 700 Bay St., Toronto, Ontario M5G 1Z6, tel. 416/326–0111 (voice/TDD for the hearing-impaired) or 800/387–4456 (voice/TDD). To obtain the booklet in
French, call 800/387–4456 (*voix*/ATS).

Toronto with Ease is a free booklet available from the Metropolitan
Toronto Convention and Visitors Association (*see* Government Information Offices, *above*). Or call the Ontario March of Dimes (tel.
416/425–0501), which will be happy to mail the booklet to you if you
send the organization postage and handling.

Two free publications are available from the U.S. Consumer Information Center (Pueblo, CO 81009): "New Horizons for the Air Traveler with a Disability" (include Dept. 608Y in the address), a U.S.
Department of Transportation booklet describing changes result-
ing from the 1986 Air Carrier Access Act and from the 1990 Americans with Disabilities Act, and the Airport Operators Council's
Access Travel: Airports (Dept. 5804), which describes facilities and
services for people with disabilities at more than 500 airports worldwide.

Travelin' Talk Directory (*see* Organizations, *above*) was published
in 1993. This 500-page resource book ($35 check or money order with
a money-back guarantee) is packed with information for travelers
with disabilities. Twin Peaks Press (Box 129, Vancouver, WA 98666,
tel. 206/694–2462 or 800/637–2256) publishes the *Directory of Travel Agencies for the Disabled* ($19.95), listing more than 370 agencies
worldwide. Add $2 for shipping.

Hints for Older Travelers

Organizations **The American Association of Retired Persons** (AARP, 601 E St., NW, Washington, DC 20049, tel. 202/434–2277) provides independent travelers who are members of the AARP (open to those age 50 or older; $8 per person or couple annually) with the Purchase Privilege Program, which offers discounts on lodging, car rentals, and sightseeing, and the AARP Motoring Plan, which furnishes domestic trip-routing information and emergency road-service aid for an annual fee of $39.95 per person or couple ($59.95 for a premium version). AARP also arranges group tours, cruises, and apartment living through **AARP Travel Experience from American Express** (400 Pinnacle Way, Suite 450, Norcross, GA 30071, tel. 800/927–0111 or 800/745–4567).

Two other organizations offer discounts on lodgings, car rentals, and other travel products, along with such nontravel perks as magazines and newsletters: the **National Council of Senior Citizens** (1331 F St. NW, Washington, DC 20004, tel. 202/347–8800 (membership $12 annually); and **Mature Outlook** (6001 N. Clark St., Chicago, IL 60660, tel. 800/336–6330; $9.95 annually).

Note: Mention your senior-citizen identification card when booking hotel reservations for reduced rates, not when checking out. At restaurants, show your card before you're seated; discounts may be limited to certain menus, days, or hours. If you are renting a car, ask about promotional rates that might improve on your senior-citizen discount.

Educational The nonprofit **Elderhostel** (75 Federal St., 3rd Floor, Boston, MA Travel 02110, tel. 617/426–7788) has offered inexpensive study programs for people 60 and older since 1975. Held at more than 1,800 educational and cultural institutions, courses cover everything from marine science to Greek myths and cowboy poetry. Participants usually attend lectures in the morning and spend the afternoon sightseeing or on field trips; they live in dormitory-type lodgings. Fees for programs in the United States and Canada, which usually last one week, run about $300, not including transportation.

Publications *The 50+ Traveler's Guidebook: Where to Go, Where to Stay, What to Do* by Anita Williams and Merrimac Dillon ($12.95, St. Martin's Press, 175 5th Ave., New York, NY 10010) is available in bookstores and offers many useful tips. "The Mature Traveler" (Box 50820, Reno, NV 89513, tel. 702/786–7419; $29.95), a monthly newsletter, contains many travel deals.

Hints for Gay and Lesbian Travelers

As you will see throughout this book, metropolitan Toronto is a city of neighborhoods: Italian, Chinese, East Asian, Greek, Jewish, Portuguese, Caribbean, and some 100 more. The true heart of the gay and lesbian community can be found near the corner of Church and Wellesley streets, just a few blocks east and north of Eaton Centre (or east and south of Bloor and Yonge streets).

Toronto has one of the largest populations of gays and lesbians in North America, and inarguably the largest in Canada. It would be dishonest to flatly proclaim that the city is heaven for gays and lesbians—the occasional gay-bashing, whether in verbal political struggles against extending health benefits to same-sex couples, or even the rare act of violence—are not unknown. Still, there are openly-gay school trustees and city councillors, and it is fair to say that gay and lesbian travelers will probably find Toronto to be a surprisingly safe and welcoming destination.

The first thing to do is pick up a free copy of *XTRA!*, a biweekly newspaper for the community, which is available up and down the streets around the Church–Wellesley area, noted above. If you want a copy *before* you arrive in Toronto, you can order one for $2 by writing *XTRA!* (Box 7289, Station A, Toronto, Ont. M5W 1X9, tel. 416/925–9872); if you call, the newspaper will provide a verbal list of local events, businesses, and meeting places.

Also consult the *Pink Pages*, an annual reference directory (found in various bookstores and bars) for Toronto's gay and lesbian community, and other free newspapers, such as *Lexicon* and *Rites*.

Most gay and lesbian bars are located in the Church–Wellesley area; for specific information on events and activities when you are in Toronto, contact the **519 Community Centre** (519 Church St., tel. 416/392–6874), where you can ask about events, bars, and more. The most popular gay beach in the Toronto area is Hanlan's Point, at the northwest tip of the Toronto Islands.

Lesbian and Gay Pride Day takes place on the last Sunday of June each year, usually attended by over 100,000 people; it is Toronto's third-largest parade, after the Caribana and Santa Claus parades. And don't forget **Buddies in Bad Times** (*see* Theater in Chapter 7) an often-inspired theater company, dedicated to gay and lesbian themes.

Organizations The **International Gay Travel Association** (Box 4974, Key West, FL 33041, tel. 305/292–0217, 800/999–7925, or 800/448–8550), which has 700 members, will provide you with names of travel agents and tour operators who specialize in gay travel. The **Gay and Lesbian Visitors Center of New York, Inc.** (135 W. 20th St., 3rd Floor, New York, NY 10011, tel. 212/463–9030 or 800/395–2315; $100 annually) mails a monthly newsletter, valuable coupons, and more to its members.

Tour Operators and Travel Agencies The dominant travel agency in the market is **Above and Beyond** (3568 Sacramento St., San Francisco, CA 94118, tel. 415/922–2683 or 800/397–2681). Tour operator **Olympus Vacations** (8424 Santa Monica Blvd., #721, West Hollywood, CA 90069; tel. 310/657–2220) offers all-gay-and-lesbian resort holidays. **Skylink Women's Travel** (746 Ashland Ave., Santa Monica, CA 90405, tel. 310/452–0506 or 800/225–5759) handles individual travel for lesbians all over the world and conducts two international and five domestic group trips annually.

Publications The premier international travel magazine for gays and lesbians is *Our World* (1104 N. Nova Rd., Suite 251, Daytona Beach, FL 32117, tel. 904/441–5367; $35 for 10 issues). "Out & About" (tel. 203/789–8518 or 800/929–2268; $49 for 10 issues, full refund if you aren't satisfied) is a 16-page monthly newsletter with extensive information on resorts, hotels, and airlines that are gay-friendly.

Further Reading

Don't miss Michael Ondaatje's award-winning *In the Skin of a Lion*, about Toronto in the 1940s and 1950s. The best literary and geographic history of the area is *Toronto Remembered* by William Kilbourn. *Toronto Observed*, by William Dendy and William Kilbourn, is an award-winning book on Toronto's 100 most interesting buildings. Eric Arthur's *No Mean City* is a penetrating look at the city's 19th-century architecture.

Robertson Davies wrote a series of novels about the supernatural, set in Toronto. One is *Fifth Business*.

Margaret Millar's *Wall of Eyes* and Hugh Garner's *Death in Don Mills* are mystery/thrillers set in the area.

Austin Clarke's *Nine Men Who Laughed* and *The Storm of Fortune* are novels about immigrants from the West Indies to Toronto. Mordecai Richler's *The Inconquerable Atuk* is about the life of an Inuit (Eskimo) in Toronto; the picture it paints of the city is exceedingly dated, but it's an uproarious example of the author's youthful satiric work.

The best encapsulation of today's Toronto, albeit fictional, is Margaret Atwood's *Cat's Eye*. It is highly entertaining, as well written as her other fine books—including the dystopian *Handmaid's Tale*, and *Life Before Man*—and punctures all the city's pretensions and foibles with a devastatingly satiric vision. Harry J. Pollack's *Gabriel: A Novel* is an autobiographical novel about a Toronto man involved in the literary life. Other suggested titles include *Hunger Trace* by Adrienne Clarkson, and *A Casual Affair: A Modern Fairytale* by Sylvia Fraser.

Arriving and Departing

From the United States by Plane

Flights are either nonstop, direct, or connecting. A **nonstop** flight requires no change of plane and makes no stops. A **direct** flight stops at least once and can involve a change of plane, although the flight number remains the same; if the first leg is late, the second waits. This is not the case with a **connecting** flight, which involves a different plane and a different flight number.

Airports and Airlines With a handful of exceptions—such as planes from Newark, Montreal, Ottawa, and London, Ontario, that land at Toronto's tiny **Island Airport**—flights into Toronto land at the **Lester B. Pearson International Airport,** so named in 1984 to honor Canada's Nobel Peace Prize–winning prime minister of three decades ago. It's commonly called "the Toronto airport" or "Malton" (after the once-small town where it was built, just northwest of the city), but it's just as often called "impossible," since its terminals are inadequate for the number of travelers who use it. Waits for bags are often lengthy—although the free carts are a human touch—and Pearson can be dreadfully overcrowded, both coming and going. Terminal 1, which opened in 1964 to handle 3 million passengers, handled over *10 million* in 1990. The sorely needed Terminal 3 opened in early 1991 after many delays, and it is the only airline terminal in the world to ban smoking (with a few exceptions, such as in pubs). And, thank heavens, the ugly and uncomfortable Terminal 2 has undergone a $52 million renovation, which included replacing the endless walks with moving sidewalks and adding skylights and atria.

Toronto is served by **American** (tel. 800/433–7300), **Delta** (tel. 800/843–9378), **Northwest** (tel. 800/225–2525), **United** (tel. 800/241–6522), **US Air** (tel. 800/428–4322), **Air Canada** (tel. 800/422–6232), and **Canadian Airlines International** (tel. 800/387–2737). A low-cost airline, **Canada 3000** (tel. 416/674–2661) flies mainly between Toronto and major Canadian cities, such as Vancouver, Edmonton, and Winnipeg, but it also flies in and out of a half-dozen cities in Florida, including Orlando. (Florida residents should check this one out!)

Flying Time Flying time from New York is about 1 hour; from Chicago, about 1½ hours; from Miami, 3 hours; from Los Angeles or San Francisco, 5 hours. One should know that Toronto's Pearson airport, in deference to the tens of thousands of nearby residents who must suffer the regular roar of jets, has an evening curfew, and one cannot expect to land there much after 11 PM or before 8 AM. Travelers who are arriving from the West Coast will therefore not be able to get flights after 2 or 3 PM. A handful of airlines offer the infamous "red-eye" service, which leaves western cities after midnight, local time, and arrives in Toronto about 8 or 9 AM, sometimes via Chicago.

Cutting Costs The Sunday travel section of most newspapers is a good source of deals. When booking, particularly through an unfamiliar company, call the Better Business Bureau and your local or state Consumer Protection Bureau to find out whether any complaints have been registered against the company; pay with a credit card if you can; and consider trip-cancellation and default insurance (*see* Insurance, *above*). A helpful resource is *Airfare Secrets Exposed*, by Sharon Tyler and Matthew Wonder (Universal Information Publishing, $16.95), available in bookstores.

Promotional Less expensive fares, called promotional or discount fares, are
Airfares round-trip and involve restrictions, which vary according to the route and season. You must usually buy the ticket—commonly called an APEX (advance purchase excursion) when it's for international travel—in advance (seven, 14, or 21 days are usual), although some of the major airlines have added no-frills, cheap flights to compete with new bargain airlines on certain routes.

With the major airlines the cheaper fares generally require minimum and maximum stays (for instance, over a Saturday night or at least seven and no more than 30 days). Airlines generally allow some return date changes for a $25 to $50 fee, but most low-fare tickets are nonrefundable. Only a death in the family would prompt the airline to return any of your money if you cancel a nonrefundable ticket. However, you can apply an unused nonrefundable ticket toward a new ticket, again with a small fee. The lowest fare is subject to availability, and only a small percentage of the plane's total seats will be sold at that price. Contact the U.S. Department of Transportation's Office of Consumer Affairs (I–25, Washington, DC 20590, tel. 202/366–2220) for a copy of "Fly-Rights: A Guide to Air Travel in the U.S." *The Official Frequent Flyer Guidebook* by Randy Petersen (4715-C Town Center Dr., Colorado Springs, CO 80916, tel. 719/597–8899 or 800/487–8893; $14.99, plus $3 shipping and handling) yields valuable hints on getting the most for your air travel dollars. Also new and helpful is *202 Tips Even the Best Business Travelers May Not Know* by Christopher McGinnis, president of the Travel Skills Group (Box 52927, Atlanta, GA 30355, tel. 404/659–2855; $10 in bookstores).

Consolidators Consolidators or bulk-fare operators—"bucket shops"—buy blocks of seats on scheduled flights that airlines anticipate they won't be able to sell. They pay wholesale prices, add a markup, and resell the seats to travel agents or directly to the public at prices that still undercut the airline's promotional or discount fares (higher than a charter ticket but lower than an APEX ticket, and usually without the advance-purchase restriction). Moreover, some consolidators sometimes give you your money back. Carefully read the fine print detailing penalties for changes and cancellations. If you doubt the reliability of a company, call the airline once you've made your booking and confirm that you do, indeed, have a reservation on the flight.

Discount Travel Clubs	Travel clubs offer members unsold space on airplanes, cruise ships, and package tours at as much as 50% below regular prices. Membership may include a regular bulletin or access to a toll-free hot line giving details of available trips departing from three or four days to several months in the future. Most also offer 50% discounts off hotel rack rates, but double-check with the hotel to make sure it isn't offering a better promotional rate independent of the club. Clubs include **Discount Travel International** (114 Forrest Ave., Suite 203, Narberth, PA 19072, tel. 215/668–7184; $45 annually, single or family), **Entertainment Travel Editions** (Box 1014 Trumbull, CT 06611, tel. 800/445–4137; price ranges $28–$48), **Great American Traveler** (Box 27965, Salt Lake City, UT 84127, tel. 800/548–2812; $29.95 annually), **Moment's Notice Discount Travel Club** (425 Madison Ave., New York, NY 10017, tel. 212/486–0503; $45 annually, single or family), **Privilege Card** (3391 Peachtree Rd. NE, Suite 110, Atlanta, GA 30326, tel. 404/262–0222 or 800/236–9732; domestic annual membership $49.95, international, $74.95), **Travelers Advantage** (CUC Travel Service, 49 Music Sq. W, Nashville, TN 37203, tel. 800/548–1116; $49 annually, single or family), and **Worldwide Discount Travel Club** (1674 Meridian Ave., Miami Beach, FL 33139, tel. 305/534–2082; $50 annually for family, $40 single).
Publications	The newsletter "Travel Smart" (40 Beechdale Rd., Dobbs Ferry, NY 10522, tel. 800/327–3633; $44 a year) has a wealth of travel deals in each monthly issue. The monthly "Consumer Reports Travel Letter" (Consumers Union, 101 Truman Ave., Yonkers, NY 10703, tel. 800/234–1970) is filled with information on travel savings and indispensable consumer tips.
Enjoying the Flight	Fly at night, if you're able to sleep on a plane. Because the air aloft is dry, drink plenty of fluids while on board. Drinking alcohol contributes to jet lag, as do heavy meals. Bulkhead seats, in the front row of each cabin—usually reserved for people who have disabilities, are elderly, or are traveling with babies—offer more legroom, but trays attach awkwardly to seat armrests, and all possessions must be stowed overhead.
Smoking	Smoking is now banned on all domestic flights of less than six hours' duration in the United States and on all Canadian flights, including flights to and from Europe and East Asia.
From the Airport to Center City	Although Pearson is not far from the downtown area (about 32 km, or 18 mi), the drive can take well over an hour during Toronto's weekday rush hours (7–9 AM and 3:30–6:30 PM). Taxis and limos to a hotel or attraction near the lake can cost $30 or more. You may negotiate a fare, but the meter *must* be used, and the passenger pays whichever amount is less. Many airport and downtown hotels offer free buses to their locations from each of Toronto's three terminals. Travelers on a budget should consider the express buses offered by **PW (Pacific Western) Transportation Service** (tel. 416/672–0293), which link the airport to three subway stops in the southwest (Islington) and north-central (Yorkdale; York Mills) areas of the city. Buses depart every 40 minutes from the airport, and from those subway points to the airport, beginning around 5 AM and ending around midnight; the cost is $6–$8 one-way, $10–$12 round-trip.

An even better alternative is the bus service to and from several downtown hotels (including the Harbour Castle Westin, Royal York, Holiday Inn Crowne Plaza, Marriott Eaton Centre, Delta Chelsea Inn, and Ramada Inn), which can be picked up at any hotel every 20 minutes, from around 5 AM to around 11 PM. Buses even stop at the Bus Terminal at Edward and Elizabeth streets; the cost is approximately $11 one-way, $19 round-trip.

Should you rent a car at the airport, be sure to ask for a street map of the city. Highway 427 runs south, some 3.6 miles to the lakeshore. Here you pick up the Queen Elizabeth Way (QEW) east to the Gardiner Expressway, which runs east into the heart of downtown. If you take the QEW *west*, you'll find yourself swinging around Lake Ontario, toward Hamilton, Niagara-on-the-Lake, and Niagara Falls.

From the United States by Train and Bus

Amtrak (tel. 800/872–7245) runs a daily train to Toronto from Chicago (a 10-hour trip), and another from New York City (11 hours). From Union Station you can walk underground to many hotels—a real boon in inclement weather.

Greyhound (tel. 800/231–2222) and **Grey Coach** (tel. 416/393–7911) both have regular bus service into Toronto from all over the United States. From Detroit, the trip takes five hours; from Buffalo, two to three hours; from Chicago and New York City, 11 hours. Buses arrive at 610 Bay Street, just above Dundas Street.

From the United States by Car

Drivers should have proper owner registration and proof of insurance coverage. There is no need for an international driver's license; any valid one will do.

Drivers may be asked several questions at the border crossing, none of them terribly personal or offensive: your place of birth; your citizenship; your expected length of stay. Border guards will rarely go beyond that. Expect a slight wait at major border crossings. Every fourth or fifth car may be searched, and this can increase the wait at peak visiting times to 30 minutes. However, a recent explosion of cross-border shopping has seen thousands of Canadians shooting across the border every month to take advantage of cheaper gas, food, and appliances, so expect the Detroit–Windsor and Buffalo–Fort Erie crossings to take even longer, especially on weekends and holidays.

The wonderfully wide Highway 401—it reaches up to 16 lanes as it slashes across metropolitan Toronto from the airport on the west almost as far as the zoo on the east—is the major link between Windsor, Ontario (and Detroit), and Montreal, Quebec. It's also known as the Macdonald–Cartier Freeway but is really never called anything other than "401." There are no tolls anywhere along it, but you should be warned: Between 6:30 and 9:30 each weekday morning and from 3:30 to 6:30 each afternoon, the 401 can become dreadfully crowded, even stop-and-go. Plan your trips to avoid these rush hours.

Those who are driving from Buffalo, New York, or Niagara Falls should take the Queen Elizabeth Way (fondly called the QEW or Queen E), which curves up along the western shore of Lake Ontario and eventually turns into the Gardiner Expressway, which flows right into the downtown core.

Yonge Street, which divides the west side of Toronto from the east (much like Manhattan's Fifth Avenue and Detroit's Woodward), begins at the Lakefront. Yonge Street is called Highway 11 once you get north of Toronto, and continues all the way to the Ontario–Minnesota border, at Rainy River. At 1,896.2 km (1,178.3 mi), it is the longest street in the world (as noted in the *Guinness Book of World Records*).

The distances are, from New York City, 851 km (532 mi); from Washington, DC, 899 km (562 mi); from Miami, 2,741 km (1,713 mi); from Montreal, 558 km (349 mi); from Detroit, 378 km (236 mi); from Chicago, 854 km (534 mi); from St. Louis, 1,310 km (1,023 mi); from Denver, 2,485 km (1,553 mi); from Los Angeles, 4,384 km (2,740 mi).

From the United Kingdom by Plane

Toronto is served by several airlines that fly daily from London's Heathrow and Gatwick airports. **British Airways** and **Air Canada** have regularly scheduled flights out of Heathrow. Air Canada has the most flights daily—three—two of them direct, and a third that stops at Montreal's Mirabel airport. **KLM** and **Air France** also fly between London and Toronto, the former stopping in Amsterdam on the way, the latter in Paris. Gatwick is the home of many charters, often at heavily discounted prices.

The flying time from London to Toronto is approximately seven hours and 45 minutes, to which one must add (or subtract) the five-hour time difference between the Mother Country and Her Former Colony.

Staying in Toronto

Important Addresses and Numbers

Tourist Offices The **Metropolitan Toronto Convention and Visitors Association** has its office at Queen's Quay Terminal (207 Queen's Quay W, Suite 509, M5J LA7, tel. 416/368–9821). Booths providing brochures and pamphlets about the city and its attractions, as well as accommodations, are set up in the summer outside the Eaton Centre, on Yonge Street just below Dundas Street, and outside the Royal Ontario Museum.

The **Traveller's Aid Society** is not just for the down-and-out. This is a nonprofit group whose 130 volunteers can recommend restaurants and hotels, and distribute subway maps, tourist publications, and Ontario sales tax rebate forms. *In Union Station, the society is located in Room B23, on the basement level (there is also a booth on the Arrivals level); tel. 416/366–7788. Open daily 9 AM–9 PM. In Terminal 1 at Toronto's Pearson International Airport, the society has its booth on the Arrivals level, directly across from the exit, just past Customs, near Area B; tel. 416/676–2868. Open daily 9 AM–10 PM. In Terminal 2, the booth is located between International and Domestic Arrivals, on the Arrivals level; tel. 416/676–2869. Open daily 10 AM– 10 PM. In Terminal 3, the booth is located on the Arrivals level, right outside the Domestic door; tel. 416/612–5890. Open daily 9 AM–10 PM.*

Embassies The **Consulate General of the United States** (360 University Ave., just north of Queen St., M56 1S4, tel. 416/595–1700).

The **Consulate General of Britain** (777 Bay St., at the corner of College St., M56 2G2, tel. 416/593–1267).

For all other consulates—there are dozens of countries represented in Toronto—look up "Consulate Generals" in the white pages of the phone book.

Emergencies Dial 911 for **police** and **ambulance**.

Physicians and Dentists. Check the Yellow Pages or ask at your hotel desk. Also, call *Dial-a-Doctor* (tel. 416/492–4713) or the *Dental Emergency Service* (tel. 416/924–8041).

24-Hour Pharmacies. *Pharma Plus Drugmart* (Church St. and Wellesley Ave., about a mile from New City Hall, tel. 416/924–7760). *Lucliff Place*, 700 Bay and Gerrard Sts. (tel. 416/979–2424). *Shoppers Drug Mart* (2500 Hurontario St., Mississauga, near the airport, tel. 905/277–3665).

24-Hour Pet Emergency Service. *Veterinary Emergency Clinic*, 201 Sheppard Ave. E, about a half-mile east of Yonge St., and a few blocks north of Highway 401, tel. 416/226–3663.

Road Emergencies. The *CAA* (the Canadian version of AAA) has 24-hour road service (tel. 416/966–3000).

24-Hour Gas Stations and Auto Repairs. *Texaco Stations*, at 153 Dundas St. W, behind New City Hall, near Bay St.; 333 Davenport, just south of Casa Loma; and 601 Eglington Ave. E, west of the Ontario Science Center. *Cross Town Service Center*, 1467 Bathurst St., at the corner of St. Clair Ave. W, is well-known and respected for both gas and repairs. *Jim McCormack Esso*, 2901 Sheppard Ave. E, in the Scarborough area, heading toward the Metro Zoo. *Guido's Esso*, 1104 Albion Rd., not far from the airport.

Poison Information Center. *The Hospital for Sick Children* (tel. 416/598–5900) or for the hearing-impaired (tel. 416/813–5900).

Other Numbers
Concert Line. For a list of upcoming musical events, primarily rock and pop, tel. 416/870–1045. The same number also provides ski reports, traffic information, and sports updates.

Road Report. Call the CAA, tel. 416/771–3035.

Ski Information and Weather. Tel. 416/362–4151.

Soul in Canada. Tel. 416/763–8350. This 24-hour answering service, checked every half-hour, helps black visitors get to know the large, vibrant community of color in Toronto. Since 1988, the service has eagerly assisted singles, couples, and tours with making hotel reservations and sightseeing.

Weather Information. For a taped three-day forecast, phone 416/676–3066, 24 hours a day. If you want to hear a human voice, try 416/676–4567.

Camera Repairs. Sun Camera Service Ltd. (2150 Steeles W, just east of Keele St., tel. 416/669–6355) has been in business for over three decades; it also repairs camcorders.

24-Hour Restaurants. Golden Griddle (Jarvis and Front Sts., tel. 416/865–1263), Fran's Restaurant (20 College St., just a few steps west of Yonge St., tel. 416/923–9867).

Telephones

Phones work as they do in the United States. Drop 25¢ in the slot (the machine eagerly accepts American change, unlike U.S. phones, which spit out Canadian money), and dial the number. There are no problems dialing direct to the United States; U.S. telephone credit cards are accepted. For directory assistance, dial 411.

Mail

The Canadian mail service leaves a great deal to be desired. Indeed, many in Canada like to say that "Postal Service" is an oxymoron—a contradiction in terms. Within Canada, postcards and letters up to 30 grams cost 43¢. From 30 to 50 grams, the cost is 69¢. Other items, including oversize envelopes, cost 88¢ for 50–100 grams. Letters and postcards to the United States cost 50¢ for up to 30 grams, 74¢ for 30–50 grams; oversize envelopes and postcards cost $1.13 for 50–100 grams. International mail and postcards run 88¢ for up to 20 grams, $1.33 for 20–50 grams, $2.20 for 50–100 grams. All these prices may rise by a few cents in early 1995.

Mail may be sent to you care of General Delivery, Toronto Adelaide Post Office, 36 Adelaide St. E, Toronto, Ont. M5C 1J0. American Express clients—cardholders and those who purchase traveler's checks or travel services—may pick up mail (with proper I.D.) without charge at American Express, 12 Richmond St. E, Toronto, Ont. M5C 1M5.

Opening and Closing Times

Most retail stores are open Monday–Saturday 10–6, and they now have the right to open on Sunday as well (*see* Highlights, *above*). Downtown stores are usually open until 9 PM. Some shops are open Friday evenings, too. Shopping malls tend to be open 9:30 AM to 9 or 9:30 PM.

Banks are open Monday to Thursday 10–3 and Friday 10–6. Some banks and trust companies open as early as 8:30 AM and on Saturday as well, and some remain open as late as 8 PM.

The main civic and national holidays observed in Toronto are: New Year's Day; Good Friday, Easter Sunday, and Easter Monday; Victoria Day—the fourth Monday in May; the country's birthday—Canada Day, or Dominion Day—on July 1; Simcoe Day—the first Monday in August; Labor Day—the first Monday in September; Thanksgiving— the second Monday in October (note that this is more than five weeks earlier than the U.S. Thanksgiving; the harvest and the frost arrive much earlier in Canada); Remembrance Day on November 11; Christmas Day; and since the old Blue Laws prevent shopping until *the day after* Boxing Day, this means that December 27 is the big sale day.

Getting Around Toronto

Most of Toronto is laid out on a grid pattern. The key street to remember is Yonge Street (pronounced "young"), which is the main north–south artery. Most major cross streets are numbered east and west of Yonge Street. In other words, if you are looking for 180 St. Clair Avenue West, you want a building a few blocks *west* of Yonge Street; 75 Queen Street East is a block or so *east* of Yonge Street.

At press time, the fare for buses, streetcars, and trolleys was $2 *in exact change*. However, one can purchase 10 adult tickets/tokens for $13, which lowers the price per journey a bit. All fares will undoubtedly rise at least a nickel during the first week of 1995, if not before. Two-fare tickets are available for $3 for adults. Visitors who plan to stay in Toronto for more than a month should consider the **Metropass,** a photo-identity card that costs $67 for adults, plus $2.75 extra for the photo. (And, yes, probably a few bucks more than that as of January 1995). Children (2–12) pay only 50¢, though, and may purchase eight tickets for only $2.50.

Families should take advantage of the savings of the so-called **Day Pass.** It costs $5 and is good for unlimited travel for one person, Monday–Friday after 9:30 AM, and all day Saturday. On Sunday and holidays, it's good for up to six persons (maximum two adults), for unlimited travel. These fares could go up slightly by early 1995. For information on how to take public transit to any street or attraction in the city call 416/393–4636 from 7 AM to 11:30 PM.

A very useful **Ride Guide** is published by the Toronto Transit Commission each year. It shows nearly every major place of interest in the city and how to reach it by public transit. These guides are available in most subways and many other places around the city.

The subway trains stop running at 2 AM, but the Toronto Transit Commission runs bus service from 1 to 5:30 AM on most major streets, including King, Queen, College, Bloor, Yonge, and as far north as Sheppard, Finch, and Steeles.

By Subway There is little argument that the Toronto Transit Commission runs one of the safest, cleanest, most trustworthy systems of its kind anywhere. (It keeps winning international awards, which must mean something.) There are two major subway lines, with 60 stations along the way: the **Bloor/Danforth Line,** which crosses Toronto about 3 miles north of the Lakefront, from east to west, and the **Yonge/University/Spadina Line,** which loops north and south, like a giant "U," with the bottom of the "U" at Union Station. Tokens and tickets are sold in each subway station and at hundreds of convenience stores along the many routes of the TTC. Get your transfers just after you pay your fare and enter the subway; you'll find them in machines on your way down to the trains.

By Bus All buses and streetcars accept exact change, tickets, or tokens. Paper transfers are free; pick one up at the time that you pay your fare.

By Taxi The meter begins at $2.20, and includes the first .2 kilometer. Each additional .2 kilometer is 20¢—as is the fare for each additional passenger in excess of four. The waiting time "while under engagement" is 20¢ for every 33 seconds—and in one of Toronto's horrible traffic jams, this could add up. Still, it's possible to take a cab across downtown Toronto for little more than $5. The largest companies are **Beck** (tel. 416/449–6911), **Co-op** (tel. 416/364–8161), **Diamond** (tel. 416/366–6868), and **Metro** (tel. 416/363–5611).

By Car Seat-belt use is mandatory in the province of Ontario; although there was a negative response in the United States, where this is often seen as an infringement on one's right to die, the vast majority of Canadians welcomed this governmental move some years ago. The law applies to everyone in the car, and hefty fines have been known to be given. And that means infants as well; holding one upon the lap is as illegal as it is risky. Canada went metric some years ago, so gas is sold by the liter, and signs are in kilometers. The "100 km" signs on various highways are not an invitation to accelerate but, rather, a warning not to go more than 60 miles per hour.

Pedestrian crosswalks are sprinkled throughout the city; they are marked clearly by overhead signs and very large painted Xs. All a pedestrian has to do is stick out a hand, and cars screech to a halt in both directions. And they must do it, too. Naturally, if you happen to be the pedestrian, don't be foolish; wait until the traffic acknowledges you, and begins to stop, before venturing into the crosswalk. You'll be amazed at your power.

Right turns on red lights are nearly always permitted, except where otherwise posted. You must come to a complete stop before making the turn.

Guided Tours

Orientation Tours

Toronto Harbour and Islands Boat Tours are provided by **Boat Tours International** (tel. 416/364–2412) on attractive, sleek, Amsterdam-style touring boats, with competent tour guides. The hourly tour visits the Toronto Islands, with lovely views of the Toronto cityscape. Boats leave from the Queen's Quay Terminal daily from early May through mid-October, noon–5; tours leave as late as 7 during the summer months. Other boats depart from the Harbour Castle Westin. Fares are $9.95 adults, $7.95 students and senior citizens, $5.95 children 4–14.

Toronto Tours (tel. 416/869–1372) also provides one-hour boat tours of the Toronto harborfront for similar prices from mid-May through October. It also runs an informative 90-minute tour aboard a restored 1920s trolley car; the tour goes by both city halls, and through the financial district and the historic St. Lawrence area (*see* Tour Operators, *above*).

Executive Coach Services (tel. 416/740–3339) runs an impressive two-hour "Greater Toronto City Tour," with commentary. It includes the CN Tower, SkyDome, Harbourfront, the city halls, Eaton Centre, Chinatown, Yorkville, the Parliament Buildings, Casa Loma, and the University of Toronto, all in a comfortable minibus. (Cost: $25 adults, $20 children 12 and under.) The company picks up from most city hotels. (It also runs daily tours to Niagara Falls.)

Gray Line Sightseeing Bus Tours (tel. 416/594–3310) leave from the Bus Terminal (Bay and Dundas Sts.) and spend 2½ hours visiting such places as Eaton Centre, both city halls, Queen's Park, the University of Toronto, Yorkville, Ontario Place, and Casa Loma—the latter, for a full hour. Costs run about $22 for adults, $20 for senior citizens, and $16 for children under 11.

Toronto Heli-Tours, Ltd. (tel. 416/364–8653) gives you a bird's-eye view of the city and environs, day and night.

Special-Interest Tours

Antours (tel. 416/424–4403) provides several tours of Niagara-on-the-Lake, which include lunch and tickets to major performances at the Shaw Festival.

The **Bruce Trail Association** (tel. 416/690–4453) arranges day and overnight hikes around Toronto and environs.

The **Chinatown Walking Tour** (tel. 416/599–6855) strolls through the heart of North America's largest Chinatown, featuring a tea ceremony, an herbalist, and dim sum lunch.

Ghostwalk (tel. 416/690–2875) covers two centuries of ghostly folklore while visiting Toronto sights.

Great Lakes Schooner Company (tel. 416/461–3875) lets you see Toronto's skyline from the open deck of the tall ship *Challenge*, among other excursions.

The world-class Royal Ontario Museum offers **ROMWALK** (tel. 416/586–5513), with such tours as "Citadels of Wealth" and "Cabbagetown." Take a long look at Toronto's historical development, and the many steps taken to preserve its unique heritage.

Sculpture in Toronto (tel. 416/537–3627) explores the works of world-famous Canadian and international artists. The tour includes a visit to SkyDome, with its fine sculpture collection.

Sundance Balloons International Inc. (tel. 905/889–5505) takes you up and away from it all on a spectacular tour of the region in a hot-air balloon.

June–September, **Toronto Architecture Tour** (tel. 416/922–7606) offers a "Downtown Toronto Walking Tour," a two-hour tour of the area's architectural gems, including works by I. M. Pei and Ludwig Mies van der Rohe.

The **Toronto Stock Exchange** (tel. 416/947–4676) has tours of its exciting facilities at 2 PM Tuesday–Friday; it is open 9–4:30, in case you only wish to watch the trading process. Go to 2 First Canadian Place at the northeast corner of King and York streets.

Call the **Metropolitan Toronto Convention and Visitors Association** (tel. 416/203–2500 or 800/363–1990) for more information on special-interest tours.

Tipping

Restaurants. Fifteen percent of the total bill is what most waiters and waitresses expect.

Taxis. We have always found the taxi and airport limousine drivers in Toronto to be a decent, polite lot, so a tip of 10% to 15% is usually in order.

Porters and doormen. Around 50¢ a bag; $1 or more in luxury hotels.

Room service. In moderate hotels, $1 per day; in luxury hotels, $2.

American money is always welcome (a U.S. $1 tip is worth about C$1.25–C$1.35), so don't worry if you run out of Canadian money.

Smoking

Nonsmokers may be pleased to learn that Toronto's stringent "no smoking" regulations apply to all public areas, sections of most restaurants, and even in all taxis.

Lodging

Home Exchange You can find a house, apartment, or other vacation property to exchange for your own by becoming a member of a home-exchange organization, which then sends you its annual directories listing available exchanges and includes your own listing in at least one of them. Arrangements for the actual exchange are made by the two parties to it, not by the organization. For more information contact the **International Home Exchange Association** (IHEA, 41 Sutter St., Suite 1090, San Francisco, CA 94104, tel. 415/673–0347 or 800/788–2489). Principal clearinghouses include: **Homelink International** (Box 650, Key West, FL 33041, tel. 800/638–3841), with thousands of foreign and domestic listings, publishes four annual directories plus updates; the $50 membership includes your listing in one book. **Intervac International** (Box 590504, San Francisco, CA 94159, tel. 415/435–3497) has three annual directories; membership is $62, or $72 if you want to receive the directories but remain unlisted. **Loan-a-Home** (2 Park La., Apt. 6E, Mount Vernon, NY 10552, tel. 914/664–7640) specializes in long-term exchanges; there is no charge to list your home, but the directories cost $35 or $45 depending on the number you receive.

Apartment and Villa Rentals If you want a home base that's roomy enough for a family and comes with cooking facilities, a furnished rental may be the solution. It's generally cost-wise, too, although not always—some rentals are luxury properties (economical only when your party is large). Home-exchange directories do list rentals—often second homes owned by prospective house swappers—and some services search for a house or apartment for you (even a castle if that's your fancy) and handle the paperwork. Some send an illustrated catalogue and others send photographs of specific properties, sometimes at a charge; up-front registration fees may apply.

Among the companies are **Property Rentals International** (1 Park West Circle, Suite 108, Midlothian, VA 23113, tel. 804/378–6054 or 800/220–3332); **Rent-a-Home International** (7200 34th Ave. NW, Seattle, WA 98117, tel. 206/789–9377 or 800/488–7368); and **The Invented City** (*see* IHEA, *above*). **Hideaways International** (767 Islington St., Box 4433, Portsmouth, NH 03802, tel. 603/430–4433 or 800/843–4433) functions as a travel club. Membership ($99 yearly per person or family at the same address) includes two annual guides plus quarterly newsletters; rentals are arranged directly between members, not by the club staff.

Credit Cards

The following credit-card abbreviations are used: AE, American Express; D, Discover; DC, Diners Club; MC, MasterCard; V, Visa.

2 Exploring Toronto

Well, now you're in Toronto, and probably in the downtown area. It's rather confusing, isn't it? We're not talking about Avenue A, B, and C here, or 33rd, 34th, and 35th streets, either, so to begin with we're on somewhat shaky ground.

But once you establish that Lake Ontario runs along the south of the city, and that the fabulous Harbourfront Centre complex is there, as well as the ferry to the lovely Toronto Islands, you are well on your way to orienting yourself.

It's a shame to turn your back on our now-blossoming waterfront, but when you do, you meet the striking, often magnificent high-rise buildings that give Toronto so much of its skyline. Banks, banks, and banks: Yes, the church may have stood the highest and proudest in most western towns since medieval times, but today it is the god Mammon who towers over what was once called (both mockingly and with reverence) Toronto the Good. (May we remind you that there were no movies shown on Sundays until the late 1950s and no Sunday newspapers until the late 1970s.)

Every one of the major banks of Canada, which are far wealthier and more powerful than most of their U.S. counterparts, has its headquarters in downtown Toronto, between University Avenue and Yonge Street.

This preoccupation with massive buildings first expressed itself in the black 54-story tower of the **Toronto-Dominion Bank** (T-D Centre), designed by the justly admired German-American architect Mies van der Rohe. There are four towers there now, eclipsed by I. M. Pei's silver and mirrorlike **Bank of Commerce** building, right across the street.

Only a few years later—and only a few feet away—came the **Bank of Montreal**'s tower, covered with handsome marble and now holder of the title "Tallest Building in the Whole British Commonwealth." In the end, Toronto's most stunning bank building would be not the tallest but the most extraordinary: the **Royal Bank Building,** designed by the very gifted Torontonian Boris Zerafa. Born in Cairo to parents of Italian and English descent—which is late 20th-century Toronto in a nutshell—Zerafa is also the designer of Toronto's Richmond–Adelaide Centre, and his firm of Webb Zerafa Menkes & Housden designed the fascinating **Scotiabank Tower,** which opened in 1989.

Although the Scotiabank Tower's architecture is impressive it would be hard to beat the Royal Bank for sheer beauty. Its golden exterior, coated with fully 2,500 ounces of real gold (purchased when it was only $100 an ounce) in order to keep the heat in and the cold out (or vice versa, depending on the season), truly defines the skyline of Toronto. It's "a palette of color and texture as well as mass," in Zerafa's own words; "It has a cathedral feeling, due to natural light." It is certainly worth a visit.

After seeing all the bank buildings, the next best place to get a sense of orientation would be, without doubt, the **CN Tower.** One local wag suggested that the 180-story, 130,000-ton structure was built to teach Canadian men humility. Perhaps. But for all its basic ugliness, the CN Tower is the ideal place to get a sense of the layout of Toronto. The food here is terrible, but those of you who enjoy an overpriced drink now and then should make a reservation and head up the tower any clear day between noon and 5.

Back on terra firma, imagine the downtown area of Toronto as a large rectangle. The southern part is, as you already know, Lake

34

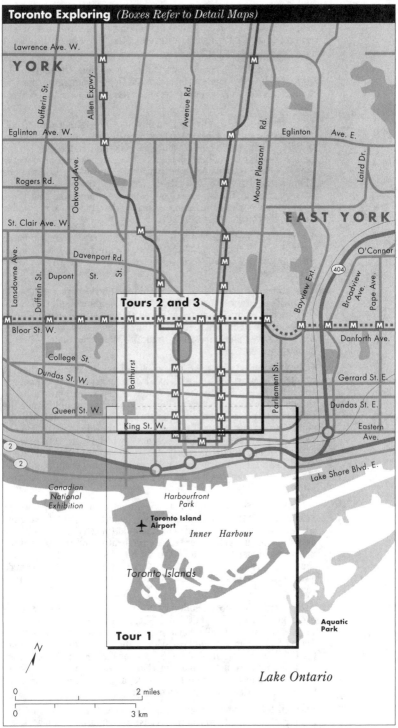

Ontario. The western part, shooting north to Bloor Street and beyond, is Spadina Road, near the foot of which stand the CN Tower, Harbourfront, and the spectacular new SkyDome Stadium. On the east, running from the lakefront north for hundreds of miles (believe it or not), is Yonge Street, which divides the city in half. University Avenue, a major road that parallels Yonge Street, for some reason changes its name to Avenue Road at the corner of Bloor Street, next to the Royal Ontario Museum. A further note: College Street, legitimately named since many of the University of Toronto's buildings run along it, becomes Carlton Street where it intersects Yonge Street, then heads east.

Tour 1: The Waterfront, St. Lawrence, the Financial District, and the Underground City

Numbers in the margin correspond to points of interest on the Tour 1 map.

Since, as we noted, Toronto has a waterfront as its southernmost border, it seems logical that we begin there. And it shouldn't be too hard to get there, since it's just south of Union Station. Unfortunately, only a handful of the city's major north–south streets—Bay, Jarvis, and York streets—go right to Lake Ontario from the city center. A new streetcar line between Union Station and the lakefront came into operation in the summer of 1990. It stops at Harbourfront, and continues on westward to Spadina Avenue, before looping back to Union Station—which is the beautiful terminus of both the University and Yonge north–south subway lines, and where trains leave for Stratford, Niagara-on-the-Lake, and Niagara Falls. The very fact that this new streetcar line was built at all underlines civic awareness of the growing importance of the central waterfront, both residentially and recreationally.

It was not always thus. Indeed, until quite recently, Toronto was notoriously negligent about its waterfront. The Gardiner Expressway, Lakeshore Boulevard, and a network of rusty rail yards stood as hideous barriers to the natural beauty of Lake Ontario. The city wished it could drop the expressway underground, but an estimated cost of several billion dollars put a rapid halt to that discussion.

Well over a decade ago, thank heaven, the various levels of government—city, metropolitan, provincial (Ontario), and federal (Ottawa)—began a struggle to change this unfortunate situation. By that time, most of the area just south of the Gardiner Expressway and Lakeshore Boulevard was overflowing with grain silos, various warehouses, and most unattractive (and unsweet-smelling) towers of malt, used by local breweries.

Part of the answer was the building of a handsome hotel, the Harbour Castle Westin (which, until the fall of 1987, was a Hilton hotel), and an attractive tower of condominiums. The hotel has an exterior, glassed-in elevator that offers guests a view of the waterfront and the Toronto Islands.

Toronto Islands ❶ Just behind the giant Harbour Castle Westin is the embarkation point for ferries to the **Toronto Islands,** surely one of the highlights of any trip to the city—especially from May to October. It takes only eight minutes for the quaint little ferries to chug across the tiny bay. The islands make up one of the world's great parks.

The four thin, curved, tree-lined islands—Centre, Ward's, Algonquin, and Hanlan's Point—have been attracting visitors since 1833, four years before Victoria became queen and just a year before the

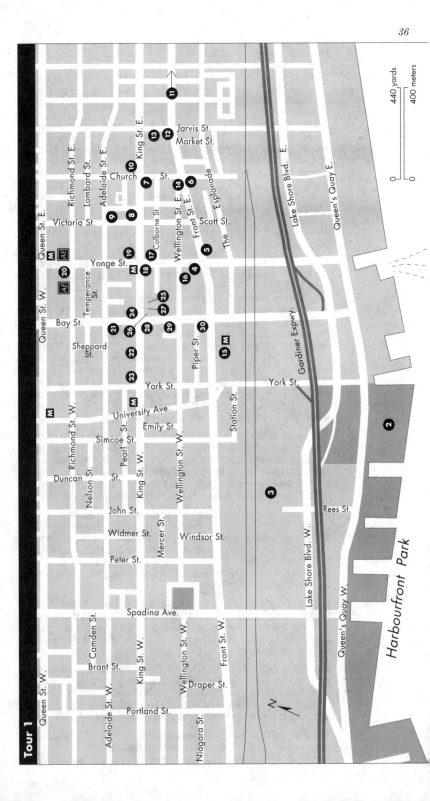

Tour 1

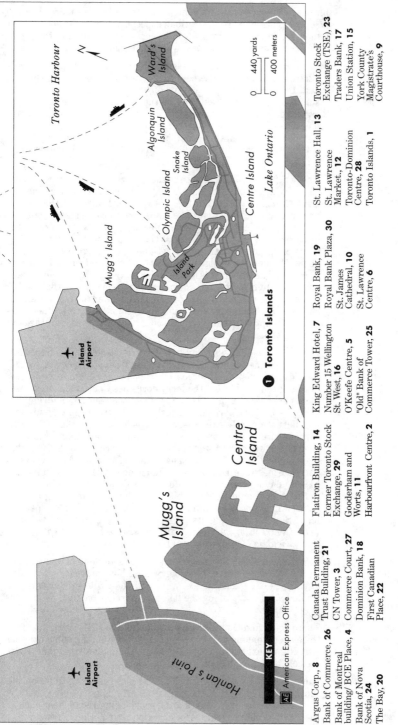

1 Toronto Islands

Argus Corp., **8**
Bank of Commerce, **26**
Bank of Montreal building/BCE Place, **4**
Bank of Nova Scotia, **24**
The Bay, **20**

Canada Permanent Trust Building, **21**
CN Tower, **3**
Commerce Court, **27**
Dominion Bank, **18**
First Canadian Place, **22**

Flatiron Building, **14**
Former Toronto Stock Exchange, **29**
Gooderham and Worts, **11**
Harbourfront Centre, **2**

King Edward Hotel, **7**
Number 15 Wellington St. West, **16**
O'Keefe Centre, **5**
"Old" Bank of Commerce Tower, **25**

Royal Bank, **19**
Royal Bank Plaza, **30**
St. James Cathedral, **10**
St. Lawrence Centre, **6**

St. Lawrence Hall, **13**
St. Lawrence Market, **12**
Toronto-Dominion Centre, **28**
Toronto Islands, **1**

Toronto Stock Exchange (TSE), **23**
Traders Bank, **17**
Union Station, **15**
York County Magistrate's Courthouse, **9**

KEY

AE American Express Office

town of York changed its name to Toronto. And the more than 550 acres of parkland are irresistible, especially during the hot summer months, when downtown Toronto seems to be melting as rapidly as the ice cream cones sold everywhere on the islands.

Be warned: The crowds always head to Centre Island, since that's where most of the amusements are located. It gets so crowded, in fact, that no bicycles are allowed on the ferry to that island during summer weekends. Take one of the equally frequent ferries to Ward's or Hanlan's, both of which are quiet, delightful places to picnic, sunbathe, read under a tree, or simply escape the city. You'll enjoy spectacular views of Toronto's majestic skyline, especially as the setting sun turns the Royal Bank Tower and other downtown skyscrapers to gold, silver, and bronze.

The beaches on Ward's tend to be the least crowded. They're also the cleanest, although there have been problems with the cleanliness of Lake Ontario's water over the past decade. Except for the hottest days in August, the Great Lake tends to be uncomfortably chilly, so bring appropriate clothing. You'll be wise to rent a bike for an hour or more and work your way across the interconnected islands. (Students of the petty politics of the petit bourgeois might enjoy hearing about the endless controversy over the hundred or so homes on Ward's and neighboring Algonquin Island that many city politicians have been fighting to tear down for years. Some argue that having people living in a much-used park makes it safer to visit; others insist that the "squatters" are using up precious parkland. Whoever is "right," it appears that the homes on the islands are safe for the next decade, at least.)

If you are traveling with children, Centre Island is the one to check out first. Signs everywhere read "Please Walk on the Grass," which should charm visitors to pieces, even before they begin to explore. A few hundred yards from the ferry docks lies **Centreville,** an amusement park that's supposed to be a turn-of-the-century children's village. The concept works wondrously well: True, the pizza, fries, and hot dogs are barely edible—pack a lunch!—but on the little Main Street there are charming shops, a town hall, a little railroad station, and more than a dozen rides, including a restored 1890s merry-go-round with over half a dozen hand-carved animals. And there's no entrance fee to the modest, 14-acre amusement park, although you'll have to pay a nominal charge for each ride or buy an all-day pass. Perhaps most enjoyable for children is the free **Far Enough Farm,** which is near enough to walk to. It has all kinds of animals to pet and feed, ranging from piglets to geese, cows to birds. *Tel. 416/363-1112. Centreville: open weekends Apr. 30–May 15 and Sept. 10–25; daily Victoria Day (mid-May)–Labor Day.*

All transportation on these islands comes to you compliments of your feet: No cars are allowed anywhere. Your nostrils will wonder at the lack of exhaust fumes, while your feet will wonder why you walked all the way along the boardwalk from Centre to Ward's Island (1.5 mi).

There you'll find **Gibraltar Lighthouse,** built back in 1808, making it the oldest monument in the city that is still standing on its original site. Right next to it is a pond stocked with rainbow trout, and a concession for buying bait and renting rods.

Sandy beaches circle the islands, the best ones being those on the southeast tip of Ward's, the southernmost edge of Centre, and the west side of Hanlan's. There are free changing rooms near each of these areas, but no facilities for checking your clothes. Swimming in the various lagoons and channels is prohibited. The winter can be bitter cold on the island, but snowshoeing and cross-country skiing with downtown Toronto over your shoulder will be irresistible to many. In the summer, there are rowboat and canoe rentals, tennis courts, gardens, playgrounds, and a wildlife sanctuary.

The ferries run irregularly during the winter: every hour or so until 10 or 11 AM, and then every few hours thereafter. In the summer, from early June to Labor Day, ferries leave from the foot of Bay Street every half-hour from 8 AM to 4 PM, Monday to Friday, to Ward's Island and Hanlan's Point; they leave to the more popular Centre Island every 15 minutes, from 10 AM to 10 PM.

On summer weekends, ferries leave every 15 minutes to Centre Island as usual, but switch to every 45 minutes after 10 PM until 11:30 PM. Ferries to both Ward's Island and Hanlan's Point depart every half-hour from 11 AM–6:30 PM and every 45 minutes from 7 PM to 11:30 PM.

The cost one-way is $3 adults, $1.50 senior citizens and students, $1 children under 15. For a recording, giving the schedule and prices, call 416/392–8193; for other information, call 416/392–8186.

Harbourfront Centre ❷ Back at the ferry docks on the mainland, your next move should be to **Harbourfront Centre.** This is a trip that is well worth planning ahead—check *Now, eye,* and *Toronto Life* magazines, as well as daily newspaper listings, to see what concerts, dances, art shows, festivals, etc., are taking place there, and build your visit around them.

For many years, as we said, Toronto had good reason to be ashamed of its God-given, man-taken-away waterfront. Today Harbourfront Centre has become a 100-acre culture-and-recreation center, drawing over 3 million visitors each year. Stretching from just west of the Harbour Castle Westin for nearly a mile to Bathurst Street, the complex has become the scene of fabulous entertainment, exquisite buildings, glorious attractions—a true match for San Francisco's Pier 39 and Baltimore's Inner Harbor. Sadly, there have been numerous problems with funding this wonderful concept: All three levels of government—federal, provincial, and local—are fighting over who should pay and what may have to be closed. Still, even if some of the attractions are lost in the bureaucracy, this is still one of the highlights of Toronto.

Highlights are many. The **Queen's Quay** (pronounced "key") **Terminal** is a must: The 57-year-old food warehouse was transformed in 1983, at a cost of over $60 million, into a magnificent eight-story structure with delightful specialty shops, eateries, and the handsome 450-seat Premiere Dance Theatre. The very popular **Harbourfront Antique Market** takes place every day but Monday. The approximately 70 dealers may triple in number each Sunday. *390 Queens Quay W, at the northeast corner of Queen's Quay and Spadina, tel. 416/260–2626. Open Tues.–Fri. 11–6, Sat. 10–6, Sun. 8–6.*

Contemporary art exhibits of painting and sculpture, architecture and video, photography and design, now take place at the **Power Plant,** just west of Queen's Quay. (The building started in 1927 as a power station for an ice-making plant; you can spot it by the tall red smokestack.)

York Quay Centre has concerts, live theater, readings, even skilled artisans at work in open craft studios. A shallow pond at the south end is used for canoe lessons in warmer months, and as the largest artificial ice-skating rink in North America in more wintry times.

The Nautical Centre nearby has many private firms offering lessons in sailing and canoeing, and vessels for rent.

Here are some of the seasonal highlights: *Late January:* an Ice Canoe Race. *February:* two weekends of Winterfest. *April:* an Easter program. *May:* the Milk International Children's Festival and the Canoe Festival. *June:* a Jazz Festival. *July:* Canada Day celebrations and a Parade of Lights. *August:* the Zingy Dingy Boat Race and Teddy Bears Fair. *September:* a youth-oriented Labor Day weekend. *October:* the world-acclaimed Authors' Festival, a Harvest Festival, and Francophone Week. *November:* the Swedish Christmas Fair. *December:* Festive Trees, the Cavalcade of Lights, and a New Year's Eve Party.

Harbourfront Centre is within walking distance of Union Station. Drivers should head for the foot of Bay Street or Spadina Avenue and park in one of the many lots. For information on the Queen's Quay stores, call 416/203–0510; the Harbourfront Centre Hotline, listing all events happening at the Centre, is 416/973–3000. There's now a streetcar that swings around from Union Station to Harbourfront Centre, and on to Spadina Avenue. If you take a subway to Union Station, you don't need a transfer; just look for signs for the free streetcar to Harbourfront.

❸ From Harbourfront Centre, it's a short walk to the **CN Tower,** an attraction second only to Eaton Centre.

The CN Tower, the tallest free-standing structure in the world, is tall with a cause: So many high buildings had been built over the past few decades that lower radio and TV transmission towers were having trouble broadcasting over them.

And so the tower stands, rather arrogantly, on Front Street near Spadina Avenue, not far from the waterfront. It's fully 1,815 feet, 5 inches high and it really is worth a visit, *if the weather is clear.* And it's in the *Guinness Book of World Records.*

Four elevators zoom up the outside of the $57 million tower, which weighs 130,000 tons and contains enough concrete to build a curb along Highway 401 from Toronto to Kingston, some 163 miles to the west. The ride takes but a minute, going at 20 feet a second, a rate of ascent similar to that of a jet-plane takeoff. But each elevator has only one floor-to-ceiling glass wall, preventing vertigo.

The **Skypod,** about two-thirds up the tower, is seven stories high, and it has two observation decks, a nightclub, and a revolving restaurant. It also has oodles of microwave equipment that is not open to the public but is its true *raison d'être.*

Level 2 is the **outdoor observation deck,** with an enclosed promenade, and an outdoor balcony for looking straight down at the ground. Level 3 of the Skypod, the **indoor observation deck,** has not only conventional telescopes, but high-powered peritelescopes that almost simulate flight. Also here is a unique Tour Wand System, which provides an audio tour of the city of Toronto. A minitheater shows a presentation on the CN Tower.

The **Space Deck,** which is 33 stories higher, costs around $2.25 extra; at an elevation of 1,465 feet, it is the world's highest public observation gallery. But even from the Skypod below, you can often see Lake Simcoe to the north, and the mist rising from Niagara Falls to the south. All the decks provide spectacular panoramic views of Toronto, Lake Ontario, and the Toronto Islands.

CN Tower, 301 Front St. W, tel. 416/360–8500. Observation deck $12 adults, $8 senior citizens and children 13–16, $6 children 5–12, children under 5 free. Peak visiting hours: between 11 AM and 4 PM, especially on weekends. Open summers, Mon.–Sat. 9 AM–midnight, Sun. 10–10; for the rest of the year, Sun.–Thurs. 10–10, Fri. and Sat. 10 AM–11 PM.

After a decade of a quite charming simulated space-shuttle journey to other planets, two new attractions opened at the base of CN Tower in mid-1994. **MindWarp Theatre** ("reality with a twist") begins with a witty video starring a manic magician and concludes with "Devil's Mine Ride," an award-winning video adventure that takes you up and down an abandoned mine shaft. *Admission: $8 adults, $6 children 4–12. Combination ticket packages (with the CN Tower) are available.*

The other new presentation is **Q-ZAR,** "the futuristic live-action laser game," in which you try to seek, find, and deactivate opposing team members for points, using the world's most advanced laser equipment. *Tel. 416/360–8500 for more information. Admission: same as for MindWarp, above.*

St. Lawrence From Harbourfront Centre and the CN Tower, you may wish to experience the area of **St. Lawrence,** where the 19th century meets the 21st, before you head back into the 20th century of the financial district. Back when the city fathers divided up the city, in 1834, they gave each district a saint's name. They christened the area that lay farthest to the south, extending from the lake up to King Street and from Yonge Street east to Parliament, St. Lawrence.

Much like the waterfront before Harbourfront Centre, it was for years a depressing, tacky section of old, dirty buildings, factories, and railway tracks. But like so many parts of this city, it has been born again, as any area with a saint's name should be capable of doing.

During any walk through the St. Lawrence area, you will jog between the centuries: from strikingly beautiful, centuries-old buildings to the new St. Lawrence project, just south of the Esplanade, designed to house close to 10,000 people. It's part of Toronto's genius, this peaceful coexistence of classy condominiums and low-cost (alias subsidized) housing. No, downtowns do not necessarily have to be dead, dirty, and dangerous.

This area is where Toronto began, as the village of York, back in 1793. Start at the northwest corner of Yonge and Front streets at the **Bank of Montreal building,** an early example of ostentatious bank architecture. Built in the mid-1880s by the architects Darling & Curry, it is a significant city landmark. Note the richly carved Ohio stone, and don't miss the Hermes figure supporting the chimney near the back of the building. It's a beauty. Be sure to walk through the Galleria of **BCE Place,** a modern complex built around this magnificent heritage building and now the home of the wildly popular **Hockey Hall of Fame** (*see* Sightseeing Checklists, *below*). The new complex stretches from Front Street up to Wellington Street and from Yonge Street over to Bay Street.

On the southeast corner of Yonge and Front streets is one of the major showcases for live theater, opera, and ballet in the city: the gigantic **O'Keefe Centre.** Another block east, at the corner of Church Street, is the two-theater complex of the **St. Lawrence Centre,** which has a number of repertory companies and many concerts year-round (*see* Concert Halls and Theaters in Chapter 7).

❼ Walk up to King Street and admire the attractive (and ritzy) **King Edward Hotel,** built in 1903 and recently refurbished in grand fashion. Note the details both inside and out; the architect was none other than E. J. Lennox, who also designed Old City Hall, Massey Hall, and Casa Loma.

Looking north from King Street, on the west side of Toronto Street, **❽** is the very understated head office of **Argus Corporation,** one of Canada's major conglomerates. It was originally built in 1853 as a **❾** post office. Still farther to the north is the **York County Magistrate's Courthouse,** built in 1852 and restored in 1982.

❿ At the corner of Church and King streets stands **St. James Cathedral** (Anglican), with its noble, gothic spires. The steeple is the tallest in Canada—even if the bank towers dwarf it now—and its illuminated spire clock once guided ships into the harbor (which was once far closer; everything south of Front Street is landfill). This is the fourth St. James Cathedral on this site; the third one burned down in the Great Fire of 1849.

Continue east to Trinity Street and walk south. The first distillery **⓫** in Canada—**Gooderham and Worts**—celebrated its 185th birthday in 1987. The massive limestone building is still used today to make rum spirits from molasses. The brothers-in-law started their company as a flour mill but soon began making alcohol out of the surplus grain.

Return along Front Street to the corner of Jarvis Street. There it **⓬** is—the **St. Lawrence Market.** Built in 1844 as Toronto's first city hall (what other city has four extant?), it now has an exhibition hall upstairs where the original council chambers stood. It continues to serve the citizens of the city, although in a more delicious fashion— as a food market. It grew up around the city hall at the turn of the century. (Who says governments never produce anything?)

Renovated in 1978, the market is renowned for its wide range of foods—from kiwi fruit to Ontario cheddar, from homemade bread to conch meat. Its four dozen stalls are open each Tuesday through Saturday, and are an ideal place to create lunches for the Metro Zoo, Canada's Wonderland, or the nearby Toronto Islands—three places where the excellence of the attractions in no way guarantees excellence in cuisine.

The plain brick building just across Front Street, on the north side, is another superb farmer's market, but it is open only on Saturdays. As early as 4 AM, the finest produce from farms just north of Toronto pours into this cornucopia.

Walk just behind the market, one block north, and you'll find, on the south side of King Street, another treasure: the second city hall of To- **⓭** ronto, today called **St. Lawrence Hall.** This is Victorian architecture at its finest (built in 1850). Erected originally for musical performances and balls, this is where Jenny Lind sang and where P. T. Barnum first presented the midget Tom Thumb. For the last several years, it has been the home of the National Ballet of Canada. Take time to admire its interior and its exterior; it is an architectural gem.

Back on Front Street, heading west toward Yonge Street and the heart of downtown, you'll encounter a building that has relatives in **⓮** pie-shaped lots all over North America—the **Flatiron Building.** There it stands, on the little triangle of Wellington, Church, and Front streets. It was erected in 1892 as the head office of the

Gooderham and Worts distilling company, and it is now a prestigious office building. You may wish to take a ride in its original elevator.

One more treat before we head into Toronto's financial district: As you walk west along the sweet little park that sits behind the Flatiron Building, look back at the witty mural by Derek Besant (on the west side of the Flatiron Building). It's a giant painting of a painting of windows, drawn around the real windows of the structure; it looks as though it's been tacked up on the wall and is peeling off. It plays tricks with your eyes, makes children and adults giggle, and is a pleasant way to end your walk through St. Lawrence.

Financial One doesn't always recommend visits to a train station, but **Union**
District **Station** is special. On the south side of Front Street, between Bay
⓯ and York streets (and across from the handsome Royal York Hotel), Union Station is a most historic building, though it is of this century. It was designed back in 1907, when trains were still as exciting as space shuttles are today, and it was opened in 1927 by the Prince of Wales. As the popular historian Pierre Berton has written, its planning recalls "the love lavished on medieval churches." Of course, the latter used to take centuries to build; this shrine to Our Lady of the Train was put up in less than two decades.

Put up? More like erected. Established. Created. Try to imagine the awe of the immigrants who poured into Toronto between the two world wars by the tens of thousands, staring up at the towering ceiling of Italian tile or leaning against one of the 22 pillars, each one 40 feet tall and weighing 75 tons. Walk along the lengthy concourse and study the mellow reflection in its walls. Get a sense of the beauty of the light flooding through the high, arched windows at each end of the mammoth hall.

When you look up, you almost expect to see a rose window; instead, you can read the names of the towns and cities of Canada that were served by the two railroads that used Union Station when it first opened. Many of those places are no longer served by trains, which take too long in a world that now seems to travel at the speed of light. That the remarkable structure still remains, its trains (and, more recently, hundreds of very modern subway cars) still chugging back and forth several levels below its glorious canopy, is no thanks to the many local politicians of the 1970s who wanted it torn down. But once again, Torontonians rallied, petitioned, and won the day.

As you come out of Union Station, walk back to Yonge Street and the beautiful **Bank of Montreal** building, at the northwest corner of Front Street. Just steps north of it is a shabby row of shops, which are among the oldest surviving commercial buildings in the city. Many of the original Georgian facades have been drastically altered, but the one- and two-story buildings give you a sense of the scale of buildings from the 1850s and are the last remnants of the early business community of the then brand-new city of Toronto. In 1993, the striking, giant **BCE Place** was built around and above the old bank.

Make a left turn at the first intersection, which is Wellington Street
⓰ West. **Number 15** is the oldest building on this walk, an elegant stone bank designed in the Greek Revival style. It's one of the earliest (1845) projects of William Thomas, the talented architect who also designed the St. Lawrence Hall, which we recently visited.

Head back a few steps to Yonge Street and go north again, away from Front Street. On the northeast corner of Yonge and Melinda
⓱ streets, at 67 Yonge Street, is **Traders Bank,** the first "skyscraper" of the city when it went up in 1905–06, complete with an observation

deck. It's fun to see what was considered the CN Tower of the turn of the century. The next building to the north (69 Yonge St.) was built in 1913, and it helped turn the intersection into a grouping of the tallest buildings in North America, outside of Manhattan. After more than 75 years, it is still owned by **Canadian Pacific,** the largest private employer in Canada (planes, trains, hotels, and more).

⑱ Just across the street, at the southwest corner of King and Yonge streets, is the **Dominion Bank** building (1 King St. W), erected in 1913 by the same architects who designed the voluptuous Bank of Montreal building we saw at Yonge and Front streets. It's a classic Chicago-style skyscraper and is well worth a visit inside. Climb the marble-and-bronze stairway to the opulent banking hall on the second floor, and enjoy the marble floor, marble walls, and the ornate plaster ceiling, which features the coats of arms of the then nine Canadian provinces. (Newfoundland did not join the Confederation until 1949). No, they most certainly do not build places like this anymore.

⑲ On the northeast corner of Yonge and King streets (2 King St. E) is the original **Royal Bank** building, also put up in 1913. Note the distinctive cornice, the overhanging roof, the decorative pattern of sculpted ox skulls above the ground-floor windows, and the classically detailed leaves at the top of the Corinthian columns. Greek culture lives!

Walking several blocks farther north along Yonge Street, you reach the original Simpsons department store, on the northwest corner of Richmond Street West and Yonge Street (176 Yonge St.). In the fall of 1991, Simpsons was bought by The Hudson Bay Company; it is ⑳ now called **The Bay.** Built in 1895, it was one of the city's first buildings with a steel-frame construction. There are attractive terracotta decorations in the section closest to Yonge Street, which went up in 1908; the part along Richmond Street, near Bay Street, added in 1928, is a fine example of the Art Deco style, popular between the two world wars.

Continue a few steps west to Bay Street, a name synonymous with finance and power in Canada, as Wall Street is in the United States. Head south (left), back toward the lakefront. Just south of Adelaide ㉑ Street, on the west side of Bay Street, is the **Canada Permanent Trust Building** (320 Bay St.). Built in the very year of the stock-market crash (and we don't mean the 1987 one), it's a skyscraper in the New York wedding-cake style. Look up at the ornate stone carvings both on the lower stories and on the top, where carved, stylized faces peer down to the street below. Walk through the imposing vaulted entrance with its polished brass doors, and note that even the elevator doors in the foyer are embossed brass. The spacious banking hall has a vaulted ceiling, marble walls and pillars, and a marble floor with mosaic borders. Those were the days—or so they thought.

Turn right (west) along King Street, and you arrive at the first of the towering bank buildings that have defined Toronto's skyline over ㉒ the past two decades. This is **First Canadian Place** (100 King St. W), built in the early 1970s by the firm of Bregman and Hamann, architects, with consultation from Edward Durrell Stone. Also called the Bank of Montreal tower, its 72 stories were deliberately faced with white marble to contrast with the black of the Toronto-Dominion Centre, to the south, and with the silver of the Commerce Court Tower. The second phase of the project, opened in 1983, houses the ㉓ ultramodern **Toronto Stock Exchange (TSE).**

The Exchange Tower (2 First Canadian Pl.) has a Visitors' Center that should be visited by anyone interested in the world of high finance. Enter the Exchange Tower and proceed to the TSE reception area on the ground floor. The nearby escalator and circular staircase lead to the Visitors' Center and observation gallery.

This is the pulse of the Canadian economy, where papers fly, traders scoot about, tickers tick away, phones ring off the hooks, and fortunes are made or lost. Here, visitors can learn about the securities industry through colorful displays, or even join in daily presentations. The attractions are many: a 100-foot public gallery, a 140-seat auditorium, recorded tours, a wall show of the TSE 300 Composite Index (an echo of the Dow Jones Average). *Tel. 416/947–4670. Admission free. Public tour daily at 2 PM. Open weekdays 9:30–4.*

㉔ On the northeast corner of King and Bay streets (44 King St. W) is the **Bank of Nova Scotia.** Built between 1949 and 1951, and partially replaced by the recently completed ScotiaBank Tower just to the east, it has sculptural panels inspired by Greek mythology above the large, exterior windows. In the lobby, there are reliefs symbolizing four regions of Canada and a brightly colored gilded plaster ceiling. The original stainless steel and glass stairway with marine motifs is attractive, as are the marble counters and floors. The north wall relief depicts some of the industries and enterprises financed by the bank.

㉕ On the southeast corner of King and Bay streets is the **"Old" Bank of Commerce Tower,** which for a third of a century was the tallest building in the British Commonwealth. Its base has bas-relief carvings, and marvelous animal and floral ornamentation around the vaulted entrance. Because the top is set back, you must look up to see the huge, carved human heads on all four sides of the building. These are "the wise old men of commerce," who are supposed to be looking out over the city.

㉖ The **Bank of Commerce** building (25 King St. W) was built in the two years following the stock-market crash of 1929, but the hard times didn't prevent the creation of a stunning interior of marble floors, limestone walls, and bronze vestibule doors decorated with masks, owls, and animals. In the alcoves on either side of the entrance are murals that trace the history of transportation. The bronze elevator doors are richly decorated, the vaulted banking hall is lit by period chandeliers, and each desk has its own lamp. What a difference from the often cold, brittle skyscrapers of today!

㉗ Just south of the "old tower," at 243 Bay Street, is **Commerce Court,** the bank's 57-story stainless-steel sister. And due west, just across Bay Street, also on the south side of King Street, are the two black
㉘ towers of the **Toronto-Dominion Centre,** the first international-style skyscrapers built in Toronto, thanks to the "less is more" man, Mies van der Rohe. The two towers went up in the mid-1960s, and they are starkly plain and stripped of ornament. The only decoration consists of geometric repetition and the only extravagance is the use of rich materials, such as marble counters and leather-covered furniture.

㉙ Immediately south of the T-D Centre towers, at 232 Bay Street, is the **former Toronto Stock Exchange** building, which, for close to half a century, was the financial hub of Toronto. Built in 1937 of polished pink granite and smooth buff limestone, it's a delightful example of Art Deco design. The stainless steel doors are a wonder, as is the wise and witty stone frieze carved above them. Don't miss the hilarious social commentary up there—the banker with the top hat marching behind the laborer, his hand sneaking into the worker's pocket. Only in Canada, where socialism has always been a strong political force, would you find such an artistic statement on the side of a stock exchange.

Walk south another block, still heading toward Lake Ontario, to the northwest corner of Bay and Front streets: There, in all its golden **30** glory, is the **Royal Bank Plaza,** built only in 1976 but already a classic of its kind. Be sure to go into the 120-foot-high banking hall and admire the lovely hanging sculpture by Jesús Raphaél Soto.

And there you have our tour of the waterfront, St. Lawrence, and the financial district, which could take anywhere from several hours to one or two days, depending on whether or not you head off to the Toronto Islands, spend several hours shopping at Harbourfront Centre, or catch some theater and meals along the way. But in all three portions of this walk, you have encountered what makes Toronto so admirable: the coexistence of the city's oldest and newest buildings, often side by side. The fact that many of the older properties have been included on the city's Inventory of Buildings of Architectural and Historical Importance proves just how determined Toronto is not to destroy its history. Only two cheers, though. There was massive destruction of great 19th-century buildings throughout the first quarter of this century; many of their still-striking facades, porticoes, and columns can be seen on the grounds of the Guild Inn, in Scarborough, about a half-hour's drive to the northeast of downtown Toronto (*see* Off the Beaten Track in Chapter 6).

If you cross Front Street to its south side and return to Union Station, you can begin another rather fascinating walk—and a very welcome one, should the weather be windy, cold, snowy, slushy, or even too hot: Toronto's Underground City.

Underground The origins of Toronto's **Underground City**—purportedly the larg-
City est pedestrian walkway in the world—go back over a generation, and it somehow all came about with very little assistance from the powers that be. As each major new building went up, the respective developers kept agreeing to connect their underground shopping areas, until it finally all came together. One can walk—and shop, eat, browse, etc.—without ever seeing the light of day, from beneath Union Station to the Royal York Hotel, the Toronto-Dominion Centre, First Canadian Place, the Sheraton Centre, The Bay, the Eaton Centre, and the Atrium. Altogether, it extends through nearly 3 miles of tunnels and seven subway stops. But these are not the depressing, even dangerous subway tunnels that one encounters in Paris, London, and New York; they are sparklingly clean, and the underground is wall-to-wall with more than 300 eateries, shops, banks, even dental offices and theaters.

One can respond with civic pride ("The world's only weather-proof city!" "The ultimate in climate control!") or with cynicism, echoing King Lear's lament over Cordelia: "Why should cars and animals have fresh air while we are forced to live, breathe, and shop underground?" But one is *not* forced, which is part of the Underground City's charm. Shop along the main streets of Toronto as you wish—but isn't it nice to know that there's a subterranean complex, running for dozens of blocks, just a few feet below you? And with Toronto's weather—so often inclement—it's kind of an insurance policy against sudden or insistent storms, or merely the exhaust fumes of cars.

The Underground City has been called a must-see for visitors, but that's debatable; Toronto overflows with attractions and first-class shopping that it's hard to recommend that one rush "downstairs."

And, indeed, there are numerous other, but far smaller, underground retail passageways: beneath Bloor Street, running east of Yonge Street; and along College Street, between Yonge and Bay streets. There are offshoots of the Underground City reaching all the way to the New City Hall and beyond. Enter the subterranean community from anywhere between Dundas Street on the north and Union Station on the south, and you'll encounter everything from art exhibitions to buskers (the city actually auditions young musicians and licenses the best to perform throughout its subway system and elsewhere) to walkways, fountains, and trees growing as much as two stories high. Because up to 50% of the complex lies underneath Toronto's multibillion-dollar financial district, you will keep bumping into men and women in business suits, browsing or on lunch breaks.

So don't see this so much as a walking tour but rather as a very pleasant option to escape sun, rain, snow, or heat. It's just another example of Toronto's architectural ingenuity—making a city that occasionally lacks a livable climate more livable.

Tour 2: From Eaton Centre to the City Halls and the Far and Middle East

Numbers in the margin correspond to points of interest on the Tours 2 and 3 map.

From the corners of Yonge and Queen streets, one can begin a tour that will include several of this city's most popular attractions, as well as some of its most interesting neighborhoods. The following walking/driving tour should make for a very pleasant day in the central and western portions of Toronto's downtown.

Eaton Centre and City Hall ❶ **Eaton Centre,** a 3-million-square-foot building that extends along the west side of Yonge Street all the way from Queen Street up to Dundas Street (with subway stops at each end), has quickly become the number one tourist attraction of Toronto. Even people who rank shopping with the flu will still be charmed, even dazzled, for this is a beautiful environment indeed.

The handsome collection of over 300 stores and services, just a few blocks from Toronto's New City Hall, was quite controversial in the late 1970s, when some Torontonians attacked it as "a sterile and artificial environment." Yet others, like Jane Jacobs, author of *Death and Life of Great American Cities,* wrote that "people like the environment of the Galleria. Its popularity has lessons for Yonge Street."

And lessons for most cities of the world, as well. From its graceful glass roof, arching 127 feet above the lowest of the mall levels, to Michael Snow's exquisite flock of fiberglass Canada geese floating poetically in the open space of the Galleria, to the glass-enclosed elevators, porthole windows, and nearly two dozen long and graceful escalators, there are plenty of good reasons for visiting Eaton Centre.

Such a wide selection of shops and eateries can be confusing, however, so here's a simple rule: Galleria Level 1 contains two food courts; popularly priced fashions; photo, electronics and record stores; and much "convenience" merchandise. Level 2 is directed to the middle-income shopper, while Level 3, suitably, has the highest elevation, fashion, and prices. **Eaton's,** one of Canada's classic department-store chains, has a nine-floor branch here. At the southern end of

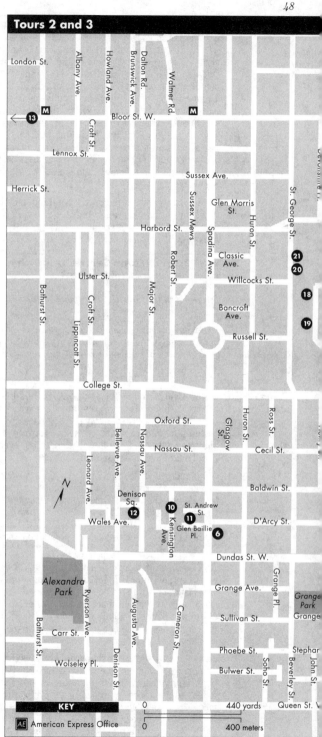

Tours 2 and 3

KEY

AE American Express Office

0   440 yards

0   400 meters

49

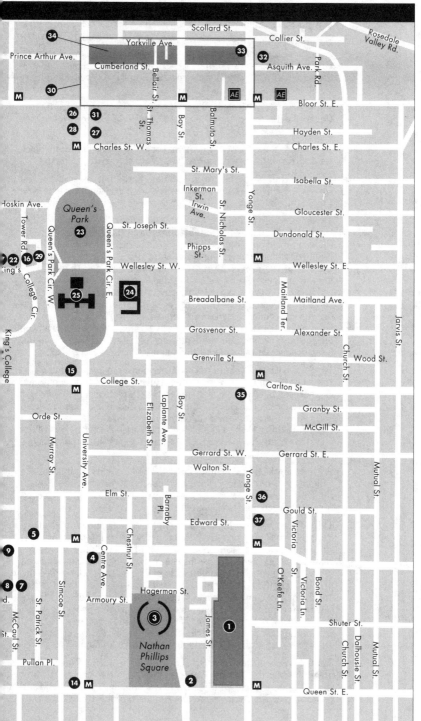

Level 3 is a skywalk that connects the centre to the seven-floor **The Bay** (formerly Simpsons) department store, across Queen Street.

Dozens of restaurants, from snack to full-service, can be found here. A 17-theater cinema complex—the initial unit of the now worldwide Cineplex chain—is located at the Dundas Street entrance. (Tuesdays are half-price days for movie tickets, and it's a cheap 90-minute break from shopping.)

There are safe, well-lighted parking garages sprinkled around the Centre, with spaces for some 1,800 cars. *Admission free. Open weekdays 10–9, Sat. 9:30–6, Sun. noon–5.*

Exit the Eaton Centre at Queen Street and walk just one long block west to Toronto's city halls. Yes, the plural is correct.

② **Old City Hall** is the beautiful building at the northeast corner of
③ Queen and Bay streets, sweetly coexisting with the futuristic **New City Hall,** just across the street, on the west side.

The creator of the old one, which opened in 1899, was none other than E. J. Lennox, who would later design Casa Loma. It was considered one of North America's most impressive municipal halls in its heyday, and since the opening of its younger sister, it has been the site of the provincial courts, county offices, and thousands of low-cost marriages. Do note the hideous gargoyles above the front steps, which were apparently the architect's witty way of mocking certain politicians of the time. The designer also carved his name under the eaves on all four faces of the building—a cry for recognition from nearly a century ago. The great stained-glass window as you enter is attractive, and the handsome old structure stands in delightful contrast to its daring and unique sibling.

The New City Hall—humorously described by many as "a urinal for the Jolly Green Giant"—was the result of a massive international competition in 1958, to which some 520 architects from 42 countries submitted designs. The winning presentation by Finnish architect Viljo Revell was controversial: two towers of differing height, and curved, yet! But there was and is a logic to it all: An aerial view of the New City Hall shows a circular council chamber sitting like an eye between the two tower "eyelids."

Within months of its opening in 1965, the New City Hall became a symbol of a thriving city, with a silhouette as recognizable as, say, the Eiffel Tower. How sad that architect Revell died before his masterwork was opened to the public.

The entire area is a living, breathing environment, with Nathan Phillips Square (named after the mayor who initiated the project) spreading across a 9-acre plaza in front of the building. It has become a true gathering place for the community, whether for royal visits, protest rallies, picnic lunches, or concerts. The reflecting pool is a delight in the summer, and even more so in the winter, when office workers come down and skate during lunch. There is a Peace Garden for quiet meditation, a striking bronze sculpture by famed British sculptor Henry Moore (*The Archer*), and a remarkable mural within the main entrance of the New City Hall, *Metropolis*, put together by sculptor David Partridge from 100,000 common nails.

Annual events at the New City Hall include the Spring Flower Show in late March; the Toronto Outdoor Art Exhibition early each July (the 34th annual one will be held in the summer of 1995); and the Cavalcade of Lights from late November through Christmas each year, when over 100,000 sparkling lights are illuminated across both city halls.

Tel. 416/392–7341 for details; for information on facilities for the disabled, 416/392–7732. Underground garage for 2,400 cars. Open to public weekdays 8:30–4:30. Free 30-minute guided tours on weekdays. Cafeteria in basement of New City Hall open daily 7:30–4.

Chinatown and the Museums Just north of the New City Hall begins Toronto's main **Chinatown,** which is the largest in all of North America—and that includes San Francisco. There are more than 100,000 Chinese living in the city, which is quite impressive, considering that just over a century ago there was only one—Sam Ching, who ran a hand laundry on Adelaide Street.

Today Chinatown covers much of the area of Spadina Avenue from Queen Street to College Street, running along Dundas Street nearly as far east as Bay Street. The old Chinatown used to be stuck behind the Old City Hall, but it was uprooted by the building of the New City Hall, and began to spread to the west. This was helped by the huge influx of Chinese immigrants, which began some two decades ago and still continues. Most come from Hong Kong, bringing money, skills, and intelligence to the already burgeoning community that had been here before.

One of the best times to explore Chinatown is on a Sunday, when, up and down Spadina Avenue and along Dundas Street, Chinese music blasts from storefronts, cash registers ring, abacuses clack, and bakeries, markets, herbalists, and restaurants do their best business of the week.

But whatever day you wander through Toronto's impressive Chinatown—we recommend that you start on Elizabeth Street, just north of the New City Hall, and walk north to Dundas Street, east toward Bay Street, and west to Spadina Avenue—you will be thrilled by the diversity, the excitement, the liveliness: the sheer foreignness of it all. (Remember the cliché: If the United States is a melting pot, Canada is a mosaic—with each piece maintaining its individuality and differences.)

On Dundas Street, you'll pass shops selling reasonably priced silk blouses and antique porcelain; silk kimonos for less than half the price elsewhere; exquisite sake sets; and women's suits made from silk. Huge Chinese characters hang over the **52nd Division police station,** a large building on the west side of University Avenue, on the south side of Dundas Street. Many of the banks still have abacuses, to help those who prefer to use 4,000-year-old "hand-held calculators" over the modern ones.

Just to the north, on St. Patrick Street, is the **Chinese Catholic Church.** Over on D'Arcy Street is the modern **Chinese home for the aged,** with charming crafts rooms, hydroponic gardens, and lots of goldfish, because an Eastern tradition has it that every time a goldfish dies, a human being is guaranteed long life.

Just to the south of Dundas Street is the **Ontario College of Art** (100 McCaul St.), one of the major institutions specializing in animation, design, advertising art, tapestry, glassblowing, sculpture, and painting in Canada. Directly across the street is **Village by the Grange** (89 McCaul St.), an apartment-and-shopping complex that contains more than a hundred shops selling everything from ethnic fast food to serious art. It's a perfect example of what more cities need in their downtown areas: a wise, careful blending of the commercial and the residential.

❾ Return to Dundas Street, and head west to the **Art Gallery of Ontario (AGO)**, which has been slowly but steadily evolving into one of the better art museums in North America. From extremely modest beginnings in 1900, the AGO is now in the big leagues in terms of exhibits and support. Its membership of over 25,000 is one of the largest among the continent's museums, and recent international exhibits of King Tut, van Gogh, Turner, Judy Chicago, William Blake, and Picasso will give you an idea of the gallery's importance, image, and profile.

In 1988, the AGO began its $28 million "Stage 3 expansion," completed in 1991. This has increased its exhibition space by nearly 50% and now includes new galleries for contemporary art, Inuit art, and an indoor sculpture court. Even before its expansion, the AGO was noted for the excellence of its art treasures.

The **Henry Moore Sculpture Centre** on the second floor has the largest public collection of the sculptor's work in the world. (Do not miss Moore's large *Two Forms*, which stands outside the AGO, at the southwest corner of McCaul Street. Adults as well as children love to climb in and around it.)

Also on the second floor is the **Samuel and Ayala Zacks Wing**, with its fine collection of 20th-century sculpture. The **Canadian Wing** includes major works by such northern lights as Emily Carr, Cornelius Krieghoff, David Milne, and Homer Watson, plus a broad selection from the Group of Seven, which is no rock group—although they *did* paint rocks—rather a group of Ontarian painters famous for developing "Canadian Impressionism." On the lower level is a hands-on room where children are invited to paint, make slides, and otherwise creatively muck about (open Sundays, summers, and holidays).

The Art Gallery of Ontario also has a growing collection of Rembrandt, Hals, Van Dyck, Hogarth, Reynolds, Chardin, Renoir, de Kooning, Rothko, Oldenburg, Picasso, Rodin, Degas, Matisse, and many others. And it also has **The Grange,** a historic house located just behind the AGO, in a large park (*see* Historic Buildings and Sites in Sightseeing Checklists, *below*). In early 1989, the AGO unveiled a new, computerized reinstallation of paintings and sketches by Tom Thomson and the Group of Seven. Installed near some of the oil sketches, there are computers and telephones that give simple messages about the paintings and related topics as well as explanatory material.

The AGO, 317 Dundas St. W, 3 blocks west of St. Patrick station of University subway line, tel. 416/979-6648. Admission: $7.50 adults, $4 senior citizens and children 12–18, children under 11 free; $15 maximum charge for families. Free Wed. 5–10; free Fri. for senior citizens. Fri. 5–10, admission is 2-for-1. Open Wed.– Sun., 10–5:30, Wed. and Fri. until 10. Closed Mon., Tues., Christmas, New Year's Day.

Across from the AGO and The Grange is Village by the Grange, as noted above. It is a perfect place to browse, either before or after a visit to the art gallery.

Check out some of the commercial art galleries on the north side of Dundas Street, across from the AGO, many of which display classical and contemporary Chinese paintings. Then head west, back through Chinatown. **Champion House** (478 Dundas St. W, near Spadina) is a good bet for lunch.

Spadina and the Marketplaces Toronto's widest street, **Spadina Avenue,** has been pronounced "Spa-*dye*-nah" for a century and a half, and we are too polite to point out that it really should be called "Spa-*dee*-na." To explain why it's 149 feet wide, double the width of almost every other vintage street in town, we have to go back to 1802, when a 27-year-old Irish physician named William Warren Baldwin came to Muddy York. He soon married a rich young woman, built a pleasant home where Casa Loma now sits, and decided to cut a giant swath through the forest from Bloor Street down to Queen Street so they could look down—literally and socially—on Lake Ontario. Alas, their view disappeared in 1874, when a thankless granddaughter sold the land at the crescent just above College Street for the site of Knox College, which moved to the University of Toronto campus several decades later. Now covered with vines, the Victorian college building still sits in the crescent, a number of the chestnut trees planted by Dr. Baldwin still standing on the west side of the crescent. Little else remains of Dr. Baldwin's Spadina, except for a handful of Victorian mansions.

Spadina, running from Queen Street north to College Street, has never been fashionable, or even worth a visit by most tourists. Way back, it was just a collection of inexpensive stores, factories that sold to you wholesale if you had connections, ethnic food and fruit stores, and eateries that gave you your 2¢ worth, usually plain.

And so it remains, with the exception of some often first-class, if modest-looking, Chinese restaurants sprinkled throughout the area. Each new wave of immigrants—Jewish, Chinese, Portuguese, East and West Indian, South American—added its own flavor to the mix, but Spadina–Kensington's basic bill of fare is still "bargains galore." Here you'll find gourmet cheeses at gourmet prices, fresh (no, not fresh-frozen) ocean fish, fine European kitchenware at half the price of stores in the Yorkville area, yards of fabric remnants piled high in bins, designer clothes minus the labels, and the occasional rock-and-roll night spot and interesting greasy spoon.

For any visitor who plans to be in Toronto for over four or five days, a few hours exploring the ins and outs of the garment district could bring great pleasure—and even greater bargains. Park your car at the lot just west of Spadina Avenue on St. Andrew's Street (a long block north of Dundas St.), or take the College or Queen streetcar to Spadina Avenue. Be warned: This area can be extraordinarily crowded on weekends, when smart suburbanites head here for top-quality luggage and handbags at unbelievably low prices; wholesale dry-goods stores overflowing with brand-name socks, underwear, and towels; designer jeans and jackets; women's evening wear, coats, sportswear, and dresses; new and used furs; and more.

We cannot resist mentioning a few of our favorites. **Fortune Housewares** (388 Spadina Ave., tel. 416/593–6999) is possibly the best kitchenware shop in Toronto. There's a good selection of cookbooks, too, and the staff is both knowledgeable and helpful. Also recommended is the new **Dragon City Food Court,** located on the southwest corner of Dundas and Spadina, where 11 independent outlets offer a variety of exotic Asian foods. It is open daily 10 AM–midnight.

⑩ And then there's **Kensington Market,** a delightful side tour off Spadina Avenue. Here, the bargains are of the more edible kind. All your senses will be titillated by this old, steamy, smelly, raucous, colorful, European-style marketplace. Come and explore, especially during warmer weather, when the goods pour out into the narrow streets: Russian rye breads, barrels of dill pickles, fresh fish on ice, mountains of cheese, bushels of ripe fruit, and crates of chickens and rabbits that will have your children both giggling and horrified.

Kensington Market sprang up just after the turn of the century, when Russian, Polish, and Jewish inhabitants set up stalls in front of their houses. Since then, the market—named after the area's major street—has become a United Nations of stores. Unlike the UN, however, these people get along fabulously with one another. Jewish and Eastern European stores sit side by side with Portuguese, Caribbean, and East Indian stores—with Vietnamese, Japanese, and Chinese establishments sprinkled throughout. Most shops are open every day except Sunday, from as early as 6 AM.

Lovers of religious architecture may wish to visit the two hauntingly ⑪ attractive old synagogues in the market area: **Anshei Minsk** (10 St. Andrew's St., just west of Spadina Ave.) and, just a few short blocks ⑫ away, the **Kiever Synagogue** (corner of Denison Sq. and Bellevue Ave.).

Afterward, you can rest in **Bellevue Square** (corner of Denison Sq. and Augusta Pl.), a lovely little park with shady trees, benches, and a wading pool and playground for kids.

⑬ **Mirvish** (or **Markham**) **Village** (*see* Shopping Districts in Chapter 3) is a small, delightful tourist area— but no tourist trap—one block west of Bathurst Street, running south from Bloor Street. It is open on Sundays.

The history is interesting: Ed Mirvish is an inspired capitalist who has run a big, ugly, barnlike bargain-basement store called **Honest Ed's** for the past four decades. The place is nothing special; Americans have its equivalent in every city (although his sheer vulgarity is disarming; the world's largest neon sign on his store screams out such sayings as "Honest Ed's no midwife . . . but the bargains he delivers are real babies"). As if to make up for the crudeness of his selling techniques (which include daily "door crashers," such as five pounds of white flour for 79¢), Mirvish saved the magnificent Royal Alexandra Theatre from destruction, and he even decided to purchase the venerable Old Vic, in London, England. When Mirvish tried to tear down all the houses on the block behind his store to build a parking lot, he was prevented by zoning bylaws. No problem: He thought up the brilliant alternative of Mirvish, or Markham, Village. By officially being declared a tourist attraction, the village could legally be open on Sundays; and so, though it is in the unfashionable Bloor/Bathurst area, it can be a lifesaver for weekend visitors with time to kill. Most stores are open daily 10–6.

Although the wonderful **Children's Book Store** has moved to Yonge Street, north of Eglinton, there are still many joys to be discovered here. The irresistible **Memory Lane** sells vintage movie posters and old comic books and magazines. **David Mirvish Books on Art,** run by Ed's son, has many remaindered books at shockingly low prices, as well as a fine collection of new volumes.

Before you turn back to Bloor Street, note the wonderful house at the corner of Markham and Lennox streets: the hexagonal corner tower, the fine leaded-glass butterfly window to one side of its front door, and the stunning oval window on the other. This is old Toronto architecture at its most attractive.

Tour 3: Academia, Culture, Commercialism, Crassness

University Avenue, running from Front Street for about 3 miles north to Bloor Street, where it changes its name to Avenue Road and continues north, is one of Toronto's few mistakes. It's horribly boring, with hospital after office building after insurance company after office building. Yet it is still an interesting start for a healthy walk, because it does have lovely flowerbeds and fountains in a well-maintained strip along its middle. Still, you may wish to drive this part of the tour.

⑭ One highlight is **Campbell House** (northwest corner of Queen St. and University Ave.), the stately Georgian mansion of Sir William Campbell, the sixth chief justice of Upper Canada. Built in 1822 and tastefully restored with elegant 18th- and early 19th-century furniture, it is one of Toronto's most charming "living museums." Costumed guides will tell you about the social life of the upper class. Note the model of the town of York as it was in the 1820s, and the original, restored kitchen sans Cuisinart. *Tel. 416/597–0227. Admission: $2.50 adults, $1.25 students and senior citizens. Guided tours only. Open weekdays 9:30–4:30; mid-May–New Year's Day, also open weekends, noon–4:30.*

⑮ College Street is the southern boundary of the **University of Toronto.** A city the size of Toronto is too large to be labeled a college town, but with a staff and student population of more than 50,000, and over 225 buildings on three campuses, the university is almost a city in itself.

It goes back to 1827, when King George IV signed a charter for a "King's College in the Town of York, Capital of Upper Canada." The Church of England had control then, but by 1850 the college was proclaimed nondenominational, renamed the University of Toronto, and put under the control of the province. And then, in a spirit of good Christian competition, the Anglicans started Trinity College, the Methodists began Victoria, and the Roman Catholics established St. Michael's; by the time the Presbyterians founded Knox College, the whole thing was almost out of hand.

But not really: The 17 schools and faculties are now united, and they welcome anyone who can pass the entrance exams and afford the tuition, which, thanks to generous government funding, is still only about $1,500 a year.

The architecture is interesting, if uneven—any place would be, too, if it had been built in bits and pieces over 150 years. We recommend a walking tour. Enter the campus just behind the Parliament buildings, where Wellesley Street ends. Go under the bridge, past the guardhouse (whose keeper will not let you pass if you are encased in an automobile), and turn right, around King's College Circle.

⑯ At the top of the circle is **Hart House,** a Gothic-style student center built during the teens of this century by the Masseys—the folks who brought us Massey-Ferguson farm equipment, Massey Hall, Vincent Massey (a governor-general of Canada), and Raymond Massey, the actor. It was once an all-male enclave; today anyone may visit the Great Hall and the library, both self-conscious imitations of Oxford and Cambridge. Check out the dining hall for its amazing stained-glass windows as well as its food, which is inexpensive and rather good.

As you continue around King's College Circle, you'll see on your **⑰ ⑱** right the Romanesque **University College,** built in 1859. Next is **Knox**

College, whose Scottish origins are evident in the bagpipe music that escapes from the building at odd hours. It's been training ministers since 1844, although the building was put up only yesterday—1915.

 You may well wish to tip your hat to the **Medical Sciences Building,** which is no beauty but is where, in 1921, Drs. Frederick Grant Banting, Charles H. Best, and others discovered the insulin that has saved the lives of tens of millions of diabetics around the world.

 Just a few hundred yards west is St. George Street and the **Robarts Research Library,** and **Thomas Fisher Rare Books Library** (*see* Sightseeing Checklists, *below*).

There is lots more to see and do around the main campus of the University of Toronto. Visit the **Public and Community Relations Office** (Room 133S, 27 King's College Circle, tel. 416/978–2021), across the field from Hart House, and pick up free maps of the school grounds. Guided one-hour walking tours are held on summer weekdays, setting out from the map room of Hart House at 10:30, 12:30, and 2:30 (tel. 416/978–5000).

Back at College Street and University Avenue, you can see the Victorian structure of the Parliament buildings to the north, with Queen's Park just north of them.

Queen's Park   There are a number of meanings to **Queen's Park,** for the native Torontonian as well as the visitor. The term can refer to a charming circular park just a few hundred yards southeast of the Royal Ontario Museum (on University Ave., just below Bloor St.). This is a grand place to rest your feet after a long day of shopping or visiting the Royal Ontario Museum. But Queen's Park also refers to the **Ontario Legislative Building,** which is nothing less than what Albany is to New York State or Lansing is to Michigan: the home of the provincial parliament. The mammoth building was opened back in 1893 and is really quite extraordinary, with its rectangular towers, triangle roofs, and circular and oval glass. Like the New City Hall, it was the product of an international contest among architects; it was won by a young Briton who was residing in Buffalo, New York.

The **Parliament building** itself looks grotesque to some, with its pink exterior and heavy, almost Romanesque style. But a close look will show the beautifully complex detail carved in its stone, and on the inside there are huge, lovely halls that echo half a millennium of English architecture. (Its pinkness does not necessarily reflect the politics of the men and women who work within the building, by the way; that's simply the color of Ontario's sandstone.)

Do go inside; the long hallways are hung with hundreds of oils by Canadian artists, most of which capture scenes of the province's natural beauty. Should you choose to take one of the frequent (and free) tours, you will see the chamber where the 130 elected representatives from across Ontario, called MPPs (Members of Provincial Parliament), meet on a regular basis. There are two heritage rooms—one each for the parliamentary histories of Britain and Ontario—filled with old newspapers, periodicals, and pictures. And the lobby holds a fine collection of minerals and rocks of the province.

On the lawn in front of the Parliament buildings, facing College Street, are many statues, including one of Queen Victoria and one of Canada's first prime minister, Sir John A. Macdonald.

Tel. 416/325–7500. Free guided tours mid-May–Labor Day, daily on the hr 9–4; frequent tours the rest of the year. On summer week-

ends, tours are every ½ hr 9–11:30 and 1:30–4. Queen's Park can be reached via University Ave. subway; get off at College St. and walk north 1 block. If you drive, there are parking lots in the area, and meters around Queen's Park Circle.

26 Just to the northwest of Queen's Park is the world-class **Royal Ontario Museum (ROM)**. Its supporters pointed out that "ROM wasn't built in a day" during a major fund-raising effort earlier this decade. How true. Although once labeled "Canada's single greatest cultural asset" by the Canada Council, the museum floundered throughout much of its existence, which began in 1912 (the same day the *Titanic* sank). It never stopped collecting—always with brilliance—reaching more than 6 million items altogether. But by the 1970s, the monstrous building had run out of room to display its glorious treasures; its roofs had started leaking; and it was deemed necessary to install a climate-control system.

What a difference just $80 million can make! Today, at last, the museum has the space it needs, and when expansion is completed sometime in the 1990s, the ROM will be the second largest museum in North America, after New York's Metropolitan Museum of Art.

What makes the ROM unique is the fact that its science, art, and archaeology exhibits are all under one roof. The **Dinosaur Collection** will stun children and adults alike. The **Evolution Gallery** has an ongoing audiovisual program on Darwin's theories of evolution. The **Roman Gallery** has the most extensive collection of Roman artifacts in Canada. The **Textile Collection** has been ranked fifth in the world in size and scope. The collection of **Chinese art and antiquities** is one of the finest this side of Beijing. And the **European Musical Instruments Gallery** has a revolutionary audio system and over 1,200 instruments dating back to the late 16th century.

The **Discovery Gallery** allows children (7 years and older) to handle objects from the ROM's collections and to study them, using microscopes, ultraviolet light, and magnifying glasses.

The **Bat Cave,** opened in early 1988, contains 4,000 freeze-dried and artificial bats in a lifelike presentation. Piped-in narration directs visitors on a 15-minute walk through a dimly lit replica of an 8-foot-high limestone tunnel in Jamaica, filled with sounds of dripping water and bat squeaks. Yes, the dinosaurs and mummies have a new rival in popularity.

In early 1992 the ROM's brilliant **Ancient Egypt Gallery** reopened, joined by the brand-new **Nubia Gallery**—the only one in North America.

Containing fascinating exhibits that range from a massive Ming tomb to an Islamic home, from Egyptian mummies to a Buddhist temple, from a towering totem pole to suits of armor, the Royal Ontario Museum is simply fabulous. The **Mankind Discovering Gallery** tells about the museum itself and helps one choose what to see.

ROM, tel. 416/586–5549. Admission: $7 adults, $4 senior citizens and students, $3.50 children 5–14; children under 4 free. Free entry to senior citizens all day Tues. (including the Gardiner and Planetarium shows); free to the rest of the public Tues. after 4:30 PM. Open mid-May–Labor Day, Mon. and Wed.–Sat. 10–6; Tues. 10–8; Sun. 11–6. For the rest of the year, closed Mon., except Easter Mon.; closed Christmas, New Year's Day. Discovery Gallery open Sept.–June weekdays noon–4, weekends and holidays 1–5; July–Aug. weekdays 11–4. Call ahead for Discovery Gallery hours; school visits often ne-

cessitate changes in schedules. To get here, take University subway to Museum stop; parking is expensive.

㉗ The **George R. Gardiner Museum of Ceramic Art** has now merged with the ROM, meaning that it costs not a penny more to visit a magnificent $25 million collection of rare European ceramics. The collection features 17th-century English delftware and 18th-century yellow European porcelain. Most popular is the second-floor display of Italian commedia dell'arte figures, especially Harlequin. *Across the street from ROM, on the east side of University Ave., just south of Bloor St., tel. 416/586–8080. Open Tues.–Sat. 10–5, Sun. 11–5; July–Labor Day, same hours except open Tues. 10–7:30. Closed Christmas, New Year's Day.*

㉘ Next door to the ROM, to its south, is the **McLaughlin Planetarium,** which attracts more than 200,000 visitors a year. There are six new 45-minute star shows each year and thrilling laser shows. Open since 1986 is the **Astrocentre,** which has hands-on exhibits, computer terminals designed for both adults and children, and an animated model of the star system. *Planetarium (tel. 416/586–5736) has the same hours as ROM, plus evening hours for star shows. Admission: Same as the Royal Ontario Museum, above. However, admission to star shows is additional: $5.50 adults, $3.50 senior citizens and students, $2.75 children under 15. Laser shows are offered Wed., Thurs., and Sun. 8:45; Fri. and Sat. 4:15 PM, 8:45 PM, and 10:15 PM. Admission to laser show: $8.50 adults, $6.50 children 6–14 at matinees. Senior citizens free on Tues. Combined admission ticket available to ROM and planetarium, should you plan to visit both on the same day. Tel. 416/586–5751 for taped description of current night sky.*

㉙ A five-minute walk due south of the planetarium will bring you to the **Sigmund Samuel Canadiana Collection,** which is also part of the ROM and may be seen at no extra charge. Here is where you can view early Canadian furnishings, glassware, silver, and six settings of furniture displayed in typical 18th- and 19th- century homes. *14 Queen's Park Crescent W, on northwest corner of University Ave. and College St. Open Tues.–Sat. 10–5, Sun. 1–5.*

㉚ After so much culture, you may wish to enjoy one of the most dynamic and expensive areas of Toronto—**Bloor and Yorkville.** A recent article in one of Toronto's newspapers began, "If Imelda Marcos came to Toronto, she would shop on Bloor St. W. This is the home of the $1,300 loafers, the $110,000 fur coat, the $350 belt, and the $14,000 travel trunk, a chic zone where style is everything and cost is no object."

Not every store on these half-dozen-plus blocks between University Avenue and Yonge Street—and the two blocks running north and parallel to them—is so costly, but when monthly rents go above $100 per square foot, one can't sell at discount rates, can one?

When Joseph Bloor made his brewery fortune and built his family home on this street over a century ago, how was he to know that his name would become synonymous with success and high fashion? Had he known, he would never have sold an inch of his property, that's for sure.

Some call it Toronto's Rodeo Drive; others call it Toronto's Fifth Avenue. (Smug Torontonians have been known to call Fifth Avenue New York's Bloor Street, but that may be pushing it.) One thing is certain: These blocks are packed with high-price stores specializing in designer clothes, furs, jewels, specialty shops, ritzy restaurants, and more.

③ **The Colonnade,** on the south side of Bloor Street, a few doors east of University Avenue, has recently undergone a $10 million face-lift. In addition to several levels of luxury residential apartments and private offices, it also has more than two floors of stores selling quality leather goods, perfumes, jewelry, and European apparel.

Along the south side of Bloor Street are stores with haute couture designs; **Creed's,** for more than seven decades *the* place for quality furs, lingerie, shoes, etc., went bankrupt in 1990, to the shock and horror of its very wealthy patrons. Still, there is **The Bay** (at the northeast corner of Bloor and Yonge Sts.), a department store with elegant, high-fashion designer clothes for men and women; **Holt Renfrew,** possibly the most stunning store in Toronto, with marble, chrome, glass, and glittering fashions for both sexes; **Eddie Bauer,** selling sturdily made and cleverly designed clothing, equipment, and accessories for all sports; **William Ashley,** which has the finest quality china, crystal, and silver available in Canada, at competitive prices; and **David's,** with the finest footwear at the highest prices. Also catch **Hermès, Chanel,** and **Tiffany's** along this wonderful classy shopping walk. **110 Bloor Street West** (near the northeast corner of Avenue Rd. and Bloor St., almost across from The Colonnade) is a dazzling complex of condos, offices, and retail shops. The high-quality **Zoe** has moved just a short block north, to 158 Cumberland.

A block north of Bloor and Yonge streets is the magnificent **③** **Metropolitan Toronto Library.** Arranged around a tall and wide interior atrium, the library gives a fabulous sense of open space. It was designed by one of Canada's most admired architects, Raymond Moriyama, who also created the Ontario Science Centre. Among the highlights is a fascinating fabric sculpture, *Lyra,* designed by artist Aiko Suzuki. Overhanging the pool and waterfall in the foyer, it was meant to create a transition from the bustle of Yonge Street to the quiet library. It took eight months to complete—the artist walking over 250 miles back and forth in her studio to create it. Glass-enclosed elevators glide swiftly and silently up and down one side of the atrium, allowing you to admire the beautiful banners that hang from the ceiling, announcing the collections on each floor.

Browsers will appreciate that fully one third of the more than 1.3 million books—spread across 28 miles of shelves—are open to the public. The many audio carrels have headphones, which you may use to listen to any one of over 10,000 albums.

The **Arthur Conan Doyle Room** will be of special interest to Baker Street regulars. It houses the finest public collection of Holmesiana anywhere, with records, films, photos, books, manuscripts, letters, and even cartoon books starring Sherlock Hemlock of "Sesame Street." *789 Yonge St., just steps north of Bloor St., tel. 416/393–7000. Open Mon.–Thurs. 9–9, Fri. 9–6, Sat. 9–5, Sun. (Oct.–Apr.) 1:30–5. To get an answer to any question, on any subject, tel. 416/393–7131.*

Back on the east side of Avenue Road, two blocks north of Bloor Street and two blocks west of the Metro Library, is a real don't-miss **③** shopping area—**Hazelton Lanes** (416/968–8600). Offering everything from Swiss chocolates to Hermès silks and Giorgio Armani's latest fashions, this is a wonderful, magical paean to capitalism. In 1989 it doubled, in size and glory, with the addition of some 80 new stores. Here is where you'll find the glamorous **Rodier, Polo, Andrew's** (a striking mini-department store), **Messori** (men's clothing), **Vintages** (fine wine), **Valentino** (women's clothing), **Gian Franco**

Ferre (a quality Italian designer for women), and much more. And don't miss the delightful skating rink (in season) and the fine cafés.

❸❹ And then there is what is still called **Yorkville,** which runs along the street of the same name, between Avenue Road and Yonge Street, but also includes Cumberland, Bellair, Bay, Scollard, and Hazelton streets. This little gathering of low-rise buildings, mostly old Victorian town houses turned into marvelous storefronts, has gone through many changes over the years: from a conservative middle-class residential district, to the gathering place for Ontario's revolutionaries, drug pushers, hippies, runaway kids, and avant-garde artists, to what it is today—a chic, expensive shopping district. (A century ago, it was a real village, just north of Toronto, with its own town hall, planked sidewalks, and horse-drawn streetcars linking it to the city's downtown.)

All along these streets—especially Cumberland and Yorkville—you will find many of Toronto's finest commercial art galleries (*see* Sightseeing Checklists, *below*). Just to the south is the best shopping in the city (with the exception of Bloor St.).

For a sense of what all this costly beauty was like before haute couture moved in, walk along Scollard and Berryman streets, just north of Yorkville Street. The rows of Victorian houses will be a rest for your overworked eyes and pocketbooks. Should you want to experience the seedy side of this rather uptight town, simply head over to Yonge Street and walk slowly south from Bloor Street as far as you desire. It's called The Strip, although it really doesn't strip anymore; there was quite a movement to clean up the area back in the 1970s. (This is Toronto, Canada, not the average American city; when one cleans up in a place like this, one starts at a much cleaner level of dirtiness.)

Still, by the time you reach Dundas Street, some 2 miles to the south, you'll have passed the (only recently tolerated) hard-core porn bookstores, the movie houses, the pinball arcades, the harmonica-playing vagabonds, the street vendors peddling jewelry, the hustlers and whores, the endless rows of fast-food dives, the occasional future politician, and the ubiquitous patroling cops (who are, in Toronto, there when you need them, though you rarely do).

No, Times Square this isn't. Back in the early 1970s, The Strip did indeed radiate a sense of vulgarity, danger, and despair; today, it has more the air of a tacky carnival. Three million dollars was spent refurbishing streets adjoining Yonge Street, adding trees, benches, outdoor cafés, and Victorian-style lampposts to create a fresher look. And, in the great tradition of keeping the downtown of Toronto healthy, many thousands of people keep moving to within a few blocks of this major street, making it more and more a living community. The massage parlors have long been closed and most heavy drug peddlers are gone. Yonge Street today is a safe area packed with people—both residents and visitors—enjoying the punk rockers, the far-out clothing shops, and the raucous music blaring from many of the storefronts. It's certainly Toronto's *liveliest* street, if also its most vulgar and least "Toronto-like."

❸❺ You really should not miss **College Park,** at the southwest corner of Yonge and College streets. This building, complete with marble walls and brass railings, was a major Eaton's department store from 1930 to the late '70s, when the chain put most of its marbles (and money) into the gigantic Eaton Centre, just a few blocks to the south. But would Toronto *dare* to tear down such an architectural wonder? Not on your life! They simply redid it brilliantly, renamed it College Park, and filled it with dozens of beautiful stores and eateries—one more example of how cities can preserve their pasts while they march proudly into the future.

Just before you reach the Eaton Centre, on the east side of Yonge Street, are two major record stores—among the largest on the North American continent—**Sam the Record Man** (347 Yonge St.) and **HMV** (333 Yonge St.), just north of Dundas. Both stores are open Monday–Thursday 9:30 AM–11 PM, Friday and Saturday 9:30–midnight, Sunday noon–6. Be sure to enjoy the four dozen listening booths at HMV.

And that's the Yonge Street walk. Do you feel dirty all over? Are you worried that we won't respect you anymore? Not at all. If it will make you feel better, think historic: You have just walked the street where Canada's first streetcar line was inaugurated in 1861; where the first section of road in British North America was macadamized and tested in 1833; and where the first subway line in all of Canada was built, in the early 1950s. Feel better now?

Tour 4: Toronto's Finest Neighborhoods

Numbers in the margin correspond to points of interest on the Tour 4: The Neighborhoods map.

The major reason for Toronto's success as a city is its inspired preservation of handsome, clean, safe neighborhoods—often just steps from the heart of its vibrant, booming downtown. Many of these neighborhoods are practically little villages in their own right (indeed, many of them began that way). But because they are sprinkled across the city, it is difficult to walk to most of them, even if every single one is well worth walking through.

What we've done is to gather together several of Toronto's most interesting neighborhoods: (1) Rosedale, (2) Forest Hill, (3) the Annex and Casa Loma, (4) the Beaches, (5) Cabbagetown, and (6) others with a distinct ethnic flavor.

Rosedale Morley Callaghan, the Toronto author who used to box with Ernest Hemingway and quarrel with F. Scott Fitzgerald, called the neighborhood "a fine and private place." Others have called it Blueblood Alley or Millionaire Row. But whatever it is called, most of it is exceptionally beautiful and, once again, just blocks from the heart of downtown Toronto.

The place is **Rosedale,** the posh residential area of Toronto and still the symbol of old money. For visitors, Rosedale is a lovely place to walk, bike, or drive and admire the handsome, oversize houses. The neighborhood is bounded by Yonge Street on the west, the Don Valley Parkway on the east, St. Clair Avenue to the north, and the Rosedale Ravine (just above Bloor St. E) to the south. It is as if Mother Nature herself planted ravines around the area to keep out the riffraff.

Some years ago, a child of the privileged wrote a pithy article entitled "Rosedale Ain't What It Used to Be," and, in fact, it ain't. Many of the old families have gone, and their mansions have been chopped up into expensive flats. Pseudo-Georgian town houses have sprouted up in side gardens, like so many weeds.

Speaking of gardens, that's where this original Suburb of the Rich and Famous got its name. Rosedale began as the country estate of Sheriff William Jarvis, one of the powers that were, back in the 1820s. He brought his wife, Mary, to settle on the 200-acre estate,

Tour 4: The Neighborhoods

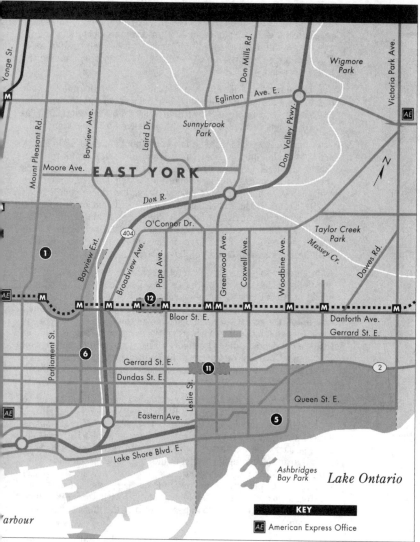

and she named her home Rosedale because of the wild roses that bloomed in profusion. Most of the roses are gone now; so are the magnificent elms that once lined Elm Avenue—including the famous Rosedale Elm, planted by Mary Jarvis herself back in 1835. Dutch elm disease hit even the estates of the very rich during the last generation.

Yet, there is surely not another metropolis in North America that maintains such an upper-class neighborhood just steps from the city's heart—a jumble of Edwardian, Victorian, Georgian, and Tudor. And massive maple trees cast their heavenly shade upon it all.

The heart of Rosedale is just a few yards north of the Castle Frank subway station on the Bloor Line. Walk up Castle Frank to Hawthorne Gardens. On the northeast corner of the two streets stands the old Seagram (as in booze) mansion, which was converted into five condominiums back in the early 1980s. Two doors north, along Castle Frank, is the impressive home of the Thomson family, the people who brought us *The London Times*, the Hudson's Bay Company, and some three dozen papers across North America, including *The Globe and Mail*. From here, follow your inclination along Elm Avenue, Milkman's Road, Craigleigh Gardens, and South Drive.

Another way to get to Rosedale (other than inheriting several million dollars) is via Roxborough Street or Crescent Road, just eight blocks north of Bloor Street, going east from Yonge Street. It is easy to find, because there is a Rosedale subway stop on the Yonge Line. Just follow the streets down and around all the ravines. Some of our favorites—all blooming with gigantic mansions—are Beaumont Road, a cul-de-sac called Old George Place, and a little park called Craigleigh Gardens. Listen carefully and you may just hear the delicate clicking of teacups as they are set down on their Wedgwood saucers.

Forest Hill The closest rival to Rosedale in prestige is an area about 2 miles to
2 the north and west of Yonge and Bloor streets called **Forest Hill**. A sense of this community can be obtained by recalling a Great Controversy back in 1982: Would the former village of Forest Hill continue to have backyard garbage pickup, or would the villagers have to (gulp!) drag their rubbish out front like everyone else in metropolitan Toronto? The City Council finally voted to continue the special service, on the principle that "invisible garbage" was one of the unwritten terms of Forest Hill's amalgamation with Toronto in 1968. In 1994, that special service appeared to bite the dust, but it had a good, long ride!

This golden square of about 940 acres is bounded by Bathurst Street on the west, Avenue Road on the east, Eglinton Avenue on the north, and St. Clair Avenue West on the south. Today Forest Hill is home to approximately 25,000 rather well-heeled people, although it numbered but some 2,100 souls in 1923 when it chose to become a village on its own. Its first reeve passed a bylaw requiring that a tree be planted in front of every house; you can see the shady results of his campaign today. At that time, there were no paved streets. Eglinton Avenue was a wagon trail, and Old Forest Hill Road was part of an old Indian path that meandered from the Humber River to Lake Ontario.

Forest Hill remained its own little village, with its own police and fire departments and school system, until it was incorporated into Toronto. Today, apart from the green street signs, it is mainly a state of mind.

You don't need a car to see Forest Hill. Either bike or walk along some of the streets, and you are in for an enjoyable hour or two. It lacks the gorgeous ravines of Rosedale, but you'll see some of this city's grandest homes and gardens. A good place to start is **Forest Hill Road,** just west of Avenue Road and St. Clair Avenue (and only a few blocks northeast of **Casa Loma**). You are now entering the thick of Forest Hill, with its handsome English manors and splendid Georgian homes. Just up the street is **Upper Canada College,** one of the country's most prestigious private schools, which has educated the likes of humorist Stephen Leacock, author Robertson Davies, the Eatons, and numerous bankers, mayors, and prime ministers.

A few blocks west of Upper Canada College is **Bishop Strachan** (rhymes with "yawn") **School.** It is one of the select private girls' schools in the city, and it is much admired, much attended, and much paid for. It's fitting that BSS shares a Forest Hill address with UCC; they both conjure up other initials: MBA, MP, MPP, and, in general, VIP.

Admire the homes along Old Forest Hill Road, then head up and down the streets that run north–south: Dunvegan, Warren, and Russell Hill. South of St. Clair Avenue, Russell Hill Road becomes a showpiece of mansions that really should be seen.

The only stores are on Spadina Road (it's Spadina Ave. south of Bloor St.), a few blocks north of St. Clair Avenue. This shopping area, with its fine shops and a superb bakery, still retains the feeling of a small village, which seems proper for the very proper people of Forest Hill.

It's a special part of Toronto, Forest Hill, and like Rosedale, a rare North American example of peacefulness, all within a short distance of Bloor and Yonge streets. Come to think of it, a lot of Forest Hill's inhabitants *own* stores at Bloor and Yonge streets. That is why they can afford to live in Forest Hill.

The Annex/ Casa Loma ❸ The origin of **the Annex's** name is hardly the stuff of romance. It was born in 1887, when the burgeoning town of Toronto annexed the area between Bathurst Street and Avenue Road—north from Bloor Street to the Canadian Pacific railway tracks, alias Dupont Street.

The Annex was still country then, so it soon became an enclave for the well-to-do. Timothy Eaton (of department-store fame) and the Gooderham family (of liquor fame) escaped the masses and built north of Bloor Street. Eaton built a handsome structure at 182 Lowther Avenue; the Gooderhams erected a lovely red castle at the corner of St. George Street and Bloor Street, now the home of the exclusive York Club.

As Queen Victoria gave way to King Edward, the old rich gave way to the new rich in the Annex, and the Eatons headed farther north. Ethnic groups came and went, until the arrival of the ultimate neighborhood wrecker—the developer. Now began a war between the 19th and the 20th centuries that continues today. Alas, much of St. George Street has been lost to high rises; and as you near the Spadina subway entrance along Lowther Avenue and Walmer Street, you'll see that many Edwardian mansions have given way to apartment buildings whose architecture will forever remain 1960-ish—and *very* ugly.

Still, the Annex, with its hundreds of attractive old homes, can be cited as a prime example of Toronto's success in preserving lovely, safe streets within blocks of the downtown area. Even today, many examples of late 19th-century architecture can be enjoyed on Admiral Road, Lowther Avenue, and Bloor Street, west of University Avenue. Round turrets, pyramid-shape roofs, and conical and even comical spires are among the pleasures shared by some 20,000 Torontonians who live here—professors, students, writers, lawyers, and all the others who rightly find the area a vibrant place to live.

While the Annex is not number one on any visitor's checklist, it is an important part of the city, and it is lovely to visit. At the western end of the Annex—at Bathurst and Bloor streets—you come to Mirvish (or Markham) Village, described in Tour 2. And at the northern tip is the ultimate version of Your Home as Your Castle: Casa Loma.

❹ Casa Loma (1 Austin Terr.; on Spadina Rd., just south of St. Clair Ave. W and the St. Clair Ave. subway stop) is truly a stunner: an honest-to-goodness 20th-century castle, with 98 rooms; two towers; secret panels; long, creepy passageways; and some of the best views of Toronto—all just a short distance from the heart of the city.

The medieval-style castle was built shortly before the Great War by Sir Henry Pellatt, a soldier and financier who spent over $3 million to construct his dream (that's 1913 dollars, remember), only to lose it to the taxman just over a decade later. Today it's owned by the city of Toronto and has been operated by the Kiwanis Club of West Toronto since 1937, with profits going to aid its various charities.

Adults and children will be intrigued by the giant pipe organ; the reproduction of Windsor Castle's Peacock Alley; the majestic, 60-foot-high ceiling of the Great Hall; and the mahogany and marble stable—reached by a long, underground passage—with porcelain troughs worthy of Kohler. And architecture lovers will be fascinated by the rooms from English, Spanish, Scottish, and Austrian castles, which Sir Henry picked up during trips across Europe. The architect E. J. Lennox, who also designed Toronto's Old City Hall and King Edward Hotel, has created a remarkable structure; in a world of Disneyland-type plastic models, Toronto's "house on the hill" is a real treat.

There are no more guided tours of Casa Loma—you now get automatic tape recordings. That's all for the best, as you can drift through at your own speed while the children rush off to the stables or towers. You'll walk a good mile by the time you're done, so wear sensible shoes. *Tel. 416/923-1171. Admission: $8 adults, $4.50 senior citizens and children 6-16, 5 and under free with adult. Open daily 10-4; closed Christmas Day and New Year's.*

The Beaches One of the most charming of all the neighborhoods that make up what we call metropolitan Toronto is to the east of downtown, reached by the Queen Street streetcar. Called both the Beach and **❺ The Beaches,** the area is bounded by Kingston Road to the north, the Greenwood Raceway to the west, Victoria Park Avenue to the east, and the lake to the south. But The Beaches is really an *attitude*, as much as it is a neighborhood. The chance to live in a small town outside Toronto, with easy access to the city via public transport and even easier access to Lake Ontario, has attracted tens of thousands of residents over the years.

A soldier from London, Joseph Williams, first settled the area back in 1853, having arrived in Toronto with the 2nd Battalion Rifle Brigade five years earlier. His 25-acre grant was named Kew Farms, after London's Kew Gardens, and it was there that he raised vegetables, selling them along with pies and pickles at the St. Lawrence

Market on Saturday mornings. (That market is discussed in Tour 1.) When Williams chose to turn his property into a park in 1879, he called it **Kew Gardens.** It was soon flooded by hundreds of hot and sticky Torontonians attracted by the advertisements for "innocent amusements" and the prohibition of "spiritous liquors." Only Canadians would be drawn to such promised innocence!

The youngest son of the *paterfamilias,* suitably named Kew Williams, built a handsome house of stone with a circular staircase and a tower. It stands in Kew Gardens today, The Beaches' own modest version of Casa Loma, serving as home to the park's keeper.

The cottages that once stood on the lakeshore vanished with the waves in 1932, at which time Kew Gardens, Scarborough Beach Park, and Balmy Beach were incorporated into one large park. But on a leisurely walk along the charming streets that run north from the lake to Queen Street, you will still find—and be charmed by—hundreds of New England–style clapboard-and-shingle houses, often standing next door to formal stucco mansions in the Edwardian tradition.

Ride east to the end of the 501 Queen Street streetcar line, to what's called the Neville Park Loop. From here, stroll down to the lake, and walk west toward the city along the delightful, safe, and often crowded (in the summer) boardwalk. Remember, July and August are the only months when one does not risk frostbite when dipping a toe into Lake Ontario. But merely sunbathing can be magical beside The Beaches' boardwalk, which is graced by huge, shady trees. And if you get too warm, there is the free Olympic-size **Somerville Pool** at Woodbine Avenue.

A return walk back up to Queen Street, window shopping along the way, is well worth the time, before grabbing the 501 car westbound and back into the last decade of the 20th century.

Cabbagetown Anyone with less than a week to spend in Toronto may wish to put this way down on their list of must-dos, but anyone with the time and a healthy interest in what makes the city of Toronto so healthy (and interesting) really should take an hour or so to walk through ❻ Cabbagetown—a cozy neighborhood just east of the downtown area.

We're not talking about major historic landmarks here, but it has the charm of street after street of 19th-century houses, giant trees, and the loveliness of its natural boundaries—two fascinating cemeteries and the Don Valley, now slashed through by the parkway of the same name.

Cabbagetown was originally populated by poor Irish immigrants, who gave it its very prosaic name: They used to grow cabbages in their front yards. Today, that name is used with almost wistful irony; the "white painters" eventually descended on the area, brushes and hammers waving, turning houses that sold in the $25,000 range just two decades ago into ones that will fetch $250,000 and more. In other words, Cabbagetown is yet another good example—along with Yorkville (in the Bloor/Avenue/Yonge district) and the St. Lawrence area (near Front/Church/Jarvis)—of the insistent gentrification of Toronto's downtown.

And so, the area that the late Cabbagetown-born-and-bred writer Hugh Garner once described as "the world's largest Anglo-Saxon slum" has Cinderellaed into one of the most popular areas in the city. (Being within walking distance from the Eaton Centre, at least in good weather, hasn't hurt.)

The borders of Cabbagetown are not terribly well defined. They extend roughly from Parliament Street on the west (about a mile due east of Yonge St.) to Broadview Avenue on the east, and from Bloor Street (aka The Danforth) on the north to Queen Street East on the south.

Our tour will point out only the highlights, but we think that you might well find the entire neighborhood of interest, especially if you are fond of small-scale domestic Victorian architecture.

The "main street" of Cabbagetown is Parliament, so we'll begin there, at the southeast corner of Carlton Street (alias College St., but on the east side of the city). The street was so named because the first government buildings were built near its foot in the closing years of the 18th century.

Walk south from Carlton and Parliament streets, through the busiest part of the Parliament Street commercial area. Most of the buildings on the west side date from the 1890s, though the fronts of the stores are more recent.

Turn left on Spruce Street, which is the first block you come to. The little brick cottage at **No. 35,** set far back from the street, was built in 1860–61 and was once the home of the dean of Trinity College Medical School. Note the fence, as well, which also dates from the last century.

From 1856 to 1914, the entire block to your south was the site of the Toronto General Hospital (which now stands, along with most of the city's other major and modern hospitals, along University Ave., south of College St.). The building at **41 Spruce Street** was built in 1871, served until 1903 as a medical school, and has now been recycled as part of a residential development. Its history is outlined on the Toronto Historical Board plaque on its front lawn.

Continuing east, to the corner of Spruce and Sumach streets, you'll see **Spruce Court** on the northwest corner. It's one of the earliest and most attractive of Toronto's low-income housing projects. Constructed for the Toronto Housing Company between 1913 and 1926, the individual units not only provided modern conveniences and street access but also opened to a grassy courtyard. Today, it's a residential cooperative, and the humanity of the city continues to flourish.

Around that corner to the right, at **289 Sumach Street,** is the building that once housed the Ontario Women's Medical College, built in 1889 and a forerunner of Women's College Hospital. (Yes, fellow feminists, Toronto was slow to educate female doctors.) The attractiveness of this brick-and-stone building demonstrates well the success with which Victorian architects and builders managed to integrate institutions into streetscapes that were basically residential.

Now, turn around and walk north on Sumach Street. After crossing Spruce Street, look to your right, on the attractive row of small houses at **119–133 Spruce Street.** Erected in 1887, this terrace of workers' cottages is typical of the form of residential architecture built (to every scale) in Toronto between 1875 and 1890. The style, Second Empire, is typified by the high mansard roof punctuated by dormers with marvelous details, such as carved wooden brackets and metal decorative devices.

Continue north on Sumach Street back to Carlton Street, where you'll see some of the area's largest homes. (Note the redbrick surface of the street to the east.) Among the most outstanding is **No.**

288, a solid brick house with white stone trim in the Second Empire style built in 1882. The house next door, **No. 286,** was built the following year; it has the familiar Toronto-style steep gable and bargeboard trim. Check out the wrought-iron cresting over the round bow window.

The handsome residence at **No. 297** is unusual for the area and is more like the stately homes of the Annex area of Toronto. Its interior, fully restored and exquisitely furnished, has been in more magazine pictorials than Elizabeth Taylor. Its neighbor at **295 Carlton Street** is an earlier house of Victorian Gothic design. It was originally the home of an executive of Toronto's first telephone company—be aware that the wondrous machine was invented by Alexander Graham Bell in Brantford, Ontario, just over an hour west of Toronto—and it had one of the first telephones in the entire city. It didn't cost a quarter to make a call back then.

Continue west on Carlton Street to Metcalfe Street, which, thanks to all its trees, fences, and unbroken rows of terraces, is one of the most beautiful streets in Toronto. On the sidewalk, on the east side nearest Carlton Street, is a utility-hole cover from the Victorian era, bearing the date 1889.

Proceed north to look at **37 Metcalfe Street,** a house that is unique due to its various additions. The renovations over the years (1891 and 1912) have created an array of beaux-arts classical forms, superimposed on the side of a simple but picturesque Victorian home. It's a fine example of the architectural diversity of the entire area.

Look north again. At the northeast corner of Metcalfe and Winchester streets is the handsome Romanesque **St. Enoch's Presbyterian Church,** erected in 1891. Its scale and style blend nicely with that of the surrounding homes of the same period. Today, it is the home of the Toronto Dance Theatre.

Turn left now, and walk west along Winchester Street, back to Parliament Street. As you amble along, admire the repeated sunburst patterns of carved wood in many of the gables and the very large amount of stained glass, much of it original, some of it recently installed by lovers of Victoriana.

At the southeast corner is the most prominent building in the area, the venerable but (alas) decaying **Winchester Hotel.** The old wing on the Winchester bears the plaque "Winchester Hall" and was put up in 1881; the large corner part was built seven years later.

South of the hotel stands an imposing row of large Victorian houses, numbered **502–508 Parliament Street.** Erected in 1879, they are among the largest and most elaborately decorated Second Empire structures still standing in Toronto.

To the north, at the northwest corner of Parliament and Wellesley streets—you can't miss them, sadly—loom the overwhelming apartment towers of **St. James Town,** built in the 1960s and reviled ever since. They wiped out many streets that had been lined with houses like the ones we have been walking by. Yes, Toronto, too, has been occasionally victimized by progress.

On the east side of Parliament Street, just north of Wellesley Street, is **St. James Cemetery,** which is worth a visit. This beautiful final resting place was laid out in the 1840s, making it the eternal home of many of the most prominent early citizens of the then town of York and the site of some of the most interesting funereal statuary in Toronto. While you are there, observe the small yellow-brick Gothic

Chapel of St. James-the-Less, built in 1858 and considered to be one of the most beautiful church buildings in the entire country.

Turn right and walk east along Wellesley Street. Be sure to take note of **No. 314,** built in 1889–90, with its stonework around the windows and carved stone faces above the door and in the keystones.

Farther east, turn north up the lane marked **Wellesley Cottages.** This row of workers' houses was built in 1886–87 by a carpenter of the time. Much of Toronto's most inexpensive housing of the 19th century was built in this simplified Gothic style, faced with wood lath and stucco. They may look unchanged to you, but some have been extensively modernized.

Back on Wellesley Street, walk north up the lane just east of number 402 to see the **Owl House,** named after the figure on a small terracotta plaque under one of its windows. This interesting little house was built in 1893–94.

Wellesley Street comes to an end at **Wellesley Park,** which was, from 1848 to 1888, the site of the area's only major industry, the P. R. Lamb Glue and Blacking Factory, just the thing one wouldn't want next door. Today, it's a small, pleasant neighborhood park and playground, framed by parts of the Don Valley, the Necropolis Cemetery, and the row of houses to the south, for whose occupants the park is a large and lovely front lawn.

Proceed south through Wellesley Park, and turn right along Amelia Street to Sumach Street. Walk south, past Winchester Street, and make a left (east) into **Riverdale Park.** The large stone gateposts on your left were the entrance to the Riverdale Zoo, a public zoo operated by the city from 1894 to 1974, when they finally moved all the animals—and brought in several thousand more—to the magnificent Metro Toronto Zoo, in Scarborough. It will warm your heart to know that this area was laid out on landfill that was dumped by prisoners of the Don Jail, as part of their work program.

It's now **Riverdale Farm,** one of Toronto's most delightful—and free—attractions, and a very special treat for children. Here is where they can find Jasmine and Snappy the Goat; Dolly Clydesdale, her daughter Christie (chickens), and son Rooster; and Eddie and Flo Mule.

The old birdhouse on the grounds is the last remnant of the old zoo, but the most interesting structure is the original, 19th-century Pennsylvania German–style barn, built in 1858 and moved to the farm in 1975. Inside are various implements, such as a light sleigh from the turn of the century and an exact replica of a Conestoga wagon, the kind used by German-speaking immigrants to this country early in the last century.

Bring along bathing suits for the very young children: There's a wading pond in the lovely park adjacent to the farm.

The Riverdale Farm, 201 Winchester St., near Wellesley and Parliament Sts., tel. 416/392–0046. Open daily 9–4.

The **Necropolis** ("city of the dead") **Cemetery** lies just to the north of Riverdale Farm. The nonsectarian burial ground is filled with many of Toronto's early pioneers. Among the most famous (and notorious): Toronto's first mayor, William Lyon Mackenzie, who led a revolt against the city in 1837; Samuel Lount and Peter Matthews, two of Mackenzie's followers, who were hanged for their part in that rebellion; and George Brown, founder of the *Globe* newspaper and one of the fathers of Canada's confederation.

The beautiful chapel, gate, and gatehouse of the cemetery, erected in 1872, constitute one of the most picturesque groupings of small Victorian buildings in all of Toronto. The Necropolis is also known for its great variety of trees, flowering shrubs, and rare and exotic plants.

Other Neighborhoods As we never get tired of pointing out, part of Toronto's magic, and surely one of its major reasons for its success as a "city that works," is its quite extraordinary collection of neighborhoods. Here are a few others worthy of mention.

➐ **A Polish community.** The beauty of High Park is described at length in Sightseeing Checklists, below; let us merely say that one of North America's loveliest parks is but 3 or 4 miles due west of Bloor and Yonge streets, along the Bloor subway line. But just east of the park is a long street running north–south: **Roncesvalles Avenue.** This is the commercial heart and soul of Toronto's Polish community, filled with butcher shop after butcher shop, each selling homemade sausages just like grandmother should have made, if she had had the skill and time. (Consider buying a few to grill in High Park.)

On the west side of the park is Runnymede Road. Here, and along Bloor Street West, you move both west and east across Europe: Both **➑** **German** and **Ukrainian** shops come into view, selling fine food and clothing.

➒ **An Italian community.** From the College and Bathurst streets area, west to Dufferin Street and beyond, and north all the way to the city limits of Steeles Avenue, is the ever-widening Italian neighborhood, its numbers making Toronto one of the largest Italian communities outside the mother country. The streets here are filled with the passion and excitement of that great, vibrant Mediterranean culture—especially **St. Clair Avenue,** from Bathurst Street west to Dufferin Street. Here are many fine Italian restaurants and stores, including several that sell excellent ices and ice creams.

➓ **A West Indian community.** West Indians and their fascinating food shops can be found along Eglinton Avenue, just east of Dufferin Street, and down along Bloor Street West near Christie Street. They can also be found along Bathurst Street, north from Bloor Street. Their snack bars selling *roti*—spicy Jamaican meat patties—can be found most everywhere in Toronto nowadays.

⑪ **An East Indian community.** East Indians are also fairly widely dispersed, although there is one quite concentrated row of Indian shops and restaurants—and movie houses—along Gerrard Street East, near Greenwood Avenue, a few miles east of Yonge Street.

⑫ **A Greek community.** The Danforth. This is a strange name for a street, but it is stranger still in its crazy-quilt ethnicity: Once English-settled (although it was named after Asa Danforth, an American contractor who cut a road in the area back in 1799), it is now Italian, Greek, East Indian, Latin American, and, increasingly, Chinese. But it is still called "Greek town," with its late-night taverns, all-night fruit markets, and some of the best ethnic restaurants in Toronto.

There are now well over a quarter-million Greek Canadians; more than 150,000 of them live in Ontario, and more than half of those live in metropolitan Toronto. They created such major Canadian enterprises as Devon Ice Cream and Diana Sweets restaurants, and they gave the world internationally acclaimed opera star Teresa Stratas. For more than a decade, in fact, Toronto provided a home and a professorship (at York University, in the northwest part of the city,

near Finch and Keele Sts.) for exiled Andreas Papandreou, who was
Greece's socialist prime minister during much of the 1980s.

In the summer of 1982, 50 street signs in the Little Athens area of
the Danforth, between Logan and Woodycrest avenues, went bilingual (English and Greek). When you've had a little too much
souvlaki and Greek wine, the signs can help you find your way home.

What to See and Do with Children

Free
Attractions
The **Hilton,** at University Avenue and Richmond Street, and the
Harbour Castle Westin, at the foot of Bay Street, both have outdoor,
glass-enclosed elevators, which provide hair-raising rides and spec-
tacular views of the city.

The **ferry boat** to the **Toronto Islands** offers a stunning panorama of
downtown Toronto. The islands themselves offer swimming and biking (bikes can be rented) in the summer, skiing in the winter, and
the delightful **Far Enough Farm** in Centreville (*see* Tour 1, *above*).

The **Riverdale Farm** in Cabbagetown is a working farm with animals
and a wading pond (*see* Tour 4, *above*).

High Park has a sweet little zoo, swimming, skating, picnicking, and
more (*see* Sightseeing Checklists, *below*).

Skating, skiing, and **tobogganing** are all available for free in most of
the major Toronto parks and ravines. And, still thinking about winter, don't forget the beautiful skating rink in front of the New City
Hall and the often-terrifying hills at Winston Churchill Park, High
Park, Earl Bales Park, and Riverdale Park.

The **Children's Bookstore** (tel. 416/480–0233), which recently moved
from Mirvish Village to 2532 Yonge Street, about six blocks north of
Eglinton, can provide an hour or more of free fun for children. It's
the largest store of its kind in the world, and it frequently holds
weekend concerts and readings in the summer. Now located in a historic old YMCA building from the 1930s, it is truly the Louvre of
children's books.

The **David Dunlap Observatory** in Richmond Hill, just north of metropolitan Toronto, and the **McLaughlin Planetarium,** right next to
the Royal Ontario Museum, both provide outer-space experiences
for preteens and teens (*see* Sightseeing Checklists, *below*).

Harbourfront Centre nearly always has free events and activities,
from painting and sculpting to concerts and plays. Just being on the
waterfront can be a thrill for children. Feeding the seagulls popcorn
or hunks of bread is endlessly interesting, especially when the gulls
catch the food in midair dives (*see* Tour 1, *above*).

Boys and Girls House is a superior library for children. The former
Spaced-Out Library on the second floor, now called the **Merril Col-
lection,** will thrill all teenage fans of science fiction (*see* Sightseeing
Checklists, *below*).

Modestly
Priced
Attractions
Apple, strawberry, and **raspberry picking** are available within a short
drive of downtown Toronto. Our favorite place is **Al Ferri's** (15 min-
utes west of the airport, near the corner of Mississauga Rd. and
Steeles Ave., tel. 905/455–8202). Check out a wonderful cross-bred
apple at Ferri's called the Macoun, the result of crossing a Red Deli-

cious with a MacIntosh. Glorious! For a free list of places to pick fruits and vegetables in the vicinity of Toronto, call 416/965–7701.

The *Haida,* at Ontario Place, is a giant World War II destroyer that children love to explore (*see* Sightseeing Checklists, *below*).

The **Art Gallery of Ontario** has a hands-on room that is marvelously creative and entertaining. Right behind it is the fascinating, historic **Grange** house. In front of the gallery is a Henry Moore sculpture that children love to climb (*see* Tour 2, *above*).

The **Royal Ontario Museum,** with its fantastic dinosaurs, towering totem pole, and other child-oriented exhibits, is ideal for children from three to 18 and their parents (*see* Tour 3, *above*).

Casa Loma. *See* Tour 4, *above.*

The Puppet Centre, near Yonge Street and Highway 401, has more than 400 puppets from all over the world.

Cullen Gardens and Miniature Village. Even preschoolers—especially preschoolers—just love this place, to be found less than an hour east of the Metro Zoo. Here are some 150 tiny, perfect shops, houses, farms and cottages, and miniature trains that zoom under bridges and stop at a ministation. This minuscule world is exquisitely landscaped with small shrubs, little cars zipping along highways, and even a burning house, complete with firefighters, flames, and smoke! The charming site is especially recommended during the months of December and January, when there is an annual Festival of Lights—with fully 100,000 of them gleaming everywhere. *Take Hwy. 401 east, exiting at Hwy. 12, drive north approximately 4.3 mi, through Whitby, turn west on Taunton Rd., tel. 416/294–7965. Admission: $9 adults, $7 senior citizens and students, $4 children 3–12, children under 3 free. Open Feb.–Dec., daily 10–10; Jan., Wed.–Sun. 2–9; closed Christmas. There are live Christmas shows through Dec., and Santa can be visited until Dec. 24.*

More Expensive Attractions
The **Ontario Science Centre** is a must for children, especially those five and older (*see* Sightseeing Checklists, *below*).

The **CN Tower** and the **Tour of the Universe** in its basement are not cheap, but they're a real treat for everyone, especially children (*see* Tour 1, *above*).

Black Creek Pioneer Village is a great place for children (*see* Sightseeing Checklists, *below*).

In their respective seasons, there are numerous events that are great for children: most especially, the **Frostfest** and **Winterfest** (January); the **Fort York Festival** (May); **Caravan** and **International Festival** (June); **Caribana** and **International Picnic** (July); the **Canadian National Exhibition** (mid-August–Labor Day); the **Bindertwine Festival** (September); the **Royal Winter Fair** and **Santa Claus Parade** (November); and the **Festival of Lights** (December).

From early April through September each year, the **Toronto Blue Jays** continue their eternal/infernal climb toward the American League pennant. Throughout the season, children 14 and younger are offered various freebies, such as bats, baseball caps, and sports bags. For ticket information, call SkyDome (tel. 416/341–1111).

The **Toronto Maple Leafs,** the only leaves that fall from October through April, can provide the occasional hockey thrill at Maple Leaf Gardens (tel. 416/977–1641).

Please bear in mind that both the Blue Jays and the Maple Leafs are ferociously popular, with 95% of all their games sold out long in advance. However, scalpers are **always** to be found outside both SkyDome and Maple Leaf Gardens, respectively (if not respectfully), and if you've got the cash, they've got the tickets.

Toronto's new NBA basketball team, the **Toronto Raptors,** will play its first season in 1995 at SkyDome; the team hopes to move to a new residence near Eaton Centre that is scheduled to open in 1996. Be assured that the Raptors' games will be sold out months in advance, just like this city's other professional sports events. Once again, scalpers will be sure to be out in force before every single game.

For theater and concerts, the **Young People's Theatre** (tel. 416/864–9732) often has excellent fare, and there are frequent performances for children at **Roy Thomson Hall** (tel. 416/593–4828) and the **Minkler Auditorium** (tel. 416/491–8877), which is up north, near Finch Street and the Don Valley Parkway.

Pricey But Worth It Just north of the city is **Canada's Wonderland,** Toronto's frozen version of Disneyland. It's uninspired but can provide a decent day's entertainment. There are many rock concerts here at the Kingswood Music Theatre. In past years, Shoppers Drug Mart has offered reduced-rate tickets with purchases amounting to more than a few dollars (*see* Sightseeing Checklists, *below*).

African Lion Safari, about an hour's drive west of Toronto, can provide marvelous entertainment, especially if the giraffe puts its head through your car window. Half-price tickets are often available in shops around the city (*see* Sightseeing Checklists, *below*).

Marineland, in Niagara Falls, is top-quality entertainment put on by an underwater zoo crew. It's a world-class park, with thrilling amusement rides, dolphin shows, and aquariums (*see* Chapter 8).

Wild Water Kingdom, not far from the airport, Black Creek Pioneer Village, and Canada's Wonderland, is a welcome recent addition to every child's dream of a water-sports center: high water slides, river rapids, giant outdoor hot tubs, a fantastic wave pool, and a delightful area for younger children to splash around in. Now the largest park of its kind in Canada, it boasts a sports complex right next to it, Emerald Green, which has minigolf, batting cages, and more. *Finch Ave. W and Hwy. 427, tel. 416/369–9453. Admission: $17 adults, $13 senior citizens and children 4–9. Open June, Thurs.–Sun. 11–6; July–the day before Labor Day, daily 10–8.*

The Metro Toronto Zoo **The Metro Toronto Zoo** was built for animals, not people. The Rouge Valley, just east of Toronto, was an inspired choice of site when it was built in the 1960s, with its varied terrain, from river valley to dense forest, where mammals, birds, reptiles, and fish have been grouped according to where they live in the wild. In most of the sections, you'll find remarkable botanical exhibits in enclosed, climate-controlled pavilions. Don't miss the 3-ton banyan tree in the Indo-Malayan Pavilion; the fan-shaped traveler's palm from Madagascar in the African Pavilion; or the perfumed flowers of the jasmine vines in the Eurasian Pavilion. The "round the world tour" takes some three hours and is suitable for any kind of weather, because most of the time is spent inside pavilions. It's been estimated that it would take four full days to see everything in the Metro Zoo, so study the map you'll get at the zoo entrance, and decide in advance what you wish to see most.

For the younger children, there is the delightful Littlefootland, a special area that allows contact with tame animals, such as rabbits and sheep. There is an electrically powered train that moves silently among the animals without frightening them. It can accommodate wheelchairs (available free, inside the main gate); all pavilions have ramp access.

Meadowvale Rd., just north of Hwy. 401, in Scarborough, a 30-minute drive from downtown or take Bus 86A from Kennedy subway station, tel. 416/392–5900 for information. Admission: $9.75 adults, $7 senior citizens and children 12–17, $5 children 4–11. Free parking in winter. Parking Mar.–Oct. $4. Family rates available. Open mid-Mar.–Labor Day, daily 9–7:30; mid-Oct.–mid-Mar., daily 9:30–4:30; closed Christmas.

Off the Beaten Track

Watching the Italian promenade. St. Clair Avenue West, running from Bathurst Street to Dufferin Street and beyond, remains the heart of this city's vibrant Italian community. On many evenings, especially Sundays, the street is filled with thousands of men and women promenading between *gelaterias*, eyeing each other, and generally enjoying their neighbors. You'll think you're in Rome.

Chinatown on a Sunday morning. Spadina Avenue, from College Street south to Queen Street, and Dundas Street, from Spadina all the way east to Bay Street, are bustling most of the time, but on Sunday mornings—all day, really—the activity is nonstop. A great time to browse, buy, and just plain enjoy.

Greektown on a Sunday. The Danforth (Bloor St. east of the Don Valley Parkway) has great Greek restaurants, gift shops, and hundreds of Greek Canadians promenading. Welcome to the Mediterranean!

There's no hotel more romantic than the **Guild Inn** (*see* Chapter 6), and no view of Toronto more wonderful than from **Centre Island at sunset.**

Sightseeing Checklists

Historic Buildings and Sites There are many attractive, even fascinating historic buildings and sites around the city of Toronto, a few of them rather far from the core of the downtown area. The following is a checklist for those who wish to make sure they see the most interesting ones. A number of these have been described before, in our Exploring chapter.

Black Creek Pioneer Village. Less than a half hour's drive from downtown Toronto is a rural, mid-19th-century village that makes you feel as if you've gone through a time warp. Black Creek Pioneer Village is a collection of over two dozen period buildings that have been moved to their current site: a town hall, weaver's shop, printing shop, blacksmith's shop, and a school, complete with dunce cap. The mill dates from the 1840s and has a 4-ton wood waterwheel that still grinds up to a hundred barrels of flour a day.

Visitors watch men and women in period costumes go about the daily routine of mid-19th-century Ontario life—cutting tin, shearing sheep, tending gardens (weather permitting), fixing and even making horseshoes, baking bread, weaving, printing a newspaper, stringing apple slices, and dipping candles. Most pleasantly, these knowledgeable souls explain what they're doing and how they do it, and they answer all questions about pioneer farm life.

Free wagon rides, a decent restaurant, and many farm animals all contribute to a satisfying outing. And in the winter, there's also skating, tobogganing, and sleigh rides. *Located in northwest metropolitan Toronto at Jane St. and Steeles Ave. By car, take Hwy. 401, then Hwy. 400 north to Steeles E, and follow signs. By bus, take Bus 35B from Jane St. subway station in Toronto's west end and/or 60B, 60D, or 60E from Finch Ave. subway station. Tel. 905/661–6610 for recorded message; 905/736–1733 for more information. Admission: $7.50 adults, $5 senior citizens, $3.25 children 5–14, $5 students with I.D.; children under 5 free, when accompanied by parents. Generally open 10–5. Phone for seasonal events, reduced winter hrs, and extended summer hrs. Closed early Jan.–school break (usually mid-Mar.).*

Campbell House. *See* Tour 3, *above.*

Casa Loma. *See* Tour 4, *above.*

Colborne Lodge. Visit this grand 19th-century home in conjunction with a trip to High Park. An architect named John Howard built this Regency-style "cottage" on a park hill overlooking Lake Ontario more than 150 years ago. Visitors will see the original fireplace, bake oven, and kitchen, as well as many of Howard's own drawings and paintings. *Colborne Lodge Dr., at south end of High Park. By subway, take Bloor St. Line west to High Park station. Tel. 416/392–6916. Admission: $3.25 adults, $2.50 senior citizens and children 13–18, $2.25 children 12 and younger. Open Jan. 1–Mar. 31, weekends noon–5; Apr. 1–Dec. 31, weekdays 9:30–4, weekends and holidays noon–5.*

Enoch Turner Schoolhouse. This building, just a few blocks east of Union Station in the St. Lawrence area, helps us remember that free public education began only in the mid-19th century. Back in the 1840s, Toronto parents paid two-thirds of teachers' salaries, and the government picked up the rest. When the Ontario legislature passed an act in 1848 authorizing cities to provide free schools (paid for by property taxes), the Toronto City Council balked at the radical concept and closed down every public school in town. A brewer named Enoch Turner was outraged by the reactionary policy of the city elders, and he created Toronto's first free educational institution. Three years later, the politicians relented and absorbed the Enoch Turner Schoolhouse into the public school system of Toronto. And so, this small red-and-yellow brick building remains, looking frightfully like today's schoolrooms, except for the ancient desks. *106 Trinity St., near corner of King St. E and Parliament St., tel. 416/863–0010. Admission free. Open weekdays 9:30–4:30.*

Fort York. This remarkable historical site is in downtown Toronto, not far from Harbourfront Centre and Ontario Place. It could well be combined with visits to either of those sites.

In 1813, a fierce battle took place between the Yankees and the Queen's Rangers regiment in what was then York (now, Toronto). **Fort York** was torched, but the Canadians rebuilt it just three years later, and it still stands, near the foot of Bathurst Street, in downtown Toronto. The eight buildings, with their brick, stone, and log frames, give visitors a good sense of what it was like to be a British soldier stuck out in the boondocks nearly two centuries ago.

You'll see the blockhouses, where dozens of men froze to death in their beds over the years, and the mess, where women still bake bread in the giant stone fireplace. There's a model of the famous battle from the War of 1812, and, year-round, men get rigged up in the uniforms of the era, call themselves the Fort York Guard, and perform 19th-century drills, complete with artillery salutes. Children will enjoy climbing on the various cannons, and tour guides are both knowledgeable and friendly. *By car, take Lakeshore Blvd. W to Strachan Ave. (pronounced "strawn") north, and head east on Fleet St. By subway, take Bloor St. train west to Bathurst St., then the streetcar south to Garrison Rd. exit. The Bathurst St. #511 streetcar also goes here. Tel. 416/392-6907. Admission: $4.75 adults, $3 senior citizens and children 13-18, $2.75 children 6-12. Open Oct. 1-May 15, Tues.-Fri. 9:30-4, weekends and holidays 10-5; May 16-Sept. 30, Tues.-Sun. 9:30-5. Closed Jan. 1, Good Friday, and Dec. 25-26.*

Gibson House. It's the Little House in the Suburbs, convenient for people driving anywhere near Highway 401 and Yonge Street. The 10-room country house was built in 1851 by one of the supporters of William Lyon Mackenzie's 1837 rebellion. True, David Gibson's original home was burned to the ground by anti-Mackenzie men while the surveyor was off in a decade-long exile in the United States (during which time he assisted in constructing the Erie Canal), but when he returned to Toronto, he built this. As in Fort York and Black Creek, there are men and women in 19th-century costumes who demonstrate the cooking and crafts of the pioneers. *5172 Yonge St., about 1 mi north of Sheppard Ave. and Hwy. 401, tel. 416/395-7432. Admission: $2.50 adults, $2 students and senior citizens, $1.50 children 2-12, $6 families; senior citizens free Wed. Open Tues.-Fri. 9:30-5, weekends noon-5; also open on holiday Mon.*

The Grange. This fine living museum is located just behind the Art Gallery of Ontario. In 1911, a prominent lady donated her historic house (1817) to what was then the Art Museum of Toronto. It's been restored as a "Gentleman's House" of the mid-1830s, and it should not be missed. The columned Georgian front and the delicately balanced wings that flow from the sides of its porch only hint at the joys of the interior: Carefully refurnished in English regency style, it is a virtual stage set for "Upstairs/Downstairs," complete with music room and a row of bells to call the servants from the basement kitchen. Costumed hostesses bake bread in the 19th-century brick ovens and give out slices, and children can dress up in aprons and bonnets. *317 Dundas St. W, just west of University Ave., tel. 416/977-0414. Admission free with admission to Art Gallery ($7.50 adults, $4 senior citizens and children 12-18, children under 12 free, $15 maximum charge for families). Open Wed.-Sun. 10-5:30, Wed. and Fri. until 10. Closed Mon., Tues.*

Mackenzie House. This is in a deceptively modest row of houses, just blocks from the Eaton Centre. Its owner, William Lyon Mackenzie, was born in Scotland at the end of the 1700s and immigrated to Canada in 1820. He began a newspaper that so enraged the powers that be (they were known as "the Family Compact"—a powerful, smug group of politicians, *not* an economy car) that they broke into his print shop and dumped all his type into Lake Ontario. Undismayed, Mackenzie was elected the first mayor of Toronto, even designing the coat of arms of the new city. When he wasn't reelected in 1836, he gathered about 700 supporters and marched down Yonge Street to try to overthrow the government. They were roundly defeated, and Willie had to escape to the United States with a price on his head. When the Canadian government finally granted him amnesty, a dozen years later, Mackenzie was promptly elected to the legislative assembly—suggesting a daring on the part of Torontonians that few would imagine today—and began to publish another newspaper. By this time, though, Mackenzie was so down on his luck and cash that some friends passed the hat and bought him and his family the house we suggest you visit. His grandson, William Lyon Mackenzie King, became the longest-lasting prime minister of Canada.

Mackenzie enjoyed the place for but a few sickly and depressing years: He died here in 1861. Today it has been lovingly restored as a National Historic Site and is operated as a museum and library. There are dozens of 19th-century furnishings and treasures, even the wild man's printing press. *82 Bond St., two blocks east of Yonge St. and a few steps south of Dundas St., tel. 416/392-6915. Admission: $3.50 adults, $2.75 senior citizens and children 13-18, $2.50 children 4-12. 1-hr group tours cost about $3. Open Tues.-Fri. 9:30-4, weekends and holidays noon-5.*

Montgomery's Inn. This restored inn—one of the few attractions in the west end of Toronto—was built in the early 1830s by an Irish immigrant, and it is a good example of the Loyalist architecture of the time. Costumed staff go about quilting, rug hooking, and cooking traditional foods. There are many tours, and a daily afternoon tea, 2–4:15, which costs $2. *4709 Dundas St. W, a brief walk from Islington subway stop, tel. 416/394-8113. Admission: $2.50 adults, $1.50 students and senior citizens, $1 children, $6 maximum per family. Open Tues.-Fri. 9:30-4:30, weekends 1-5.*

Old City Hall/New City Hall. *See* Tour 2, *above.*

Queen's Park. *See* Tour 3, *above.*

Spadina. Pronounced spa-*dee*-na, as the avenue should be but never is, it is filled with arts and artifacts of a prominent Toronto family. First built in 1866, it is now a glorious living tribute to the Victorian and Edwardian eras, featuring French porcelain vases, handsome furniture, crystal chandeliers burning softly with natural gas, fine paintings, and magnificent gardens. *285 Spadina Ave., next to Casa Loma, tel. 416/392-6910. Admission: $5 adults, $3.25 senior citizens and children 13-18, $3 children 6-12. Slight discount for those with Casa Loma receipt. Open June-Dec., Tues.-Fri. 9:30-5, weekends noon-5; Jan.-May, Tues.-Fri. 9:30-4, weekends noon-5.*

Todmorden Mills Historic Site. A number of the city's oldest buildings have been restored on their original sites, all in open parkland that is a marvelous place to picnic. The name Todmorden Mills comes from England, as did the settlers who built these structures. There are two pioneer houses, a brewery (1821), a paper mill (1825), and the old Don Train Station, built in 1891 to serve two once-great railroads, the Canadian National and Canadian Pacific. *67 Pottery Rd., just off the Bayview Ave. Extension, tel. 416/425-2250. Admission: $2.25 adults, $1.75 students and senior citizens, $1.25 children 6-12. Open May-Sept., Tues.-Fri. 10-4:30, weekends and holidays 11-4:30; Oct.-Dec., Mon.-Fri. 10-4; closed weekends.*

Union Station. *See* Tour 1, *above.*

Museums and Observatories As befits the largest city in Canada, as well as the capital of the province of Ontario, metropolitan Toronto has many major museums. These range from one of the world's great museums—the Royal Ontario Museum—to the superb Ontario Science Centre to the tiny but fascinating Museum of the History of Medicine.

Art Gallery of Ontario. *See* Tour 2, *above.*

An astonishing museum, **The Bata Shoe Museum Collection,** opened in May 1992 on the east side of University, across the street from the

Royal Ontario Museum. Created by Sonja Bata, the wife of the genius who built Bata Shoes into a billion-dollar worldwide conglomerate, this new museum contains more than 8,500 shoes, ranging from wooden thongs from 2500 BC to Queen Victoria's favorite footwear, and much more.

During 1995, this fascinating collection is scheduled to move to a permanent home in a new building at the corner of Bloor and St. George streets, a few blocks west. Until then, it is in the Colonnade. *131 Bloor St. W, tel. 416/924–7463. Admission: $3 adults, $1 senior citizens and students. Open Tues.–Sun. 11–6. 2 hrs free parking available.*

Bell Canada Building. Just north of the Old City Hall is a modest display of early telephones that go back to the time of Alexander Graham Bell, who actually invented the darned thing in a town just west of Toronto. You may enjoy seeing the phone book of 1879, which listed 30 houses in Toronto, as well as the offices of 18 doctors and a single dentist. *483 Bay St., in basement; tel. 416/599–6990. Admission free. Open weekdays 9–5.*

Beth Tzedec Museum. Located within an attractive Conservative synagogue of the same name, it is the only museum of Jewish artifacts in Toronto. It has special exhibits, as well as fine regular displays of ancient coins and glass, silver coins from ancient Greece and Rome, medieval Sabbath spice boxes, and even a centuries-old chair on which infant boys would be circumcised. Tours can be arranged. *1700 Bathurst St., about 4 blocks south of Eglinton or 3 mi northwest of Royal Ontario Museum, tel. 416/781–3511. Admission free. Open Mon., Wed., Thurs. 11–5, Sun. 10–1.*

Canadian Automotive Museum. Just over a half-hour drive east of Toronto is this remarkable place with more than five dozen weird and antique vehicles on display. See a 1911 Cadillac Speedstar, a 1912 Rolls Royce limo, and great failures of automobile history. *99 Simcoe St. S, in Oshawa; take Hwy. 401 east to Simcoe and go north, just past John St., tel. 905/576–1222. Admission: $5 adults, $4.50 senior citizens and students, $3.50 children 6–11, children under 5 free. Open weekdays 9–5, weekends and holidays 10–6; closed Mon. Labor Day–Easter.*

Canada's Sports Hall of Fame. For many years this charming place sat next to a super-popular hockey museum; now it stands alone in the Sports Hall of Fame Building on the north side of Exhibition Stadium on the CNE grounds downtown, at Dufferin and Lakeshore. There are three floors of exhibits on Canadian sports heroes through history, and two touch-screen computers with autobiographies, highlights of careers, and quizzes. *Tel. 416/260–6789. Admission free. Open daily 10–4:30.*

David Dunlap Observatory. Constructed in 1935, this is both a museum of photos of sunspots, nebulae, and galaxies and the largest observatory in all of Canada—and it is only 15 miles north of downtown! Visitors are admitted only in large groups on Saturday nights, from mid-April to early October, but individuals or small groups who call for reservations may join the next tour that has space. Visitors climb a ladder and peek through the 25-ton telescope at the planet, star, or moon that is "playing" that night. It can get extremely chilly under the unheated dome, even in midsummer, so dress warmly for your close encounter. To get to the observatory, go north on Highway 404 (the northern continuation of the Don Valley Parkway, alias the DVP) past the city limits of Steeles; get off at 16th Avenue. Go west (left) to Bayview, then north (right) on Bayview. Make the second left (west) onto Hillsview Drive; it's No. 123. (That's only 1.9 miles north of Highway 7; don't panic). Or, you can take the Bayview "GO" bus at the Finch Avenue subway stop, and ask to be dropped off at Hillsview Drive. *123 Hillsview Dr., tel. 905/ 884-2112. Admission: $2.50 adults, $1.25 senior citizens and children under 12. Open Wed. 10-11:30 AM; also Sat. eve. during summer. Tour hrs vary; from mid-Apr. to early Oct., they usually begin ½ hr after sunset.*

H.M.C.S. *Haida*. On the grounds of Ontario Place, across from the Canadian National Exhibition, this World War II destroyer is now a floating museum. It is irresistible for children of all ages. *Tel. 416/ 314-9755. Admission: $1.50. Open third May weekend-Labor Day 10:30-7.*

Hockey Hall of Fame and Museum. Open since 1961, this shrine has everything from the original Stanley Cup, donated in 1893, to displays of goalie masks, skate and stick collections, jerseys of the great players, and video displays of big games. If you wish to see Wayne Gretzky's feet cast in bronze, this is the place to catch them. For many years, this exhibition hall was located on the CNE grounds, but since 1993, it has been found, and treasured, in a stunning new location: the BCE Place, at the northwest corner of Yonge and Front streets, in a century-plus-old stunning Bank of Montreal building, molded into a gorgeous new structure. Public parking is available under the BCE building, or you can walk to it from the King and University subway stops. And thanks to its larger location, it also has a copy of the Montreal Canadiens' dressing room, chairs from the old Madison Square Garden, and much more. *30 Yonge St., tel. 416/360-7765. Admission: $7.50 adults, $5.50 senior citizens and children under 13. Open Mon.-Wed. 9-6, Thurs. and Fri. 9 AM-9:30 PM, Sat. 9-6, Sun. 10-6.*

Lakeview Generating Station. A living museum located in the west end, this giant thermal-electric station produces more power than Niagara Falls' stations. Visitors see coal converted to energy in furnaces towering 17 stories overhead. *Lakeshore and Dixie Rds., a 15-min drive west of downtown; tel. 416/222-2571. Tours weekdays 9:30-4:30. Children should be over 10.*

Marine Museum of Upper Canada. Exhibits cover the War of 1812, fur-trade exploration, and so on. On display are canoes, a diving suit, relics from sunken ships, and a wireless room from the 1930s. Outside the museum is a 1932 steam tugboat in dry dock. *Located inside Exhibition Place on the CNE grounds, near Dufferin St. and Lakeshore Blvd., tel. 416/392-1765. Take Bathurst St. #511 streetcar from Bathurst/Bloor subway stop. Admission: $3.50 adults, $2.75 senior citizens and children 12-18, $2.50 children under 12. Open Jan.-Mar., weekends noon-5; Apr.-Dec., Tues.-Fri. 9:30-4, weekends and holidays noon-5.*

McMichael Canadian Collection. Though 20 miles northwest of Toronto, this popular art gallery attracts more than 300,000 visitors a year. The building, constructed from native stone and hand-hewn timber, houses the art of the Group of Seven painters and some of their contemporaries. These talented young men turned to the Canadian landscape for inspiration in the early decades of this century. At a time when 19th-century British styles were still holding the colonies in an artistic stranglehold, this struggle to capture the passion and fury of the raw and powerful Canadian landscape was a great leap forward. In addition to seeing the paintings, you won't want to ignore the 100 acres of river valley around the gallery buildings—an ideal spot for picnics. *Drive west on Hwy. 401 to Hwy. 400, then north to Kleinburg exit, tel. 905/893–1121. Admission: $6 adults, $3 senior citizens and students, $13 families. Open Nov.–May, Tues.–Sun. 10–4; June–Oct. daily 10–5.*

Metro Toronto Police Museum and Discovery Centre. Highlights are a replica of a 19th-century police station, a wide selection of firearms, and displays of some of the city's most infamous crimes. Since it recently moved into the main foyer of striking new police headquarters, just one block west of the famous Maple Leaf Gardens where the popular professional hockey team plays, the museum has become "heavy on discovery." You can now study your fingerprints. Oodles of interactive displays include everything from information on drugs to "Did You Know?" quizzes. Other exhibits are computers to help track down missing children, a 1914 paddywagon, and crash car videos. There's even a brand-new Harley Davidson to jump on, and a car sliced in half, so that kids can climb in and out, hear a dispatcher squawk at them, and check out the computer on the dashboard. *40 College St., ½ block west of Yonge, tel. 416/324–6201. Admission free. Open daily 9–9.*

Ontario Science Centre. It has been called a museum of the 21st century, but it's much more than that. Where else can one stand at the edge of a black hole, work hand-in-clamp with a robot, or land on the moon? Even the building itself is extraordinary. Three linked pavilions float gracefully down the side of a ravine at Eglinton Avenue East, near the Don Valley Parkway, and each overflows with exhibits that make space, technology, communications, and life itself irresistible. Early 1992 brought a marvelous new space exhibit called "Challenger." A dozen minitheaters show films that bring the natural world to life. Live demonstrations—of lasers, glassblowing, papermaking, electricity, etc.—take place regularly throughout the day, so check the schedule when you arrive at the center, and plan your time accordingly. And be sure to check out the Living Earth exhibit, thrilling visitors since 1993.

You need at least two hours to scratch the surface; you may want to spend an entire day. Children will love this place, probably more than any other in Toronto, but adults will be enthralled, too. There is a cafeteria, a restaurant, and a gift store with a cornucopia of books and scientific doodads. *770 Don Mills Rd., about 11 km (7 mi) from downtown. By car, head west from Eglinton Ave. exit of Don Valley Pkwy. By public transportation, take Yonge St. subway from downtown to Eglinton station, and transfer to Eglinton E bus. Get off at Don Mills Pkwy. stop. Tel. 416/696–3127 (for recording), 416/429–4100 (for further information). Admission: $7.50 adults; $5.50 children 11–17, $3 senior citizens and children 5–10; family rate of $17 for up to 2 adults and 6 children; free after 5 PM. Parking $4. Open daily 10–6, Fri. 10–9.*

Puppet Centre. *See* What to See and Do with Children, *above.*

Redpath Sugar Museum. Located on the waterfront, a few blocks east of where the ferries depart for the Toronto Island, this museum has displays of sugar harvesting, vintage sugar tools, and an enjoyable 20-minute film, *Raising Cane.* The curator is available to answer questions. *95 Queen's Quay E, by the water, tel. 416/366–3561. Admission free. Open weekdays 10–noon and 1–3.*

Royal Ontario Museum. This spectacular collection is described at length in Tour 3, above, as are its siblings, the **McLaughlin Planetarium,** the **Sigmund Samuel Canadiana Collection,** and the **George R. Gardiner Museum of Ceramic Art.**

Art Galleries Toronto is a highly cosmopolitan art center, second only to New York in North America. Over 300 commercial art galleries are listed in the Yellow Pages, offering every kind of art for viewing and sale, from Picasso to Warhol, from representational to abstract, from Inuit to Indian. The following is a list of some of the best and most respected galleries. The entertainment section of the Saturday *Globe and Mail* has several pages of listings and reviews of current shows. Most galleries have free copies of the monthly booklet *Slate*, which includes a gallery guide to Toronto. Visitors may want to stroll from gallery to gallery in either of two major districts—the Yorkville area, especially just behind the exclusive Hazelton Lanes complex, and the Queen Street area, west of University Avenue. Most galleries are open Tuesday through Saturday, 10–5:30 or 6.

Bau-Xi Gallery, across the street from the Art Gallery of Ontario (340 Dundas St. W, tel. 416/977–0600), was founded by Paul Wong, an artist and dealer from Vancouver. It provides a window on contemporary Canadian West Coast art (some from Ontario, as well), much of it affordable.

The Drabinsky Gallery (86 Scollard St., tel. 416/324–5766) was created by the man who runs the Pantages, where *The Phantom of the Opera* plays eternally, as well as the North York Performing Arts Centre, with its long run of *Show Boat*. With its attractive, rosy-maple floors and such major artists as Harold Town and Alex Colville, this is an important new addition to the Yorkville art scene.

Gallery Dresdnere (12 Hazelton Ave., tel. 416/923–4662), created by an ex-Montrealer, shows a fine selection of Canadian abstract and conceptual paintings, as well as graphics and wall hangings.

Gallery One (121 Scollard St., tel. 416/929–3103), is one of the mainstays for large-format abstract expressionists in Canada and the United States, as well as for representational landscape art from western Ontario and Inuit art. Color-field painters, from Larry Poons to Jules Olitski, are exhibited here.

Gallery Moos (622 Richmond St. W, tel. 416/777–0707) was opened by German-born Walter Moos 30 years ago to promote Canadian art. He is a discerning, reliable dealer, whose gallery has Picassos, Chagalls, Miros, and Dufys, as well as such internationally admired Canadians as Gershon Iskowitz, Ken Danby, Sorel Etrog, and Jean-Paul Riopelle.

Glass Art Gallery (21 Hazelton Ave., tel. 416/968–1823) is the only gallery of its kind in Canada. It is a thrilling showroom of stained glass, laminated and crystal sculpture, and other avant-garde work.

The Isaacs/Inuit Gallery (9 Prince Arthur Ave., tel. 416/921–9985) was started by the respected Av Isaacs to showcase fine art and crafts produced in the Canadian Arctic. It is the finest gallery of its kind anywhere. Prints, drawings, sculpture, wall hangings, and antiquities are all beautifully displayed.

Jane Corkin Photographic Gallery (179 John St. off Queen St., tel. 416/979–1980) has proven that photography is a major art form. Featuring everyone from André Kertesz to Richard Avedon, this gallery is one of the most fascinating in town, showing hand-painted photos, documentary photos, and fashion photography.

Klonaridis, Inc. (80 Spadina Ave., near King St., tel. 416/360–7800) is run by a young dealer of discerning taste who displays local talent and imports some of the newest and best from New York and elsewhere south of the border. A must-see place for those interested in new, exciting art.

Mira Godard Gallery (22 Hazelton Ave., tel. 416/964–8197), which came from Montreal to Toronto in 1972, carries such major French-Canadian artists as Borduas and Riopelle, as well as established Canadian artists like Alex Colville, Kenneth Lochhead, David Milne, Jean-Paul Lemieux, and Christopher Pratt.

Miriam Shiell Fine Art Ltd. (16A Hazelton Ave., tel. 416/925–2461) located not far from the Sable-Castelli, is a wittily designed space for displaying expensive work from the United States and abroad, as well as that of several established Canadians. One can see Dufy and Matisse, Noland and Olitski, as well as Inuit art.

The Museum for Textiles (55 Centre Ave., attached to the Chestnut Park Hotel, tel. 416/599–5321) is located one block east of University, just south of Dundas, not far from Eaton Centre. It has 10 fascinating exhibition rooms, with cross-cultural displays, contemporary galleries, and such things as men's costumes from North Nigeria.

Nancy Poole's Studio (16 Hazelton Ave., tel. 416/964–9050) is a small, intimate space, almost exclusively exhibiting Canadian contemporary painting and sculpture, generally representational. The artists include Jack Chambers, the astonishing Canadian Indian stone-carver Joe Jacobs, and the fine contemporary painter John Boyle.

Olga Korper (17 Morrow Ave. N off Dundas, ½ mi west of Dufferin St., tel. 416/538–8220) is one of the most accessible and knowledgeable dealers in Toronto, and she is a trailblazer who has discovered many important artists. This is a fine place for beginning collectors to visit.

Open Studio Printmaking (520 King St. W, 3rd Floor, tel. 416/368–8238) shows original prints of modern Canadian artists.

Prime Gallery (52 McCaul St., north of Queen, tel. 416/593–5750) has crafts from across Canada, including avant-garde ceramics, functional teapots, wall sculpture, and jewelry.

Sable–Castelli Gallery (33 Hazelton Ave., tel. 416/961–0011) is the result of the Jared Sable gallery's amalgamation in 1974 with the renowned Castelli galleries of Manhattan. Since then, he has exhibited established American artists such as Warhol, Oldenburg, Johns, and Rosenquist, as well as innovative young Canadian artists who use strong expressive imagery.

S. L. Simpson Gallery (515 Queen St. W, tel. 416/362–3738) has new Canadian paintings, and mixed media.

Thomson Gallery (on the 9th floor of The Bay's Tower, just south of the Eaton Centre) houses the impressive collection of the billionaire who owns Simpsons, The Bay, and three dozen newspapers, including the *Globe and Mail*.

Wynick-Tuck Gallery (80 Spadina Ave., tel. 416/364–8716) represents contemporary Canadian artists whose work expresses a wide range of untrendy, often imagistic concerns. Many of them have become well established, attesting to the gallery's influence.

Ydessa Hendeles Art Foundation (778 King St., 2 blocks west of Bathurst St., tel. 416/941–9400) is now, more than ever, a wonderful, major showcase for contemporary international art.

Parks and Gardens Toronto was originally a series of little villages, each one treasuring its tiny common or park. The metro area now has some 3 million souls, but residents still think in the old village way, saving from development as much parkland as is possible. The parks are more than just grass; they are great places to jog, bike, picnic, see flowers, even bird-watch. Some have skating rinks, tennis courts, and playing fields.

Edwards Gardens. Thirty-five acres of beautiful hillside gardens flow into one of the city's most popular ravines. Paths wind along colorful floral displays and exquisite rock gardens. Refreshments and picnic facilities are available, but no pets are allowed.

The great ravine walk begins at Edwards Gardens (entrance on the southwest corner of Leslie St. and Lawrence Ave. E). Head south through **Wilket Creek Park** and through the winding Don River valley. Pass beneath the Don Valley Parkway and continue along Massey Creek. After hours of walking (or biking, or jogging) through almost uninterrupted parkland, you'll end up at the southern tip of **Taylor Creek Park** on Victoria Park Avenue, just north of the Danforth. From here you can catch a subway train back to your hotel.

High Park. Toronto's equivalent of London's Hyde Park or Manhattan's Central Park (but with no political ranting and few muggings) is 3 or 4 miles from downtown, but it is certainly worth a visit—especially in the summer, when there are many special events, including free productions of Shakespeare. One of the highlights is **Grenadier Pond,** a small lake in the southwest corner. Named after the British soldiers who used to drill on its frozen surface in the last century, it is home today to thousands of migrating birds. You can fish in its well-stocked waters, either from the shore or from a rented rowboat. There are Sunday afternoon concerts in summer and supervised skating in winter. The **High Park Zoo** is a far cry from the Metro Zoo, but it's a lot closer, and it's free. It's modest enough that even young children won't tire walking among the deer, Barbary sheep, peacocks, rabbits, and the only truly native Torontonians extant—raccoons. Other highlights of the park are a large swimming pool, tennis courts, fitness trails, and hillside gardens with roses and sculpted hedges.

Take the Bloor Street subway west to the High Park station, or the College Street streetcar to the eastern end of the park. There's limited parking along Bloor Street, just north of the park, and along the side streets on the eastern side.

Highland Creek ravines. Since these are almost in their natural state, they are considered the most beautiful in Toronto—ideal for cross-country skiing, biking, and jogging. There are two parks that follow Highland Creek, **Colonel Danforth Park** and **Morningside Park.** The Colonel Danforth trail begins south of Kingston Road, on the east side of Highland Creek bridge. Morningside Park is accessible off Morningside Avenue, between Kingston Road and Ellesmere Avenue. Both parks can be entered from the grounds of Scarborough College, 1265 Military Trail, in Scarborough. The **Toronto Field Naturalists** (tel. 416/968–6255) lead over 150 outings every year, mainly within these ravine systems.

Humber Valley. This parkland in Toronto's west end is well worth a hiking/jogging/biking tour. It stretches along the Humber River ravine, from north of the city limits (Steeles Ave.) all the way down to where the Humber flows quietly into Lake Ontario.

James Gardens, a lovely formal garden, can be reached from Edenbridge Drive, east of Royal York Road. Adjoining it to the south is **Scarlet Mills Park,** one of North America's only wildflower reserves. Both parks are open daily until sunset, with lots of free parking.

Kortright Centre. This delightful conservation center is a must— and it's just a groundhog's shadow away from Canada's Wonderland, and only 15 minutes north of the city. Attractions here include three aquariums, bird feeders everywhere, and some 12½ miles of hiking trails—half of them open during the winter. Walk through the magnificent woods here and see signs of foxes, coyotes, mice, rabbits, deer, wild turkeys, pheasants, chickadees, finches, and (non-baseball) blue jays. If you visit this place in winter, bring your own cross-country skis and snowshoes and dress warmly. *Drive north along Hwy. 400, exit west at Major Mackenzie Dr. (at Canada's Wonderland), continue 1.9 mi to Pine Valley Dr., then south (left) briefly. Tel. 905/832–2289. Admission: $4.50 adults, $2.50 senior citizens and students, children under 4 free. Open daily 10–4.*

Nordheimer Ravine. This can be approached from a path leading from Boulton Drive, in the shadow of Casa Loma. On your right is a view of the great mansions of Forest Hill; on your left is Casa Loma, rising above a steep bank of trees. The ravine eventually opens up like a flower, and you are soon at **Churchill Park,** which, as we've noted, has the best tobogganing in the city.

Queen's Park. This small, lovely park in the heart of the downtown area is discussed in Tour 3, above. It's not worth a special trip, but it's certainly worth remembering after a day of shopping or museum-hopping.

The **Rosedale ravines** are only a few minutes' walk from the shopping mecca of Yonge and Bloor streets, in the very heart of the city. They are a series of peaceful ravines that cut through the luxurious, heavily wooded neighborhood of Rosedale. Walk north from the Castle Frank subway station along Castle Frank Road to **Hawthorn Gardens.** There you will find a short footpath to **Craigleigh Gardens.** Suddenly, this tiny, quiet park gives way to a ravine, and paths wind steeply down through a tangle of underbrush. From here you can go west, up Balfour Creek, across Mount Pleasant Road, and through **David Balfour Park** to St. Clair Avenue. Or you can walk northeast, past the Don Valley brickworks to **Chorley Park** and Mount Pleasant Cemetery, by way of the still-undeveloped Moore Park marshes. These marshes remain an excellent breeding ground for wildlife, though they lie within the core of a bustling city. Another way to explore this ravine is to start at Yonge Street and St. Clair Avenue. Walk east along St. Clair Avenue a few blocks, until you come to a bridge. On the north side of the street is a sign marked "nature trail." Believe it.

Scarborough Bluffs. This is the most scenic park along Lake Ontario, with breathtaking views from the high lakeside cliffs. **Cathedral Bluffs Park,** at the foot of Midland Avenue, also offers dramatic views.

Sherwood Park. Farther north, near Lawrence Avenue East and Mount Pleasant Road, is one of the best-kept secrets in Toronto. Sherwood Park has one of the finest children's playgrounds in the city, a lovely wading pool, and a hill that seems to go on forever. Head up Mount Pleasant Road, north of Eglinton Avenue, until you see a little street called Sherwood on the right. Go east a long block, and you're there. A ravine begins at the bottom of the hill. You can follow it across Blythwood Road, all the way to Yonge Street and Lawrence Avenue. There, subways and buses await you—and so do the beautiful rose gardens in **Alexander Muir Park.**

Sir Casimir Gzowski Park. Enjoy marvelous views of the Toronto Islands, Ontario Place, and the downtown skyline, and swim at nearby **Sunnyside Park.** Both lakefront parks are only a few blocks east of Bathurst Street, easily accessible by streetcar.

Sir Winston Churchill Park. Winter visitors—especially those with children—should try not to miss this park, located at Spadina Avenue, only a short walk from Casa Loma. In summer there's a sweet playground, a sandbox, a jogging track, and tennis courts. In winter there's a serious hill offering the most terrifying toboggan run in the city.

Tommy Thompson Park. This interesting place, known until 1985 as the **Leslie Street Spit,** is a peninsula that juts 3 miles into Lake Ontario. It was created from the sand dredged for a new port entry and the landfill of a hundred skyscrapers. (These Canadians don't waste a thing.) It has quickly become one of the best areas in the city for cycling, jogging, walking, sailing, photography, and bird-watching.

This strange, man-made peninsula immediately became the home (or stopover) for the largest colony of ring-billed seagulls in the world and for dozens of species of terns, ducks, geese, and snowy egrets.

No private vehicles are permitted, but on weekends, mid-May to mid-October, two vans operate free of charge from the parking lot. In summer, a city bus travels through the park from the corner of Queen Street and Berkshire Avenue.

If you drive, go east along Queen Street to Leslie Street, then south to the lake. The park is open weekends and holidays 9–6.

The Toronto Islands. *See* Tour 1, *above.*

Theme Parks and Amusement Areas

African Lion Safari. This fabulous drive-through wildlife park is a full hour's drive from Toronto, but it should be considered by anyone with children and access to a car.

If the idea of a giraffe sticking its head into your back seat does not warm your heart, there are air-conditioned trams that carry as many as 3,000 visitors a day over a 6-mile safari trail. Lions, tigers, cheetah, black bears, elephants, white rhinos, and zebras make this astonishingly uncommercial park truly special. And you'll be pleased to hear that its first female elephant ever was born in early 1994 and weighed a bouncing 262 pounds.

In addition to six large game reserves, there's a birds of prey flying demonstration, a parrot show, an elephant roundup, and even an *African Queen*–style boat that cruises past birds and primates. *Near Cambridge, Ont., due west of Toronto. Take Hwy. 401 west to Hwy. 6. Drive south to Safari Rd., and turn right. The trip takes about an hour. Tel. 519/623–2620. Admission, including boat and railway cruises: about $14 adults, $12 senior citizens and children 13–17, $10 children 3–12. You may want to pack a picnic, but food is available. Open Apr.– late Oct. 10–4, 10–5 on weekends and holidays. July and Aug., daily 10–5:30.*

Black Creek Pioneer Village. This re-creation of a 19th-century Ontario community is a joyous outing for the entire family. *See* Historic Buildings and Sites, *above.*

Canada's Wonderland. Yogi Bear, Fred Flintstone, Scooby Doo, and other Canadian cultural heroes are part of a $160 million theme park overflowing with games, rides, restaurants, and shops. The entertainment ranges from Broadway-style productions to pop and rock performances to dolphin shows. Canada's first world-class theme park lacks the warm evocativeness of Disneyland; and because it's here in the Frozen North, its season runs only from late April to early October. Yet the park is remarkably close to Toronto—barely 30 minutes from downtown, and only 15 minutes from the airport—and a visit here can easily be combined with a trip to Black Creek Pioneer Village.

Children will love it here, but adults should stay away unless they've been longing for brassy entertainment, stomach-churning rides, and eateries such as Yee Ribb Pytt, which serves French Fryes and Shrymps. Indeed, families should consider packing a picnic lunch and eating at the few tables (reluctantly) provided, just outside the park.

Since this place was recently purchased by Paramount, there will now be Paramount-related exhibits throughout the park, including a Walk of Fame, movie memorabilia, props from famous movies, and more. Indeed, there are many raves for its recent *Days of Thunder* exhibit, with simulated racing cars and a theater show.

Teens and many adults will be delighted to know that on the grounds of Canada's Wonderland is the high-quality **Kingswood Music Theatre** (tel. 905/832–8131), which has excellent pop and rock acts through the summer, which cost less than $10 above the park admission. The open-air facility has 5,200 reserved seats under a covered pavilion and 8,800 additional seats on the sloping lawn.

Low-cost GO express buses leave regularly from Yorkdale and York Mills subway stations. By car, take Hwy. 401 to Hwy. 400; drive north about 10 mins. to Rutherford Rd., and follow signs. Tel. 905/832–7000. Admission: about $32 adults (including all shows and rides), $16 senior citizens over 60 and children 3–6. Should you wish only grounds admission, which does not include rides: around $21 per person. Those who plan to return several times might consider an individual season pass for about $48, or a family pass for about $190 for 4 people. Check newspapers, chain stores, and hotels for half-price tickets. Open spring and fall weekends 10–8; late June–Labor Day, daily 10–10.

The Canadian National Exhibition (the CNE or "the Ex"), at the foot of Dufferin Street and Lakeshore Boulevard, attracts over 3 million people each year. It began back in 1879 as an agricultural show, and remnants of that tradition can still be found in the livestock exhibits. But in its second century, the Ex is a noisy, crowded, often entertaining collection of carnies pushing $5 balloons, tummy-turning midway rides, sexist beauty contests, live bands, horticultural and technological exhibits, and (sometimes) top-notch happenings.

Parades, dog swims, horse shows, grandstand shows with such talent as Bill Cosby, Kenny Rogers, and Whitney Houston—the Exhibition has something for all. It's often vulgar and brassy, the snacks overpriced and greasy, the rides too short and too expensive. But it can also be an enjoyable way to spend an afternoon—after all, the world's largest annual exhibition must have *something* still going for it! *Lakeshore Blvd. W at Strachan ("strawn") Ave. or off Dufferin St., just south of King St., tel. 416/393–6000. In 1995, the CNE will run Aug. 18–Sept. 4. Admission: about $8.50 adults, $4.25 senior*

citizens, $3 children under 14. Open daily 10 AM–midnight; build-
ings, 11 AM–9 PM; food building, 11–10; outdoor concessions, 11–11.
Tickets to grandstand shows available from box office or through
Ticketmaster (tel. 416/872–1111). Check local newspapers for special
daily events. Never take a car to the Ex; the parking is insufficient and
always terribly overpriced. Many buses and streetcars labeled "Exhi-
bition" travel across the city into the CNE grounds.

Centreville. *See* Tour 1, *above.*

Harbourfront Centre. *See* Tour 1, *above.*

Marineland, a park full of quality rides and dolphin/killer whale
shows, is about 90 minutes southwest of Toronto (*see* Chapter 8).

Ontario Place. Highlights of this waterfront complex, built on three
man-made islands, include the **Cinesphere** (a dome with a six-story
movie screen enclosed); several interesting shows in pods that float
above the waters of Lake Ontario; the *Haida,* a destroyer from the
Second World War that is fun to explore; and, best of all, the outdoor
Forum, where nightly performances by a fabulous singer or rock
group (or orchestra or ballet corps) take place, for astonishingly low
prices that range between $8 and $15. Here, too, you will find the
Children's Village—complete with water games, towering tube
slides, and a moon walk. This is one of the most creative playgrounds
in the world, and a must for children 3–14. Children's theater, puppet shows, clowns, and magicians are also included with admission.
The eateries are uneven, and the Imax films at the massive
Cinesphere tend to be all medium and no message (though still a
thrill). But Ontario Place is still a major summer draw to the waterfront, and irresistible to those in their early teens and younger.
South of Lakeshore Blvd., across from CNE grounds, tel. 416/314–
9900. Admission free. Open daily 10:30 AM–1 AM, late May–Labor
Day. Fireworks from six countries at 10 PM, in late June–early July;
on those days, you can pay $5–$15 for reserved seating to watch the
stunning event. Parking $5. Bumper boats, pedal boats, miniature
golf, Cinesphere, and some other attractions have nominal additional
charges.

Throughout much of the winter, the Cinesphere has been offering
70 mm films such as ET: The Extra-Terrestrial, Cliffhanger, Lawrence of Arabia, *and other bigger-than-life adventure movies and*
classics. Check daily newspapers for times, and remember that one
has not truly lived until one has seen Indiana Jones *surrounded by*
snakes on a 60 ft. by 80 ft. screen.

Wild Water Kingdom. *See* What to See and Do with Children, *above.*

Libraries and Special Collections

Boys and Girls House. When it opened in 1922, this was the first library in the British Empire that was devoted entirely to children's
books. It's still one of the best (40 St. George St., tel. 416/393–7746).
The Osborne and Smith Collections of Early Children's Books, located in the same building, is a world-renowned collection of
children's literature. Dr. Edgar Osborne, a British librarian, presented his private collection of about 2,000 children's books to the
Toronto Public Library in 1949; today there are more than 21,000.
The collection includes letters written and illustrated by Beatrix
Potter, and the oldest book is a fairy tale printed in 1476. There are
regular lectures and changing exhibits on everything from fairy ta-
les to Christmas customs of the Victorians. *Tel. 416/393–7753. Open*
weekdays 10–6, Sat. 9–5.

Metropolitan Toronto Library is one of the most beautiful and accessible public libraries in the world (*see* Tour 3, *above*).

The Merril Collection of Science Fiction, Speculation and Fantasy. Formerly the **Spaced Out Library**, this is the largest public collection of science-fiction material in the world. Although only a small percentage of the volumes is allowed to circulate, the collection includes more than 20,000 books, many of them in foreign languages, and close to 10,000 magazines, including a complete collection of *Galaxy*. *40 St. George St., on 2nd floor of Boys and Girls House, tel. 416/393-7748. Open weekdays 10–6, Sat. 9–5.*

Thomas Fisher Rare Books Library. Scholars and lovers of antique books may find this place of particular interest. Part of the University of Toronto, it has tomes and manuscripts going back to the early Middle Ages. *120 St. George St., a few blocks west of University Ave. and Royal Ontario Museum and just south of Bloor St., tel. 416/978-5285. Open weekdays 9–4:45.*

3 Shopping

Toronto prides itself on having some of the finest shopping in North America; and, indeed, most of the world's name boutiques can be found here, especially along the Bloor Street strip (between Yonge St. and Avenue Rd.) and in the Yorkville area, which covers the three streets immediately north of and parallel to the Bloor Street strip.

Although some Canadians have traditionally frowned on the concept of discount stores as vulgar and beneath them, there are many moderately priced stores around the city and a lively off-price clothing trade. Because of the weakness of the Canadian dollar, visitors obtain what amounts to an immediate discount on any purchase.

Toronto has a large artistic and crafts community, with many art galleries, custom jewelers, clothing designers, and artisans. From sophisticated glass sculpture to native and Inuit art, the many beautiful objects you'll find are ideal for gifts or for your own home. Among traditional crafts, available at antiques and specialty stores, are quilts, wood carvings, and pine furniture.

Food items that are fairly easy to transport as gifts include wild rice, available in bulk or in gift packages, and maple syrup in jars or cans.

Fur coats and hats are popular purchases with visitors from outside Canada. You can buy from a high-fashion outlet such as Creed's (on Bloor St. west of Yonge St.) or directly from a furrier in the Spadina Avenue garment district. Beaded Indian slippers and moccasins are also popular souvenirs. Distinctive **Hudson Bay** wool blankets, available only at The Bay, are an enduring Canadian tradition. The unique Tilley hat, sold by mail order or in the **Tilley Endurables** boutique at Queen's Quay Terminal, is an ideal present for sailors and adventurers: It's advertised as having been retrieved intact after being eaten by an elephant, and comes with a lifetime guarantee and owner's manual.

The better record stores stock a good selection of Canadian musicians, from Maureen Forrester and Liona Boyd to Anne Murray, Leonard Cohen, Kate and Anna McGarrigle, the Nylons, Stringband, Moxy Fruvous, and Bare Naked Ladies, as well as French-Canadian stars like Robert Charlebois, Roch Voisine, and Celine Dion. Similarly, good bookstores will introduce you to Canadian authors such as Margaret Atwood, Robertson Davies, Timothy Findley, Margaret Laurence, Alice Munro, Thomas King, Mordecai Richler, Lorna Crozier, and popular historian Pierre Berton.

Most stores accept MasterCard and Visa without minimums, though if you charge a purchase under $5 you won't be too popular. Major stores also accept American Express. You'll find American cash generally accepted, although not always at the most favorable rate of exchange.

Most stores are open late on Thursdays; some, like the Eaton Centre and The Bay downtown, are open late every weekday. Liquor stores are unlikely to be open late more than one night a week, perhaps Friday, although beer stores stay open later.

The biggest sale day of the year is Boxing Day, the first business day after Christmas, when nearly everything in the city, including furs, is half price. In fact, clothing prices tend to drop even further as winter fades. Summer sales start in late June and continue through August.

Shopping Districts

The **Yorkville Avenue/Bloor Street area** is where you'll find the big fashion names, fine leather goods, important jewelers, some of the top private art galleries, upscale shoe stores, and discount china and glassware. Streets to explore include Yorkville Avenue, Cumberland Street, and Scollard Street, all running parallel to Bloor Street, and Hazelton Avenue, running north from Yorkville Avenue near Avenue Road. Hazelton Lanes, between Hazelton Avenue and Avenue Road, and the adjacent York Square are among the most chichi shopping areas in Canada, and they are headquarters for café society during the brief annual spell of warm weather. Back in the 1960s, Yorkville was Canada's hippie headquarters, a mecca for potheads, runaways, and folk musicians. Goodbye Dylan, hello Gucci.

On **Bloor Street** you'll find **Holt Renfrew,** a very high-end clothing store (Holt's has men's and children's departments as well), and Harry Rosen for men, Georg Jensen, and shoe shops like Boutique Quinto and David's.

The **Eaton Centre** is a very large galleria-style shopping center downtown, on Yonge Street between Queen and Dundas streets. With scores of large and small stores and restaurants, all sheltered from the weather, it's one of the city's major tourist attractions. Generally speaking, the lower levels are lower priced and the higher levels are more expensive. In the immediate area are Sam the Record Man, probably Toronto's most comprehensive record/CD store; The Bay department store; a smaller shopping center called **The Atrium on Bay,** which is immediately north of the Eaton Centre and not tremendously interesting; and an assortment of cut-price consumer electronics stores on Yonge Street.

Queen Street West, starting just west of University Avenue and continuing past Spadina Avenue, creeping ever westward past Bathurst Street, is a trendy area near the Ontario College of Art. Here you'll find young, hip designers; stores that stock new and used books; vintage clothes; two comic book stores, including the biggest in North America (**Silver Snail,** No. 367; see also Dragon Lady Comic Shop at No. 200); and the more progressive private galleries. People-watching is fun here, too. The action is spreading onto John Street and other cross streets, and there's a rather interesting assortment of shops in **Village by the Grange,** a development on McCaul Street south of Dundas Street, across from the Art Gallery of Ontario.

Harbourfront Centre includes an antiques market that's Canada's biggest on Sundays, when there are around 200 dealers (390 Queen's Quay W, tel. 416/340–8377. Open Tues.–Fri. 11–6, Sat. 10–6, Sun. 8–6). The **Queen's Quay Terminal** is a renovated warehouse that now houses a collection of unique boutiques, craft stalls, patisseries, and so on; it's a great place to buy gifts. There's a free shuttle bus from Union Station, but it's a fairly easy walk. Parking is expensive.

Mirvish Village, a one-block assortment of bookstores, antiques shops, and boutiques, on Markham Street south of Bloor Street, used to have the distinct advantage of being one of the few areas which was open on Sunday. (Harbourfront was another). Now, of course, the city is pretty-well wide open Sunday. If you're in Mirvish Village on any other day, though (preferably not Saturday, which is unbearably crowded), check out **Honest Ed's** bargain house at Bathurst and Bloor streets, the truly silly deep-discount store that financed the revival of London's Old Vic theater. It's a good place to buy film for your camera, by the way. The strip of Bloor Street running east from Honest Ed's to Spadina Avenue is a vibrant mix of discount bookstores, casual clothing and health-food shops, pubs frequented by students from the University of Toronto, cafés, and Hungarian restaurants; it makes a delightful walk, particularly in the evening.

Another good bet for summer Sundays is **The Beaches,** on Queen Street East, starting at Woodbine Avenue. Here you'll find lots of casual clothing stores, gift and antiques shops, and bars and restaurants, all with a resort atmosphere: A boardwalk along the lake is just to the south. Take the Queen Street streetcar; parking can be a hassle.

Spadina Avenue, from Wellington Street north to College Street, has plenty of low-price clothing for the whole family, as well as fur and leather factory outlets. **Winner's,** south of King Street, is a good discount outlet for women and children. **Evex Luggage Centre,** at 369 Spadina Avenue, south of College Street, has good discount luggage, handbags, and leather accessories.

Downtown Toronto has a vast underground maze of shopping warrens that burrow in between and underneath the office towers. The tenants of the **Underground City** are mostly the usual assortment of chain stores, and the shopping is rather dull; also, directions are poorly marked. The network runs roughly from the Royal York Hotel near Union Station north to the Eaton Centre.

If you're venturing to the suburbs, there's a large shopping center at **Yorkdale,** easily reached by subway but pointless if you've been to the Eaton Centre. The area also has a number of off-price outlets within driving distance; check ads in the *Toronto Star.*

For the visitor with time to explore outside the central area, **Little Italy,** on St. Clair Avenue West (roughly between Lansdowne and Westmount streets), has some high-fashion Milanese clothing stores like Christian Boutique (No. 1236), LaScala Men's Wear (No. 1190), Gente Boutique (No. 1228), and the more casual Cheeky (No. 1180).

Department Stores

The major department stores have branches around the city and flagship stores downtown. They accept major credit cards and have liberal return policies. However, service tends to be very slow and uninformed compared with that of boutiques, and the stores generally lack the cachet of American chains like Bloomingdale's or Macy's. The big names are **Eaton's,** in the Eaton Centre, and **The Bay** (The Hudson Bay Company), at Yonge and Bloor streets.

Specialty Shops

Antiques and Galleries Yorkville is the headquarters of the establishment antiques dealers. But there are several other pockets around town, including a strip along Queen Street East, roughly between Sherbourne Street and George Street.

The Allery (322½ Queen St. W, tel. 416/593–0853) specializes in antique prints and maps.

Art Metropole (788 King St. W, tel. 416/367–2304) specializes in limited-edition, small-press, or self-published artists' books from around the world. These works often hover between visual arts and

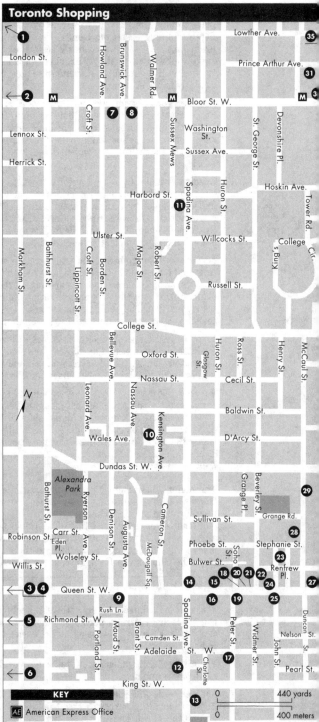

Toronto Shopping

KEY

AE American Express Office

literature. There's also a range of serious art periodicals and ephemera. It's a fascinating destination for those interested in what's happening on the fringes of the artistic community.

Glass Art Gallery (21 Hazelton Ave., tel. 416/968–1823) often has interesting Canadian and international exhibitions.

Jane Corkin Gallery (179 John St., north of Queen St., tel. 416/979–1980) specializes in photography. The more avant-garde galleries include **Cold City** (686 Richmond St. W, tel. 416/363–6681), **YYZ** (1087 Queen St. W, tel. 416/531–7869), and **Mercer Union** (333 Adelaide St. W, tel. 416/977–1412). Also check out **Toronto Photographers Workshop** (tel. 416/362–4242) and the other galleries at 80 Spadina Avenue, where you'll usually find at least one opening on a Saturday afternoon.

New Ballenford Books (98 Scollard St., tel. 416/960–0055) has Canada's largest selection of architecture titles and a gallery with usually interesting exhibits of architectural drawings and related work.

Prime Gallery (52 McCaul St., near the Ontario College of Art and the Art Gallery of Ontario, tel. 416/593–5750) has contemporary Canadian craft works, as well as art objects.

Quasi Modo (789 Queen St. W, next door to Dufflet Pastries, tel. 416/366–8370) has a quirky collection of 20th-century furniture and design. You never know what will be on display: vintage bicycles, Noguchi lamps, a corrugated cardboard table by Frank Gehry. They will order any (available) lamp for you.

Sawtooth Borders (17 Prince Arthur, just north of Bloor and west of Avenue Rd., tel. 416/961–8187) sells good-quality antique quilts. These days, it is open "by chance or appointment," to quote its charming owner.

20th Century (23 Beverley St., just north of Queen St., tel. 416/598–2172) is for serious collectors of 20th-century design, particularly furniture, lamps, jewelry, and decorative arts. Many of the pieces are museum quality, and the owners are extremely erudite.

Auctions **Christie's Auctioneers** (94 Cumberland Ave., tel. 416/960–2063).

Sotheby's (Canada) Inc. (9 Hazelton Ave., tel. 416/926–1774).

Books Toronto is rich in bookstores selling new books, used books, bestsellers, and remainders. If you need a current magazine or a paperback for the plane, there are the ubiquitous chains—Coles, Classic Bookshops, and W.H. Smith. Otherwise, we recommend:

The **Albert Britnell Book Shop** (765 Yonge St., just north of Bloor St., tel. 416/924–3321) has been a Toronto legend since 1893. The shop is now run by the third generation of the family. It has a superb search service that is getting rare. Its customers receive solicitous attention from the staff and its marvelous, British-like ambience makes for great browsing.

The **Book Cellar** (1560 Yonge St., above St. Clair Ave., tel. 416/967–5577; 142 Yorkville Ave., near Avenue Rd., tel. 416/925–9955) offers a fine choice of classical records, as well as international political and intellectual journals.

Book City has three locations (501 Bloor St. W, near Honest Ed's; Carrot Common, 348 Danforth Ave., near Chester Station; 2350 Bloor St. W, in "Bloor Village," 2 blocks east of Jane St.). It's strong on good remaindered books, has a knowledgeable staff, and offers a fine choice of magazines. It is usually open late into the evening.

The **Children's Bookstore** (2532 Yonge St., a few blocks north of Eglinton, tel. 416/480–0233) is simply magical: beautiful, large, with readings and concerts—the best-stocked bookstore of its kind on this child-obsessed globe. The staff knows and loves children and the literature they long for and need. It also has a superior collection of children's records, many of them Canadian.

David Mirvish Books/Books on Art (596 Markham St., tel. 416/531–9975) is, fittingly, smack in the middle of charming Mirvish Village. A gorgeous place, it overflows with quality books and many remainders; it has the best price in town for the Sunday *New York Times*.

Edward's Books and Art is now at four locations (356 Queen St. W, near Spadina Ave.; 2179 Queen St. E, in The Beaches; in the Park Plaza Hotel, 4 Avenue Rd., at the northwest corner of Bloor St. W; and 2200 Yonge St., south of Eglinton Ave.). All are open Sunday. This is one of the loveliest minichains in the city. It advertises huge discounts on best-sellers and remainders in every Saturday's *Globe and Mail*, as does David Mirvish.

Lichtman's News and Books is at several locations (144 Yonge St., near Adelaide St.; the Atrium on Bay St., near Dundas St.; and 1430 Yonge St., south of St. Clair Ave.). There's a good selection of books, but Lichtman's is best known for its selection of magazines and its newspapers from around the world, often only a day old.

Longhouse Book Shop (497 Bloor St. W, just west of Bathurst St., tel. 416/921–9995) stocks only Canadian titles, more than 20,000 back titles and new publications, handsomely shelved or piled high on pine tables. The respect and love for Canadian writers and writing is palpable here.

Bob Miller Book Room (180 Bloor St. W, just northwest of the Royal Ontario Museum, tel. 416/922–3557) has the best literature section in the city and a staff that has been with Bob for decades.

Pages Books and Magazines (256 Queen St. W, tel. 416/598–1447) has a wide selection of international and small-press literature; fashion and design books and magazines; and books on film, art, and literary criticism.

Old Favourites Bookshop (132 Hwy. 7, just east of Markham, tel. 905/294–3865), in a northeastern section of town, has over a quarter-million used books, magazines, and journals at fair prices.

This Ain't the Rosedale Library (483 Church St., south of Wellesley Ave., tel. 416/929–9912) stocks the largest selection of baseball books in Canada, as well as a good selection of fiction, poetry, photography, design, rock, and jazz books. The staff is well read and can offer intelligent advice when asked.

Writers & Co. (2005 Yonge St. near Davisville Ave., a few blocks south of Eglinton Ave., tel. 416/481–8432) is arguably Canada's finest literary bookstore, with hard-to-find poets, essayists, and world novelists. If you have been looking for a rare Caribbean poetry collection, a Swedish play in translation, or an Asian novella, this is the one to visit. It's a marvelous place, and they'll be happy to order any book for you.

Special-Interest Bookstores   **Bakka Science Fiction Book Shoppe** (282 Queen St. W, tel. 416/596–8161) is the largest sci-fi and fantasy bookstore in the country (8,000 new and 3,000 used titles), with rare books and posters as well.

The **Cookbook Store** (850 Yonge St., north of Bloor St., tel. 416/920–2665) has the city's largest selection of books and magazines on cooking and wine.

Glad Day Bookshop (598a Yonge St., tel. 416/961–4161) is Toronto's leading gay bookstore.

Open Air Books and Maps (25 Toronto St., just east of Yonge and King Sts., tel. 416/363–0719) offers over 10,000 travel guides, oodles of atlases and road maps, specialized travel books, and titles on nature and food.

Sleuth of Baker Street (1595 Bayview Ave., south of Eglinton Ave., tel. 416/483–3111) is the best place for mysteries and detective fiction.

Theatrebooks (11 St. Thomas St., 1 street west of Bay, running south from Bloor, near The Colonnade and the ROM, tel. 416/922–7175 or 800/361–3414) has an astounding collection of plays from around the world and large sections on every other theatrical topic.

Toronto Women's Bookstore (73 Harbord St., near Spadina Ave., tel. 416/922–8744) carries the latest feminist works on women's political and legal issues, divorce, childbirth, etc. A reading lounge is upstairs.

China, Flatware, and Crystal There are a few well-known outlets, but the best-known discounter, and bride's best friend, is **William Ashley** (50 Bloor St. W, just off Yonge St., tel. 416/964–2900). They will ship anywhere.

Clothing **The Answer Salon** (3200 Yonge St., tel. 416/483–5663) showcases designer coordinates for business and fine fashions from Canadian, American, and European designers for both work and play, in sizes 16 to 26.

Brown's (1975 Avenue Rd., south of Hwy. 401, tel. 416/489–1975) provides classic clothing for short men and women. There is also a store for men only (545 Queen St. W, tel. 416/368–5937). An offshoot is **Muskat & Brown** (2528 Yonge St., tel. 416/489–4005) for petite women.

Decollete Fashion Boutique (81 Yorkville Ave., tel. 416/323–2875) is a real find; it carries haute couture "interpretations" of both French and local designers, at prices far less than you would pay at stores just a few steps away. Decollete has another store out on Danforth, which Bloor turns into, east of the Don Valley Parkway (294 Danforth, tel. 416/466–4645).

Fetoun (99 Avenue Rd., in Hazelton Lanes, tel. 416/923–3434) is one of the latest high-fashion emporiums for the nouveau riche. If you go to a lot of charity balls, this is the place to shop.

Moores The Suit People (100 Yonge St., just 2 blocks south of Eaton Centre, tel. 416/363–5442, and a dozen other Toronto locations, including one near the airport) is a common sight in the United States, but not so in Canada; it stocks thousands of (Canadian-made) men's dress pants, sportcoats, and suits, including many famous labels and sizes ranging from extra tall to extra short and oversize, at shockingly low prices (e.g., all-wool suits that usually cost about $300, sell for less than $180). You'll find remarkably generous selections, solid quality, and surprisingly good service.

Roots (195 Avenue Rd., tel. 416/927–0041; Eaton Centre, tel. 416/977–0041) remains a real charmer that is now into its third decade in Canada, with over three dozen stores from coast to coast. It carries rustic, handsome clothes and sporty accessories for everyone in the family.

The **Queen Street West** "strip"—extending several blocks from University Avenue, west to Spadina—is a disarming row of delightful stores. Here you'll find daring new fashions, used clothes of the '50s and '60s, arcane bookstores, charming French restaurants, musty diners that take you back to your youth, quality luggage stores, eccentric antiques shops, and more. Among the Queen Street West stores for the fashion-conscious young and zany are: **Fab Gear** (312 Queen St. W, tel. 416/593–5370); **Ion** (290 Queen St. W, tel. 416/596–7296); **Fashion Crimes** (395 Queen St. W, tel. 416/592–9001); **Boomer** (309 Queen St. W, tel. 416/598–0013); and **IXL Clothing and Footwear** (202 Queen St. W, tel. 416/977–4148).

Collectibles **Painted Post** (195 Davenport Rd., tel. 416/924–5034) overflows with native art, contemporary arts and crafts, witty Canadian folk art, and even Amish rocking chairs.

Food Markets **Kensington Market** (northwest of Dundas St. and Spadina Ave.) is an outdoor market with a vibrant ethnic mix. This is where you'll find delightful and exotic Caribbean foods; great cheese, coffee, nuts, and spices; natural foods; South American delicacies; Portuguese bakeries; and charming restaurants. Saturday is the best day to go, preferably by public transit, as parking is difficult.

St. Lawrence Market (Front St. and Jarvis St., tel. 416/392–7219) is best early on Saturdays, when, in addition to the permanent indoor market on the south side of Front Street, there's a farmer's market in the building on the north side. The historic south market was once Toronto's city hall, and it fronted the lake before extensive landfill projects were undertaken.

Specialty **All the Best Breads and All the Best Cheese** (1099 and 1097 Yonge St., **Food Shops** tel. 416/928–3330) are just what it says.

The Big Carrot (on Danforth Ave., near Chester subway station, tel. 416/466–2129) is a new and pricey health-food supermarket, complete with organic butcher shop.

David Wood Food Shop (1110 Yonge St., tel. 416/968–6967) is Toronto's mini–Fortnum and Mason and is the neighborhood grocer to Toronto's old money.

Footwear **Brown's** (Eaton Centre, tel. 416/979–9270; Yorkdale, tel. 416/787–0313; and Holt Renfrew locations at 50 Bloor St. W, tel. 922–2333; Yorkdale, tel. 416/789–5377; Sherway Gardens, tel. 905/621–9900) has an excellent selection of well-made shoes, handbags, and boots.

Corbo Boutique (110 Bloor St. W, tel. 416/928–0954) has the wildest shoes in town for men and women, as well as women's clothes.

David's (66 Bloor St. W, at Bay St., tel. 416/920–1000) has a somewhat more subdued but always elegant collection.

Dorfer Shoes (165 Dupont St., tel. 416/922–9458) is *the* place to find the superior German Birkenstock shoes, at fair prices. Where else can you find an owner who simply glances at your naked feet and knows precisely what your size is and how to fit you to perfection?

Mephisto Boutique (1177 Yonge St., south of St. Clair, tel. 416/968–7026) has been making its fine walking shoes for over a quarter-century—and all from natural materials; passionate walkers swear by these shoes, and claim they never, ever wear out—even in cross-Europe treks.

Gift Ideas **Brain Buster** (Queen's Quay Terminal at Harbourfront, tel. 416/369–0471) caters to those who cannot get enough of brain-teasing games and puzzles; if you're looking for a game made in China or Albania, you'll find it here.

Filigree (1210 Yonge St., tel. 415/961–5223) has a good assortment of linens, as well as drawer liners, silver frames, and other Victorian pleasures. In the neighborhood are other gift shops selling fine glass and antiques.

Heavenly Cats (444 Yonge St., in College Park, tel. 416/591–6833; also in the TD Centre, concourse level, tel. 416/865–9903) is for shoppers who can't get enough of every cat-related object known to man or . . . cat.

Pigs (Queen's Quay Terminal, Harbourfront, tel. 416/203–7257) is just like Heavenly Cats, above, except, all the jewelry, ceramics, and clothing have a pig-related theme.

Jewelry **Secrett Jewel Salon** (150 Bloor St. W, tel. 416/967–7500) is a reputable source of unusual gemstones and fine new and estate jewelry; local gemologists consider it the best in town.

Time Out Here are a few suggestions for places to rest your feet while shopping:

Eaton Centre area. If the Centre's restaurants and fast-food joints don't appeal to you, walk two blocks north to *The Bangkok Garden* (18 Elm St.) for delicious Thai food in a luxurious atmosphere. The related bar, *The Brass Flamingo*, offers less expensive light meals, all of which are good. For an inexpensive meal, get a fabulous home-style burger at *Lick's* (Yonge St. at Dundas Sq., opposite the Eaton Centre); there's also one in The Beaches, and at Yonge Street and Eglinton Avenue. Kids will enjoy the singing counter help.

Queen Street West. We recommend *The BamBoo* (No. 312), a unique Thai-Caribbean experience with courtyard service in summer; *The Queen Mother* (No. 206), a neighborhood favorite with wholesome meals and fabulous desserts, all at reasonable prices; *The Peter Pan* (No. 373, at Peter St.); and the *Parrot Express* (No. 254), for gourmet pizza and other goodies to stay or go.

Bloor Street/Yorkville. *Arlequin Restaurant* (134 Avenue Rd.), located just yards north of all the glorious shopping on Yorkville, serves delicious soups and memorable sandwiches (such as pesto and goat's cheese, prosciutto with grilled fennel, and grilled vegetables with hummus on a pita) for only about $6. You just might laugh out loud when you see *Flo's* (10 Bellair St.), a '40s-style diner smack in the heart of Yorkville's fine shops and galleries. It's so kitschy-cum-art-deco, you may think you've been transported back to wartime. Open for breakfast, lunch, and dinner, this is a real charmer, especially if you're still in the mood for malts, milk shakes, black bean chili, and grilled-cheese-and-bacon. For Canadian ingredients interestingly prepared, try *Metropolis* (838 Yonge St., north of Bloor St.).

Spadina Avenue. You'll find top-quality Chinese or Vietnamese restaurants simply by wandering up and down Spadina, especially north of Dundas. But you certainly cannot lose with *Champion House* (480 Dundas St. W); its Peking duck is world-renowned, and its vegetarian menu is vast and superior. If you want to taste the best breads (and sandwiches) in Toronto, just walk a few blocks south of Dundas to King Street, and then another block and a half west of Spadina. *Ace Bakery* (548 King St. W) will put bocconcini, prosciutto, and pesto on a panetti bun, or serve you asiago cheese with grilled tomato and caramelized onion on homemade focaccia bread; take-out sandwiches cost under $5.

Bargaining

Toronto is *not* the Middle East, but one might haggle at flea markets, including the Harbourfront Antique Market, and perhaps in the Chinatown and Kensington Market/Spadina Avenue areas.

Refund Information

Visitors, including Canadians from other provinces, can receive a refund on the 8% Ontario sales tax for purchases over $100, as well as on the 5% sales tax on hotel and motel bills, provided they leave within 30 days. It's worthwhile if you do a significant amount of shopping. There's a form to be sent in with your receipts after you leave Ontario. You can get the form at Pearson Airport, at visitors' information booths like the one outside the Eaton Centre, at Traveller's Aid in Union Station, or from the merchants themselves.

Visitors to Canada may be surprised to encounter a highly unpopular 7% federal tax on all merchandise, services, and accommodations—the infamous GST (Goods and Services Tax). Since January 1, 1991, it has replaced Canada's earlier, 13½% tax on manufactured goods and covers many more items.

On leaving Canada, tourists are eligible for a refund of taxes paid on all accommodations, and goods purchased for export. Goods consumed or used in Canada, such as meals in restaurants or ski tickets, are not exempt from this tax.

Please remember: Reimbursement (in Canadian dollars, in this case) is immediate at all duty-free shops in airports and at border crossings, where forms are available. But returning travelers may also mail in their forms if they wish to receive a refund check in U.S. dollars. Again, tourists must spend at least $100 (Canadian) to receive the rebate—with families combining expenditures, if desired. A new pamphlet explaining this tax is available at all border crossings and at most U.S. airports.

4 Sports and Fitness

Participant Sports

A wide range of sports is available for each of Toronto's four distinct seasons. From Lake Ontario to the skiing hills just outside the city and the beautiful lakes and parks beyond, a thousand sports and recreational activities are available.

Contact the **Ministry of Tourism and Recreation** (Queen's Park, Toronto, Ont. M7A 2R2) for pamphlets on various activities. For information on sports activities in the province, phone 800/268–3735 from anywhere in the continental United States and Canada (except the Northwest Territories and the Yukon). In Toronto, contact **Ontario Travel** (tel. 416/965–4008).

A number of fine **conservation areas** circle the metropolitan Toronto area, many less than a half-hour from downtown. Most have large swimming areas, sledding, and cross-country skiing, as well as skating, fishing, and boating. Contact the **Metro Conservation Authority** (tel. 416/661–6600) and ask for the pamphlet.

Bicycling
There are over 18 miles of street bike routes cutting across the city and dozens more along safer paths through Toronto's many parks (*see* Sightseeing Checklists in Chapter 2). Bikes can be rented on the Toronto Islands. The **Martin Goodman Trail** is a 12–mile strip that runs along the waterfront all the way from the Balmy Beach Club in the east end, out past the western beaches southwest of High Park. Phone the *Toronto Star* (tel. 416/367–2000) for a map.

Metro Parks Department (tel. 416/392–8186) has maps that show bike (and jogging) routes that run through Toronto parkland. **Ontario Cycling** (tel. 416/495–4141) has maps, booklets, and information.

Boardsailing
Equipment can be rented in various areas of the waterfront. Try along Bloor Street West, near the High Park subway station.

Boating
Grenadier Pond in High Park, Centre Island, Ontario Place, Harbourfront Centre, and most of the Conservation Areas surrounding Metro Toronto rent canoes, punts, and/or sailboats.

Bowling
Don't laugh; Toronto has 5-pin, a marvelous tradition unknown to most Americans. This sport of rolling a tiny ball down an alley at five fat pins—each with a different numerical value, for a possible (impossible) score of 450—is perfect for children, even as young as 3 or 4. **Bowlerama** has lanes all over the city, including locations at 2788 Bathurst, just south of Lawrence Avenue West (tel. 416/782–1841); Newtonbrook Plaza, 5837 Yonge Street, just south of Steeles (tel. 416/222–4657); and Bowlerama Rexdale, not far from the airport, at 115 Rexdale Boulevard, near Kipling (tel. 416/743–8388). This can provide an entertaining few hours on a rainy day.

Fishing
One does not have to go very far from downtown Toronto to catch trout, perch, bass, walleye, salmon, muskie, pike, and whitefish. Contact Communication Services, Wildlife Information, **Ministry of Natural Resources** (Queen's Park, Toronto, Ont. M7A 1W3, tel. 416/965–4251).

Within Metro Toronto itself, fishing is permitted in the trout pond at Hanlan's Point on Toronto Island, as well as in Grenadier Pond in High Park. And the salmon fishing just off the Scarborough Bluffs, in Toronto's east end, is extraordinary! Every summer there is a Great Salmon Hunt, with cash prizes. Check the *Toronto Star*, which sponsors it, for details.

There are over 100 charter boats on Lake Ontario (about $60 for a half-day). Contact **Ontario Travel** (tel. 416/965–4008). Be warned, though: Some fish caught in this province have such high levels of mercury in them that you can take your temperature at the same time that you eat them. It's sad, but water pollution (including acid rain) has taken its toll upon the edibility of many fish in Ontario.

Golf The season lasts only from April to late October. The top course is **Glen Abbey** (tel. 416/844–1800), where the Canadian Open Championships is held. Cart and green fees go up to $75 on weekends, but this course is a real beauty.

Less challenging courses—and much closer to the heart of the city—include the **Don Valley Golf Course** (Yonge St., tel. 416/392–2465), just south of Highway 401; and the **Flemingdon Park Golf Club** (Don Mills Rd. and Eglinton Ave., tel. 416/429–1740). For other courses, contact Metro Parks (tel. 416/367–8186) or Ontario Travel (tel. 416/965–4008).

Horseback Riding There are two stables within the city limits. **Central Don Stables** (Leslie St. and Eglinton Ave., tel. 416/444–4044) in Sunnybrook Park, has an indoor arena, an outdoor ring, and nearly 12 miles of bridle trails through the Don Valley. **Eglinton Equestrian Club** (near Don Mills Rd. and John St., tel. 416/889–6375) has two indoor arenas.

Just north of the city, in Richmond Hill, the **Rocking Horse Ranch** (tel. 416/884–3292) offers scenic western trail rides year-round. For booklets detailing riding establishments across the province, call **Ontario Travel** (tel. 416/965–4008) or **Equestrian Ontario** (tel. 416/495–4125). People with disabilities will be pleased to hear of the **Community Association for Riding for the Disabled** (tel. 416/667–8600), which offers riding in a park near Black Creek Pioneer Village. Children as young as 4 years old can ride here, thanks to the **Variety Club** (tel. 416/961–7300).

Hunting There is little hunting within a few hours' drive of Toronto, and even that is limited to the fall: deer, moose, and black bear. The waterfowl season is longer, extending from fall into the winter. Contact Public Information Centre, Room 1640, **Ministry of Natural Resources** (Queen's Park, Toronto, Ontario M7A 1W3, tel. 416/965–4251), or write the Ontario Federation of Anglers and Hunters (Box 1269, Campbellford, Ontario).

Ice Skating Toronto operates some 30 outdoor artificial rinks and 100 natural-ice rinks—and all are free! Among the most popular are in Nathan Phillips Square, in front of the New City Hall, at Queen and Bay streets; down at Harbourfront Centre (which has Canada's largest outdoor artificial ice rink); College Park, at Yonge and College streets; Grenadier Pond, within High Park, at Bloor and Keele streets; and inside Hazelton Lanes, that classy shopping mall on the edge of Yorkville, on Avenue Road, just above Bloor Street. For details on city rinks, call 416/392–1111.

Jogging The **Martin Goodman Trail** (*see above*) is ideal. Also try the boardwalk of The Beaches in the east end; High Park in the west end; the Toronto Islands; or any of Toronto's parks.

Sailing This can be a breeze, especially between April and October. Contact the **Ontario Sailing Association** (tel. 416/495–4240).

Skiing
Cross-Country Try Toronto's parks and ravines; High Park; the lakefront along the southern edge of the city; Tommy Thompson Park; and best of all,

Toronto Islands. All these places are free. Check the Yellow Pages for ski-equipment rentals; there are many places.

Downhill Although there are a few places where one can get a taste of this sport within metropolitan Toronto, such as **Earl Bales Park,** on Bathurst Street, just south of Sheppard Avenue, and **Centennial Park Ski Hill** (tel. 416/394–8754) in Etobicoke, the *best* alpine hills are 30–60 minutes north of the city. These include **Blue Mountain Resorts** (tel. 905/869–3799) in Collingwood, Ontario, the **Caledon Ski Club** (tel. 905/453–7404) in Caledon, **Glen Eden Ski Area** (tel. 905/878–5011) in Milton, **Hidden Valley** (tel. 705/789–2301) in Huntsville, **Hockley Valley Resort** (tel. 519/942–0754) in Orangeville, and **Horseshoe Valley** (tel. 705/835–2790) and **Snow Valley Ski Resort** (tel. 905/283–2439, a number that can be called directly from Toronto), both just outside Barrie. Phone 416/963–2992 for lift and surface conditions.

Sleigh Riding **Black Creek Pioneer Village** (tel. 905/661–6610 or 905/661–6600),
and north of 401 along Highway 400, at Steeles Avenue, is open winter
Tobogganing weekends 10–4 for skating, tobogganing, and horse-drawn sleigh rides. The best parks for tobogganing include **High Park,** in the west end, and our favorite, **Winston Churchill Park,** at Spadina Avenue and St. Clair Avenue, just two blocks from Casa Loma. It is sheer terror.

Swimming The beaches of Lake Ontario are studies in extremes: The water can be bitter cold, even through the summer, while the sand can raise blisters on the hottest days of the year. Many beaches are too polluted for safe swimming; phone the city's **public health department** (tel. 416/392–7466) for the latest report.

In the east end, **Beaches Park,** south of Queen Street and east of Coxwell Avenue, is lovely, thanks to the lengthy boardwalk, local canoe club, public washrooms, and tennis courts. Even closer to downtown—only a 20-minute streetcar-ride away, along Queen Street—are **Woodbine Beach Park** and **Ashbridges Bay Park,** both fine for sunbathing and boat-watching. To the west of downtown, another fine area, **Sunnyside Beach,** has a pool, snack bar, Jungle Gym, and washrooms.

The most pleasing beaches—and certainly the ones with the best views—are on the **Toronto Islands** (*see* Tour 1 in Chapter 2). Remember, though, Lake Ontario is rarely warm enough for sustained swimming, except in late August.

Public swimming is available in 16 indoor pools, 12 outdoor pools, and 15 community recreation centers; call the **Toronto Department of Parks and Recreation** (tel. 416/392–7259).

Tennis The city provides dozens of courts, all free, many of them floodlighted. Parks with courts open from 7 AM to 11 PM, in season, include the famous High Park in the west end; Stanley Park, on King Street West, three blocks west of Bathurst Street; and Eglinton Park, on Eglinton Avenue West, just east of Avenue Road. Call the **Ontario Tennis Association** (tel. 416/495–4215).

Hotel Health Nearly every major hotel in the metropolitan Toronto area has a de-
Facilities cent indoor swimming pool; some even have indoor/outdoor swimming pools. The best include the **Sheraton Centre,** at Queen and Bay streets, and the **Inn on the Park,** at Eglinton Avenue near Leslie Street. Many also have health clubs.

Spectator Sports

Toronto has always been an exciting sports city, but since the Toronto Blue Jays made their debut—in a snowstorm!—in 1977, the place has gone wild. (Indeed, while the Blue Jays lolled about in the basement of the American League for their first five years, nearly 8 million fans poured into the ugly, uncomfortable Exhibition Stadium, down at the CNE grounds.) Since the June 1989 opening of the extraordinary, retractable-roof SkyDome, you can just imagine how revved up this city has been for professional baseball. Of course, back-to-back World Series Championships in both 1992 and 1993 didn't hurt, either!

Auto Racing For the past several years, the **Molson Indy** (tel. 416/595–5445) has been roaring around the Canadian National Exhibition grounds, including the major thoroughfare of Lakeshore Boulevard, for three days in mid-July. You'll pay more than $85 for a three-day "red" reserved seat, but general admission for the qualification rounds, the practice rounds, and the Indy itself, can be as cheap as $10–$20, depending upon the day.

Then, there is **Mosport,** about 60 miles northeast of Toronto, where motorcycle and formula racing are held. *Take 401 east to Exit 75, then drive north to track. Tel. 416/665–6665.*

Less than a half-hour drive away is the **Cayuga International Speedway** (tel. 416/765–4461), where international stock-car races are held from May through September.

Baseball As noted, the **Toronto Blue Jays** have developed into one of baseball's most dynamic teams, and are all the more popular since their move into the SkyDome in the summer of 1989. The Jays have the most costly tickets in the Major Leagues, ranging from rotten $6 seats (near heaven) to seats for about a shocking $23. And they usually sell out nearly every single home game, so plan way ahead of your visit. There are nearly always dozens of scalpers hawking tickets to that day's game just outside the SkyDome. *A hot tip:* Arrive a bit late, say, in the second or third inning, and they will often unload their tickets at a fraction of what they would have asked a half-hour earlier. *For ticket information, tel. 416/341–1111 or 416/341–1234.*

Basketball As of late 1994, much of Toronto was in a tizzy over its new N.B.A. franchise—the newly named **Toronto Raptors** basketball team, and its dynamic new general manager, long-time Detroit Pistons hero Isiah Thomas. Its first season (1995–1996) will be played in the massive SkyDome, but by early 1996, it is expected that a glamorous new stadium, built especially for the young team, will open in the shadow of the Eaton Centre. Naturally, in this sports-crazy town, most season tickets vanished within days of the announcement of the expansion team; still, there should be no problem purchasing individual seats once the first season is underway—and there will inevitably be scalpers galore at every game. At press time, there was still no telephone line set up for individual ticket purchases.

Canoeing and Rowing The world's largest **canoeing and rowing regatta** is held every July 1, as it has been for over a century, on Toronto Island's Long Pond. *Canoe Ontario, tel. 416/495–4180.*

Football Although the Canadian Football League has been teetering on the brink of dissolution, the **Toronto Argonauts** have, in recent years, developed into annual contenders. Since the Argos were bought by a consortium of new owners—including the Canadian hockey star Wayne Gretzky and the late Canadian comic actor John Candy—in

1991, the team has gone from strength to strength, capturing both its division and the revered Grey Cup that year. International fans of sports may be aware that the CFL has now expanded into several major U.S. cities. The season runs from late June until the first week in November, when the regular season wraps up. Individual tickets range from $10 to $45. Americans might find the three downs and 110-yard field to be rather quaint, but the game is much like their own. *Tel. 416/595–1131 for tickets and information.*

Golf The permanent site of the **Canadian Open** golf championship is Glen Abbey, a course designed by Jack Nicklaus. This tournament is one of golf's Big Five and is always played in late summer. *Less than a 45-min drive west, along the Queen Elizabeth Way (QEW), tel. 416/844–1800.*

Hockey The **Toronto Maple Leafs** play 40 home games each season (Oct.– Apr.), usually on Wednesday and Saturday nights, in the big, ugly Maple Leaf Gardens. Tickets are always available at each game—at least from scalpers in front of the stadium on Carlton Street, a half-block east of the corner of Yonge and College streets. Call the office (tel. 416/977–1641) at 9 AM sharp on the day of the game. Be warned: Over the past two decades, the Maple Leafs were often a fumbling, miserable excuse for a professional team. Then came 1993 and 1994, when they came out shining and glorious, just like in their heyday in the 1960s. So, whatever the situation, tickets are nigh-on impossible to obtain, except for shockingly expensive prices from scalpers. (Would you believe $60–$100 per seat for awful views close to the ceiling?)

Horse Racing Four major racetracks are handled by the Ontario Jockey Club (tel. *Thoroughbred* 416/675–6110): two in the Toronto area; one down in Fort Erie, near *Racing* Buffalo; and another about 24 miles west of Toronto.

Woodbine Race Track is the showplace of Thoroughbreds in Canada. *30-min northeast of downtown, near airport, at Hwy. 27 and Rexdale Blvd., tel. 416/675–6110. Races late Apr.–late Oct.*

Mohawk is in the heart of Ontario's Standardbred breeding country, and it features a glass-enclosed, climate-controlled grandstand and other attractive facilities. *A 30-min drive west of Toronto, along Hwy. 401, past Milton, tel. 416/854–2255.*

Fort Erie, in the Niagara tourist region, is one of the most picturesque racetracks in the world, with willows, manicured hedges, and flower-bordered infield lakes. It has racing on the dirt as well as on grass, with the year's highlight being the Prince of Wales Stakes, the second jewel in Canada's Triple Crown of Racing. *Tel. 905/871–3200 from Toronto, 716/856–0293 from Buffalo.*

Royal Horse This highlight of Canada's equestrian season is part of the Royal *Show* Winter Fair each November. *The CNE grounds, Dufferin St., by the waterfront, tel. 416/393–6400.*

Ice Canoe Every January, five-man/woman teams haul canoes across the ice **Racing** floes off Harbourfront Centre.

Soccer Although Toronto keeps getting and losing and getting a professional soccer team, one can catch this exciting sport, as well as collegiate football, in the very handy **Varsity Stadium.** *Bloor St. W at Bedford, a block west of Royal Ontario Museum and University Ave., tel. 416/979–2186.*

Tennis The finest players in the world gather at the tennis complex on the York University campus, near Finch Avenue and Keele Street, each summer, for the **Player's International Canadian Open.** *For tickets, phone Tennis Canada, tel. 416/665-9777, or Ticketron outlets, tel. 416/872-1212.*

5 Dining

By Sara Waxman

Restaurant Critic for the Financial Post *and the* Toronto Sun, *Sara Waxman is the author of three best-selling cookbooks and a Toronto restaurant guide.*

The restaurant scene is in a state of perpetual motion. Is it the recession that causes all those openings and closings, or is everyone searching for that elusive, perfect little restaurant? Still, more new restaurants opened than closed this year in Toronto.

The formal haute cuisine establishments have all but faded into Toronto's gastronomic history, making way for bistros, cantinas, tavernas, trattorias, tapas bars, noodle bars, wine bars, and smart cafés. No new steak house has opened in a decade. Meanwhile, the cuisines of the world have appeared on Toronto's doorstep. Recipes need no passports to cross borders. Little Italy, three different Chinatowns, Little India, and, of course, the cooking of Southeast Asia—a tidal wave of Korean, Vietnamese, Laotian, Thai, and Malaysian restaurants—are taking our taste buds by storm with their assertive, clean flavors: chili, ginger, lemongrass, coconut, lime, and tamarind.

Toronto's brilliant young chefs recognize that when most customers start requesting "sauce on the side," the public's collective taste is changing; those with vision are looking over their shoulders toward California for a more creative marriage of fresh-market ingredients.

Highly recommended restaurants are indicated by a star ★ .

Category	Cost*
$$$$	over $40
$$$	$30–$40
$$	$20–$30
$	under $20

per person for a three-course meal, excluding drinks, service, and sales tax

Cafés

$$ **Marché.** Designed to resemble a European marketplace, this dining complex is actually a study in organization and creativity. The constantly changing decor contains an 18,000-square-foot vista of baskets of fruits, nuts, and vegetables; mountains of meats and fish on ice; and plates of freshly made pasta. Everything smells wonderful, thanks to the bread and pastries baking; chicken and game birds broiling; seafood and fish steaming and pan-frying; lamb and steaks grilling; and aromatic sauces simmering with tomatoes, peppers, garlic, and herbs. An immense and affordable wine list is offered, too. The selection of dining areas includes an artisan's cottage, a Parisian tavern, a French country inn, and a gazebo under spreading tree branches. To experience Marché, you must first pick up a shopping "credit card" and a tray and stroll through the marketplace, choosing as much or as little as you wish. Everything is prepared before your eyes, 365 days a year, 7:30 AM to 2 AM. As you walk through, you'll notice a mixed clientele: Black leather jackets rub shoulders with black-tie socialites, and young parents with children share dining rooms with execs with briefcases. Be prepared for long lines at peak dining hours. *BCE Place, Yonge and Wellington Sts., tel. 416/366–8986. No reservations. Dress: casual. AE, DC, MC, V.*

$$ ★ **Studio Café.** At this well-lit, comfortable café—a combination hotel coffee shop, restaurant, and contemporary glass-and-art gallery—you can experience a full Japanese breakfast; order nutritionally balanced selections lower in calories, sodium, and fat (try the exuberant presentation of chicken stir-fry with Shanghainese noodles); and indulge in trend-setting pastas such as three-cheese rigatoni with oven-roasted plum tomato. The homey braised lamb shank with buttermilk mashed potatoes, and the applewood smoked salmon sandwich with cream cheese on pumpernickel prove that there's something good here for every taste. For the kids, there's spaghetti Italiano, hot diggety dog, and more. *Four Seasons Hotel, 21 Avenue Rd. (just north of Bloor St.), tel. 416/964–0411. Reservations advised. Dress: casual but neat. AE, DC, MC, V.*

$ **Future Bakery & Café.** A European-style bakery has blossomed into a small chain of cafeterias supplied by their own dairy. Old European recipes have remained: beef borscht, buckwheat cabbage rolls, and potato cheese *varenycky* slathered with thick sour cream. This place is beloved by students for its generous portions, by homesick Europeans hungry for goulash and knishes, by the cheesecake-and-coffee crowd, by health-conscious foodies looking for fruit salad with homemade yogurt and honey, and by people-watchers looking for people worth watching from 7 AM to 1 AM. *1535 Yonge St., tel. 416/944–1253; 438 Bloor St. W, tel. 416/922–5875; 2199 Bloor St. W, tel. 416/769–5020; 739 Queen St. W, tel. 416/368–4235; St. Lawrence Market, 95 Front St. E, tel. 416/366–7259. No reservations. Dress: casual. MC, V.*

$ **Masquerade Caffe Bar.** An eclectic array of red, yellow, blue, and green sofas, chairs, and banquettes fills this Fellini-esque environment. The Harlequin pattern of the bar is echoed in the red-on-red walls. Murano glass mosaics add sparkle to the huge primary color stoves. The daily changing Italian menu may include roasted-onion soup with pesto croutons; exotic lettuce salad with tuna, cheese, olives, marinated mushrooms; a seafood or veggie antipasto; saffron and porcini risotto; divine mushroom-filled ravioli; or a choice of *panini*—Italian sandwiches on homemade breads with scrumptious meat, cheese, and vegetable fillings. Zabaglione (eggs, Marsala wine, and a bit of sugar whipped to a thick, frothy cream and poured over fresh berries) is a knockout dessert. *BCE Place, Front and Yonge Sts., tel. 416/363–8971. No reservations. Dress: casual but neat. AE, DC, MC, V.*

Canadian

$$ **Metropolis.** This funky diner, right across from the Metro Library, is a brightly painted, amiable spot that you'll want to return to. Freshly baked breads, squash and carrot soups, potato and leek pancakes, fresh fruit pies, char-grilled trout, and homemade sausages of venison are all meticulously prepared and served at prices even a Canadian can afford. *838 Yong St., tel. 416/924–4100. No reservations. Dress: casual. AE, MC, V.*

Chinese

$$ **Grand Yatt Dynasty Chinese Restaurant.** At this hotel dining room, troops of polite staff work with alacrity, making sure everyone is properly served. The brightly lit, large room with masses of artificial flowers and black lacquer chairs and tables exemplifies the Hong Kong-ization of Toronto's Chinese restaurants. Master chefs contribute to the vast menu embracing such specialties as roast duck with fresh fruit salad, shark-fin soup, deep-fried little logs of coconut milk surrounded by wok'd scallops and shrimp, and beefsteak roll with mushrooms; there's a large tank of swimming fish which are cooked to order if you're inclined toward seafood. It's a good idea to check the set menus to save money and time. *Westin Harbour Cas-*

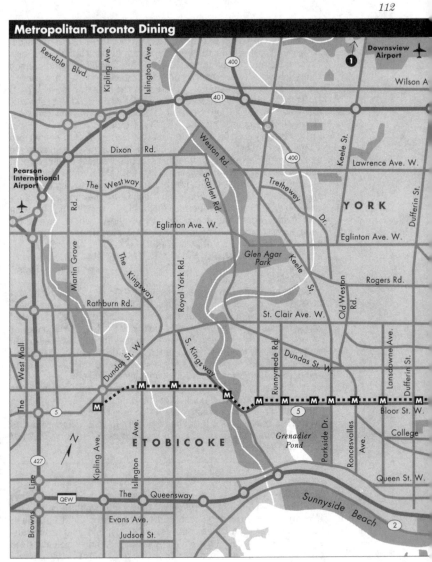

Metropolitan Toronto Dining

Auberge du
Pommier, **3**
Centre St., **1**
Centro, **6**
Chiado, **15**
Cuisine of India, **2**

Future Bakery
and Café, **11**
Grand Yatt
Dynasty Chinese
Restaurant, **16**
Grano, **9**

Herbs, **4**
Joso's, **13**
Lakes Bar & Grill, **14**
North 44, **7**
Otago, **10**

Ouzerie, **17**
Pronto, **8**
Thai Magic, **12**
Vanipha Lanna, **5**

Barolo, **26**
Bistro 990, **8**
Chinese Vegetarian
House, **13**
Giovanna Trattoria, **9**
Il Fornello, **18**
Il Posto, **4**
Jump Café & Bar, **23**
KitKat Bar & Grill, **16**
Le Bistingo, **14**
Masquerade Caffe
Bar, **20**
Marché, **22**
Metropolis, **6**
Mövenpick, **19**
Nami, **24**
Opus, **2**
Palmerston, **11**
Pazzo's Ristorante &
Grill, **10**
Prego, **5**
Renaissance Café, **1**
Roppongi, **15**
Senator Diner, **25**
Shopsy's, **21**
Splendido, **7**
Studio Café, **3**
Wah Sing, **12**
Young Lok, **17**

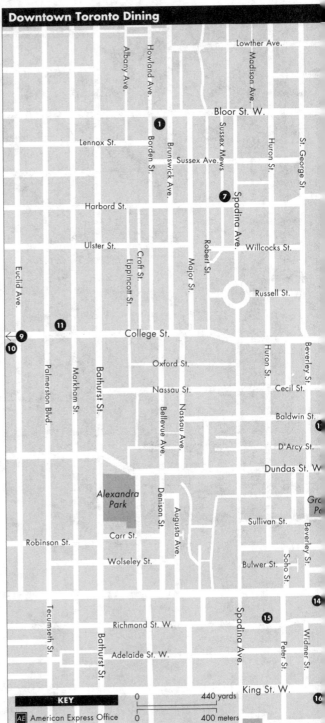

Downtown Toronto Dining

tle, 1 Harbour Sq., tel. 416/869–3363. Reservations advised. Dress: casual but neat. AE, MC, V.

$$ Roppongi. Deep, comfortable banquettes and recessed lighting in a charcoal gray room with unusual brushed metal tables give this restaurant in a downtown office tower an air of sophistication. Although Chinese cuisine is served, owner Athena Ho and several of her staff speak Japanese, and the restaurant is named after an upscale neighborhood of Tokyo. The waiters are adept at discovering exactly what you'd like to eat. Savor the crisp rolled pancakes stuffed with juicy duck meat, mushrooms, and green onions, or try the extravagant "flying fish" dish—deep-fried fish with fried wonton "sails"—that makes heads turn as it's brought to your table, or the beautiful Cantonese "goldfish swimming in a pond" entrée—minced shrimp molded in the shape of goldfish, steamed and arranged in a circle on cooked greens. Such fanciful presentations are rarely seen outside of Asia. *Karaoke begins at 10 PM. 230 Richmond St. W, tel. 416/977–6622. Reservations advised. Dress: casual but neat. AE, DC, MC, V. Closed Sat. and Sun. lunch.*

$$ Young Lok. After an afternoon at the Art Gallery of Ontario, cross the street for another kind of artistry, that of the chefs at Young Lok who prepare Cantonese and fiery Szechuan dishes with equal ease. The shrimp in black-pepper sauce, fresh lobster in black-bean sauce, crispy Mandarin duck, and whole steamed fish with garlic, ginger, and scallions are especially fine. Dim sum (small portions of dumplings and other dishes) is served weekends from 10:30 AM to 3 PM. *122 St. Patrick St., at Dundas St., tel. 416/593–9819. Reservations advised. Dress: casual. AE, MC, V.*

$ Wah Sing. Just one of a jumble of Asian restaurants clustered together on the tiny Kensington Market street, this meticulously clean and spacious restaurant has two-for-the-price-of-one lobsters (in season, which is almost always). Chopped, shell on, and fried with black-bean sauce or ginger and green onion, they're scrumptious and tender. Or try giant shrimp Szechuan-style, or choose one of the lively queen crabs from the tank. Chicken and vegetarian dishes for landlubbers are good, too. Service is pleasant, and at the end of your meal, there's a juicy, sliced orange for dessert. *41 Baldwin St., tel. 416/596–1628. Reservations required for groups of 7 or more. Dress: casual. AE, MC, V.*

Delicatessens

$ Centre St. Expatriate Montrealers have brought their expertise with smoked meat and corned beef to a modern little deli right next to the massive, suburban Thornhill Shopping Plaza. Hand-sliced, juicy, spicy beef makes a great sandwich; with a bowl of homemade cabbage soup, a slice of apple tart, or a few of Centre St.'s famous "moon cookies," you'll feel you've been well-fed. It's worth the drive north of town. *1102 Centre St., Thornhill, tel. 905/731–8037. No reservations. Dress: casual. MC, V.*

$ Shopsy's. In 1945, when the three Shopsowitz brothers came into the business started by their parents in 1921, you'd pay 8¢ for a corned beef sandwich. Today Shopsy's belongs to a food conglomerate, and such a sandwich costs $4.25. The corned beef is always freshly cooked and firm, and piled on fresh rye bread slathered with mustard, there's nothing like it. The menu is vast. Soups are satisfying, salads are huge, and hot dogs are legendary. The deli is located in the heart of the theater and business district, and there's often a wait at peak hours. *33 Yonge St., tel. 416/365–3333. Reservations only for groups of 7 or more. Dress: casual. AE, DC, MC, V.*

Diner

$ **Senator Diner.** You can appreciate this beautifully restored '40s din-
★ er from a cozy green leather booth while you munch on a great ham-
burger, fabulous crab cakes, or any one of the daily blue-plate
specials like veal cutlets or lasagna. Cakes and pies are better than
Mom made, really! On a side street in the midst of theater and shopping, the Senator is handy for a milkshake, a cappuccino pick-me-up,
or breakfast. *249 Victoria St., tel. 416/364-7517. Reservations advised. Dress: casual. AE, DC, MC, V. Closed Mon. dinner.*

Fish/Seafood

$$$$ **Joso's.** Joso Spralja—artist, musician, and restaurateur—has filled
★ his midtown, two-story restaurant with objets d'art: sensual paintings of nudes and the sea, stylized busts of women, signed celebrity
photos, and intriguing wall hangings. The kitchen prepares dishes
of the Dalmatian side of the Adriatic Sea, and the international artistic community who frequent the place adore the magnificent, unusual, and healthy array of seafood and fish. *Risotto carajoi* is Joso's
own creation of rice and sea snails simmered in an aggressively seasoned tomato sauce. Try tiger prawns from Vietnam, porgy from
Boston, salmon trout from northern Ontario, or baby clams from
New Zealand. The dish that seems most often carried aloft by
speedwalking servers is flame-grilled prawns, their charred tails
pointing skyward. *202 Davenport Rd., tel. 416/925-1903. Reservations required. Dress: casual but neat. AE, DC, MC, V. Closed Sat.
lunch, Sun.*

French

$$$$ **Auberge du Pommier.** Two groundskeepers cottages have been
merged to create this French country restaurant with murals,
whitewashed stone walls, and rough hewn ivy-covered beams. In
summer, flowers in massive containers show their glorious colors.
Invention and inspiration pervade the menu. Among the unusual appetizers is warm soufflé of goat cheese, served on bitter greens with
a creamy cider vinaigrette. The waiters provide impeccable service;
they're well versed in the intricacies of serving soy-roasted salmon
fillet with a julienne of crisp sesame vegetables and sweet-and-tart
cardamon sauce, or roast lamb loin with a crust of sun-dried toma-
toes and black olives. Dinner at this beautiful spot is worth the 20-
minute cab ride from the city center. *4150 Yonge St., tel. 416/222-
2220. Reservations advised. Jacket advised. AE, DC, MC, V.
Closed Sat. lunch, Sun.*

$$$ **Bistro 990.** A superior kitchen combined with bistro informality
make this a favorite restaurant for the '90s. Start dinner with
steamed Prince Edward Island string-cultured mussels with a red
tomato curry and cilantro, or Provençal fish soup with *rouille* and
garlic croutons; move on to traditional Bavette steak, grilled rare
and served with frites and bordelaise or Roquefort sauce; or pan-
roasted half chicken with garlic, mashed potatoes, and rosemary.
Pasta might be fusilli with peppers, tomatoes, olives, basil, and Par-
mesan. The purist kitchen uses artesian spring water for all stocks
and homemade breads. Country-style desserts, such as apple and
sun-dried cherry crumble and lemon tart, are not grand, just won-
derful. Faux stone walls stencilled with Cocteau-esque designs,
sturdily upholstered chairs, and a tiled floor create an ambience
where a jacket and tie is easily as acceptable as casual clothes. *990*

Bay St., tel. 416/921–9990. Reservations advised. Dress: casual but neat. AE, DC, MC, V. Closed Sat. lunch, Sun.

$$ Le Bistingo. In this true bistro on Queen Street—Toronto's answer to the Left Bank—George Gurnon stands "en garde" in the dining room, while co-owner Claude Bouillet commands the kitchen. Persimmon walls are hung with an arresting exhibit of Bouillet's own photographs; oak bar and floors gleam. Filled with attractive habitués, this place exudes the spirit of France. The food is superior. Try the steaming tureen of intensely flavored fish soup with croutons and rouille, or ovals of fresh goat cheese whisked with hot-pepper flakes and chives; and whether the entrée is calves' liver with onions, a half roast chicken with sweet garlic cloves, or grilled red snapper with a ragout of littleneck clams and shrimp, don't deprive yourself of warm apple tart with ice cream for dessert. *349 Queen St. W, tel. 416/598–3490. Reservations advised. Dress: casual. AE, MC, V. Closed Sat. lunch, Sun.*

$$ Herbs. Paintings of lush gardens grace the vibrantly painted walls, **★** while brown butcher paper covers floral-clothed tables. For starters, there's great bread, always a good omen. The plain menu doesn't do justice to what's on the plate. Among the litany of superb appetizers, try the silken liver pâté, seasoned with port and cognac—it comes in a tea cup, ringed with fresh figs and garlicky croutons; gravlax and smoked Arctic char, twirled on a plate with asparagus vinaigrette, are also worth sampling. The menu changes with the market, but recommended specialties include roasted pork tenderloin, napped with a glaze of fresh fig and mint; and breast of free-range pheasant roasted with fruits and berries. The *tarte-tatin* (caramelized apple cake) and the chocolate *marquis* (a rich cake of layered chocolate creams) will transport you to Paris. The young chef cooks like a dream, but dreams take time, so don't expect to eat and run. *3187 Yonge St., tel. 416/322–0487. Reservations required. Dress: casual but neat. AE, MC, V. Closed Sat. lunch, Sun.*

$$ Otago. The room is simply done—nothing that might interfere with its raison d'être: the personal, innovative, French cuisine of chef-owner Vaughan Chittock. Knowledgeable servers in blue jeans and casual shirts complement the unpretentious tone set by this young New Zealander. Appetizers and salads are visually stunning. Silken ovals of chicken liver terrine melt on the tongue, splashed with bitter chocolate dressing and textured with tiny frozen grapes that create explosions of flavor in the mouth. The lamb is outstanding. Sometimes it's a pan-roasted rack, served with a slice of sirloin, sweet breads, kidney, and tongue all bound with a rich Merlot wine sauce; sometimes the roast comes on sweet tomato confit with a dark coriander sauce. Chicken is scented with cinnamon, partnered with roasted walnuts and morels. Desserts such as coconut rum soufflé with crème anglaise heart are what sweet fantasies are made of. *1995 Yonge St., tel. 416/486–7060. Reservations advised. Dress: casual but neat. AE, DC, MC, V. Closed Sat. lunch, Sun.*

French/Mediterranean

$$$ Opus. At this darkly handsome midtown space—enlivened with clever halogen lighting and furnished with an eye to style, comfort, and big-city taste—sophisticated dishes are served with attention paid to attractive presentation. An appetizer portion of risotto with smoked chicken, fresh herbs, shittake mushrooms, and sun-dried tomatoes may precede an entrée of three fish layered with a sauce of olive oil, tomatoes, olives, and fresh basil. Or sample herbed chevre rolled in roasted peppers with a seasonal salad and truffle vinaigrette, which makes a fine introduction for fresh Canadian venison with pepper sauce or pheasant roasted with cranberry sauce and black plums. *37 Prince Arthur Ave., tel. 416/921–3105. Reservations advised. Dress: casual but neat. AE, MC, V. Closed lunch.*

$$$ **Palmerston.** Despite its unlikely storefront location in a working-class neighborhood, monied gourmets and expense-account diners flock here to book a table. If you can take the heat, eat in the kitchen and watch media-star chef Jamie Kennedy at work. In the rather spare dining room, there's an à la carte menu on which grilled flatbread (a giveaway elsewhere) with a bit of *tapenade* (olive paste spread) and feta cheese is $4.95. Warm foie gras in herb crepe with apple and calvados is divine, grouper baked with lemongrass in piquant bouillon is as perfect a rendition of fish as you'll ever find, and delicate, fresh Ontario lamb chops, partnered with ratatouille, are excellent. Upstairs, in the second-floor bistro, the $18 two-course, fixed-price menu offers steak frites, roast galantine of capon (a boneless capon breast that's rolled around a filling of mixed herbs and mushrooms and served in thick slices), grilled Atlantic salmon and hearts of romaine or soup of the day, and desserts for $4. *488 College St., tel. 416/922–9277. Reservations required. Dress: casual but neat. AE, MC, V. Closed lunch.*

Greek

$ **Ouzerie.** Grazers will find fertile pastures, and vegetarians should reach nirvana at this sun-splashed, tree-filled, Greek taverna. Go for salads and Mediterranean dips, grilled seafood platters, or skewered, grilled lamb, all drenched with the flavors of fresh lemon and olive oil. Summer nights, the music blares till the wee small hours, and a jam-packed crowd spills over to the sidewalk. Tables and chairs are very close together, so don't come here if you fear intimacy. *500A Danforth Ave., tel. 416/778–0500. Reservations not required. Dress: casual. AE, DC, MC, V.*

Indian

$$ **Cuisine of India.** It's fascinating to see Chef Shishir Sharma at work in the glass-walled, open kitchen of his casually styled, unassuming, suburban restaurant. He slaps a ball of dough with his hands, thrusts it into a smooth, round rock, and lowers it into the depths of the tandoor oven. Moments later, we're eating the puffy, crusty, buttery-center *naan*. Sharma has mastered the art of blending spices, herbs, and roots with other ingredients and achieves a delicate balance of flavors and visual appeal. He lifts a whole salmon from its marinade, fits it onto a forged steel skewer, and plunges it deep into the tandoor. A whole leg of lamb for two, halved chicken breasts, and giant shrimp can all be ordered oven-baked, too. Vegans can also enjoy elaborate dinners here. The vegetable dishes are diverse in their seasonings, and come with fragrant basmati rice. It's worth the 20-minute taxi ride from the city center to enjoy this exquisite cuisine. *5222 Yonge St., tel. 416/229–0377. Reservations required. Dress: casual but neat. AE, DC, MC, V.*

Italian

$$$$ **Barolo.** A loyal clientele loves the cozy, fresh look of white walls, golden-oak hand-carved shelves, and decorated panels that create a sense of space in this high-ceilinged dining room. Tables are arranged for maximum sociability and privacy rather than for income per square foot. The food here is *la nuova grande cucina Italiana*— traditional Italian dishes, prepared in a new, yet elegant, style. The

delectable presentations of salads, such as oak leaf and Boston lettuce, are enhanced by clusters of enoki, shittake, and coral mushrooms oozing hot buttery sauce. You'll be impressed by the splendid simplicity of the main courses, such as boneless half chicken stuffed with wild mushrooms and glazed with pink peppercorn sauce; and tiger shrimp grilled on the half shell with tender, barely cooked scallops glistening with thyme butter sauce. A hand-picked wine list of Brunellos, Barbarescos, Gajas, and rarities like Sassicaias share the cellar with a good selection of wines with down-to-earth prices. *193 Carlton St., tel. 416/961-4747. Reservations required. Jacket advised. AE, DC, MC, V.*

$$$$ **Centro.** The facade of etched glass, granite, and marble shouts hard-
★ edge. But inside it's as warm as the folksy blow-ups of owner Franco Prevedello's hometown of Asolo, in northern Italy. Massive columns that seem to hold up a bright blue ceiling, and salmon-color walls lined with comfortable banquettes help create an intimate space in this 182-seat restaurant. Many would say this is Toronto's best restaurant; regardless, it *is* the trendsetter. Every detail—from the variety of homemade breads to the incredible desserts, from the coat check to the valet parking—is overseen by Franco. You can be sure that he's tasted the ricotta and spinach gnocchi with a ragout of scallion and herb-seasoned sweetbreads, and he's approved the peppered linguine with clams, basil, and pancetta. The 2-inch-thick veal chop grilled over mesquite tingles with Sicilian seasoning; poached Atlantic salmon nestles gently in a bowl of elegant risotto and asparagus. The menu doesn't just change with each season, it seems to get better. *2472 Yonge St., tel. 416/483-2211. Reservations required. Jacket advised. AE, DC, MC, V. Closed Sun.*

$$$$ **Il Posto.** Foodies, socialites, and the who's who of the business world recognize the sophistication and ingenuity of Piero Maritano's kitchen and wife Nella's charm in the dining room. In this rather plain space tucked into the hip of Hazelton Lanes, they serve simple, traditional, excellent Italian dishes. An iced trolley of fresh fish and seafood is wheeled over for your choosing, or you may want the perfectly grilled veal chop, liver with fresh sage leaves, or angel-hair pasta with a whole lobster. The signature desserts are peeled whole oranges marinated in Grand Marnier and cake layered with fresh bananas and chocolate topped with fluffy Italian meringue. In summer, the flower-filled outdoor patio is a people-watcher's delight. *148 Yorkville Ave., tel. 416/968-0469. Reservations advised. Jacket advised. AE, DC, MC, V. Closed Sun.*

$$$ **Prego.** Tucked into a chic shopping passage between the glitz of the Renaissance Plaza and the time-worn stones of the gracefully aging Church of the Redeemer, this see-and-be-seen Italian eatery is a busy spot. Come summer, when the outdoor patio is in full bloom, it's filled with the who's who of the city's highly visible film and television industry, which has earned Toronto the name "Hollywood North." The menu has evolved into a concise litany of everyone's favorites: stone-roasted half chicken with herbs; homemade *agnolotti* (round ravioli) with stuffings like beet with burned butter sauce or butternut squash with tomato and fresh basil; pasta with sauces that are oil-based, tomato-based, or cream-based. And there's a vast display of cold antipasti including marinated vegetables and savory tortes. Chef Massimo strolls through the contemporary, muralled room, checking to see who's eating what. Next door at Enoteca della Piazza, a design award–winning wine bar, the chic and cheerful sip wine from a list of several hundred labels and nibble on *affettati misti* (thin slices of dry cured meats), smoked chicken, and marinated eggplant. *150 Bloor St. W, tel. 416/920-9900. Reser-*

vations advised. Dress: casual but neat. AE, DC, MC, V. Closed Sun.

$$$ Pronto. On the cutting edge of innovative, modern, Italian cuisine,
★ this glitzy black, mirror-and-chrome restaurant has the look of Milan. The menu marries the sunny flavors of California with solid Italian tradition and includes such specialties as pan-fried oyster mushrooms on red-oak lettuce laced with white-truffle olive oil and sophisticated pastas like lemon fettuccine with mussels and roasted garlic. A brace of boneless jumbo quails, charred to the color of mahogany, comes with whole roasted cloves of garlic, sweet and crisp snow-pea vines, and drunk-sour sun-dried cherries. But the kitchen has not lost sight of rustic tradition, and shines with homey dishes such as braised lamb shank served in a massive bowl with flageolets and greens. The trend of the future, using vegetable purées as sauces is an idea whose time has come, and not surprisingly, it has come from Pronto. *692 Mount Pleasant Rd., tel. 416/486–1111. Reservations required. Dress: casual but neat. AE, DC, MC, V.*

$$$ Splendido. This latest in a series of slick, upbeat Italian restaurants
★ is immensely popular with television, music, and film industry types. Chef-partner Arpi Magyar presents a Cal-Ital sparkling, contemporary menu. The chef coaxes ricotta and potato into plump gnocchi and serves it with splashes of white-truffle oil and chives as an appetizer or main course; he roasts farm-raised chicken in a wood-burning oven, and perches it on a *levain* bread salad, textured with currants and pine nuts. Rack of lamb is baked with honey mustard and comes partnered with homey garlic potato purée. Casual, sophisticated good taste meets the eye at every turn. Walls in warm shades of orange and blue are hung with artist Helen Lucas's glorious oversize flower paintings, mirrors are anything but square, and a glass wall marked "Cucina" separates the open kitchen from the dining room. The bar is popular for nightcaps. *88 Harbord St., tel. 416/929–7788. Reservations advised. Dress: casual but neat. AE, DC, MC, V.*

$$ Grano. What started as a bakery and take-out antipasto bar has
★ grown into a joyful collage of the Martella family's Italy. Come for animated talk, good food, and great bread in these lively rooms with faux ancient plaster walls, wooden tables, and bright chairs. There's a small espresso bar to perch at while you wait for a table or take-out. Choose, if you can, from 40 delectable vegetarian dishes and numerous meat and fish antipasti. Lucia's homemade gnocchi and ravioli are divine, as are the *tiramisù* (ladyfingers soaked in rum and espresso and mixed with chocolate bits, *mascarpone* cheese, whipped cream, and beaten egg whites) or white chocolate and raspberry pie. *2035 Yonge St., tel. 416/440–1986. Reservations advised. Dress: casual. AE, DC, MC, V. Closed Sun.*

$$ KitKat Bar & Grill. Walls are crammed with autographed memora-
★ bilia, and the kitchen is built around a massive tree. It all seems quite natural in this eclectic and eccentric Southern Italian eatery. Since it's in the middle of the theater district, pre- and post-theater hours are really busy. Choose from window tables in the front, perch at the long bar, enjoy the privacy of an old-fashioned wooden booth, or sit at a picnic table in the rear. Portions are enormous. An antipasto platter for two is a meal; pastas, seafood, roast chicken, and grilled steak are all delectable. Owner Al Carbone welcomes everyone like long-lost family. *297 King St. W, tel. 416/977–4461. Reservations advised. Dress: casual but neat. AE, DC, MC, V. Closed Sat. lunch, Sun.*

$ Giovanna Trattoria. Yes, there really is a Giovanna, and can she cook! You'll thoroughly enjoy something as simple as a half-roast chicken on a crisp Tuscan bread salad. This is but one of the new and delightful eateries recently opened during the renaissance of Little Italy on College Street. Walls are hung with works depicting the wine god Bacchus in various stages of enjoyment, and flowers are everywhere. Large groups with compatible taste buds would do well to order family-style: enormous platters of homemade fettuccine marinara, or farfel with artichokes and red-pepper cream sauce, or fusilli with prosciutto. Giovanna's cooking is light, traditional, and generous. Try the rabbit braised in traditional Italian style, paired with polenta; the succulent, grilled whole red snapper; or the veal paillard splashed with lemon and herbs. *637 College St., tel. 416/ 538–2098. Reservations advised. Dress: casual. AE, DC, MC, V.*

$ **Il Fornello.** Pizza afficionados especially love Il Fornello's 10-inch,
★ thin-crust pie, baked in a wood-burning oven. Orchestrate your own medley from over 100 traditional and exotic toppings that include braised onion, *cappicola* (spicy Italian sausage), pancetta, provolone, calamari, escargots, mussels, eggplant, and anchovies. A bottle of extra-virgin herbed olive oil graces each table. Pastas, veal dishes, and salads are available, too. Wheat-free pizza crust and dairy-free cappuccino are now on the menu—your taste buds won't know the difference. Customer clamor prompted the opening of more venues. *55 Eglinton Ave. E, tel. 416/486–2130; 86 Bloor St. W, tel. 416/588–5658; 214 King St. W, tel. 416/977–2855; 1560 Yonge St., tel. 416/920–8291; 486 Bloor St. W, tel. 416/588–9358; 1968 Queen St. E, tel. 416/691–8377; 1218 St. Clair Ave. W, tel. 416/658–8511. Reservations accepted. Dress: casual. AE, MC, V.*

$ **Pazzo's Ristorante & Grill.** An extraordinary sight in this corner café in little Italy will make you pull over and park. Huge fragments of a mural depicting sections of Michelangelo's *Creation* adorn the wall of this slick, new easygoing Italian eatery. Recommended entrées include excellent linguini with mushrooms, and crisp-skinned roast chicken with goat cheese and sage polenta. There's extra-virgin olive oil to sprinkle on lovely thin-crust pizza. Tiramisù and freshly made zabaglione both make satisfying desserts. *505 College St., tel. 416/921–9909. Reservations not accepted. Dress: casual. AE, V. Closed Sat. and Sun. lunch.*

Japanese

$$$ **Nami.** In this large, attractive, downtown restaurant, diners can choose to eat at the sushi bar, in tatami rooms with nontraditional wells under the tables, or at the *robatayaki*—a cooking grill surrounded by an eating counter. Watch the chef douse soft-shell crabs with a special sauce and put them on the grill. Scallops, shrimp, Atlantic salmon, mackerel, and ocean perch sizzle on skewers. At the sushi bar, it's a thrill to watch the chef at work: He slaps a bit of rice on his palm, tops it with *wasabi* (a spicy condiment), a shred of vegetable, and a cap of *toro*, yellowtail, or *majuro* tuna. In seconds, he handrolls cornets of salmon skin, and if sea urchin is at hand, he ties it into a neat packet with a ribbon of green onion. Each sushi design is as personal as a signature. Special $22 dinner combos at a table or booth include soup, salad, tempura, chicken yakitori (served on skewers) or a beef or salmon teriyaki dish, rice, and dessert. *55 Adelaide St. E, tel. 416/362–7373. Dress: casual but neat. Reservations advised. AE, DC, MC, V. Closed Sat. lunch, Sun.*

Mixed Menu

$$$$ **North 44.** A foyer of brushed steel nuggets outlined in black, a steel
 compass showing Toronto's longitude imbedded in a gorgeous marble floor, textured walls hung with mirrored sconces holding exotic

arrangements of fresh ginger and lilies—can Chef Marc McEwen's dishes meet the standards of this singular decor? Yes. Your taste buds will thrill to appetizers like cherrywood-smoked Atlantic salmon with crisp potato artichoke *rosti*, scallion dressing, and fresh horseradish; and who could decline a nibble of crisp tortilla spring rolls plump with barbecued chicken, vegetables, and plum-mustard chili dip? The kitchen grills Atlantic salmon to perfection, tops it with a honey-mustard crust, and partners it with sesame bok choy greens and crispy leeks. Winning combinations are spaghettini with seared scallops, grilled calamari, shrimp and sweet tomato fondue, or pan-fried gnocchi with grilled mahogany quail. Caramelized apple pecan layer cake or crème brûlée with berries are worth every luscious calorie. In the rear, a delightful private dining room seating 12–15 people has a wraparound mural of the view from a Venetian canal. *2537 Yonge St., tel. 416/487–4897. Reservations advised. Jacket optional. AE, DC, MC, V. Closed Sun. dinner.*

$$$ Jump Café & Bar. Look up through the atrium and you'll see that you're surrounded by towering skyscrapers and "Big Apple" ambience. You'll love a table at the glass wall that abuts the interior courtyard, which, from May to September, becomes a vast flower-and fountain-filled patio. Refreshing, too, is the East meets West menu with Italian top notes. Appetizers such as Mediterranean octopus with Tuscan bean salad, charred artichokes and leek in spiced olive oil, and crispy duck spring roll with cucumber noodles are favorites. The chef's pasta of the moment is *orecchiette* with spinach, forest mushrooms, roasted garlic, prosciutto, and fresh rosemary. From 5 PM to 7 PM, a smartly dressed, downtown office crowd packs the bar. *Court Level, Commerce Court East, Yonge & Wellington Sts., tel. 416/363–3400. Reservations advised. Jacket optional. AE, DC, MC, V. Closed Sat. lunch, Sun.*

$$ Lakes Bar & Grill. At this tiny, perfect, neighborhood bistro in Rosedale, you're served wonderfully spirited cuisine, unfussy and sophisticated. The open kitchen adds an air of informality, and regulars meet at the club-like bar. Favorite appetizers are properly seasoned crab cakes with zesty corn-pepper-coriander salsa, and baked goat cheese on tomato salad with *calabrese* (porous Italian bread with large holes) toast, sprinkled with olive oil, garlic, and basil. Tables are close together, and it almost seems rude not to become involved in your neighbor's conversation. The food is as friendly as the ambience. Crisp-skinned, rosemary-baked chicken nests on a fluffy plateau of buttermilk mashed potatoes; thick swordfish steak is grilled, capped with fresh tomato salsa and set on a mound of wild rice; and you won't go wrong if you choose one of the trio of daily pastas. *1112 Yonge St., tel. 416/966–0185. Reservations recommended. Dress: casual. AE, DC, MC, V. Closed Sat. and Sun. lunch.*

Portuguese

$$ Chiado. Service is bilingual (Portuguese and English) at this charming restaurant. Through open French doors, you can see polished wood floors, tables set with starched white napery, and plum velvet armchairs. Chiado's European warmth and elegance in this residential neighborhood makes it a magnet for passersby. Fish is utterly fresh. Some days you'll find tuna, whiting, and tiger shrimps, while on other days there's monkfish, sardines, squid, and salmon. A traditional Portuguese dish, *parrilhada* of fresh fish and seafood—a kind of soufflé—is carefully mixed, folded, and served from its silver tureen. Also special is the rabbit braised in Madeira wine, or steak served with fried egg and french fries. Yet the culinary boundaries do not always lie within traditional Portuguese cuisine—the char-grilled shrimp or tuna steaks are just right. Desserts, such as sweet-potato tart, pears poached in port with cream, and flan, are more homey than haute. You may prefer to end your meal with a glass of 20-year-old Muscatel Reserve. *864 College St. W, tel. 416/538–1910. Reservations required. Dress: casual but neat. AE, DC, MC, V.*

Swiss

$$ Mövenpick. Swiss hospitality, an eager-to-please staff, and a cosmopolitan atmosphere make this downtown restaurant all things to all people. Among the dinner specialties are *Zurcher G'Schnatzlets*, the famous Swiss dish of thinly sliced veal and mushrooms in a creamy white-wine sauce served with rosti (pan-fried) potatoes; *Kasseler*, a thick, smoked, juicy pork chop grilled to perfection and served with braised savoy cabbage; and Red Wine herring from Iceland marinated in wine and selected spices. The Swiss Farmers Sunday Brunch ($19.80 per person), a vast buffet of food stations, is particularly popular. You can have your eggs with ham, sausage, bacon, or rosti potatoes. Cheeses, breads, juices, cereals, and accompaniments are displayed in abundance. You can also sample more salads than you bargained for, with raw and marinated vegetables, and a variety of smoked fish and soup. Cold cuts include traditional smoked turkey and black forest ham as well as *Bundnerfleish*, a Swiss salt-cured, air-dried beef. Roast chicken, leg of lamb, and beef roasts are complimented by sautéed vegetables and fresh pastas with sauces. A dessert table burgeoning with fresh fruits, Swiss cakes, tarts, and flans ensures that your sweet tooth will be satisfied. *165 York St., tel. 416/366–5234. Reservations advised. Dress: casual but neat. AE, DC, MC, V.*

Thai

$$ Thai Magic. Bamboo trellises, cascading vines, fish and animal carvings, and a shrine to a voluptuous mermaid goddess make a magical setting for coolly saronged waiters and hot-and-spicy Thai food. Hurricane kettle is a dramatic presentation of fiery seafood soup. Whole coriander lobster sparkles with flavor, while chicken with cashews and whole dried chilies is for the adventurous. If you're in the mood for Thai, this is certainly a pretty place to indulge. *1118 Yonge St., tel. 416/968–7366. Reservations required. Dress: casual. AE, MC, V. Closed Sat. lunch, Sun.*

$$ Vanipha Lanna. Every night this tidy, colorful restaurant is
★ crowded with people who don't care if they're sitting almost cheek to cheek with strangers, or how long they have to wait for their food. They can't get enough of the clean, bright flavors, grease-free cooking, and lovingly garnished Lao-Thai presentations. The bamboo steamer of dumplings with minced chicken and seafood, sticky rice in a raffia cylinder, and chicken and green beans stir-fried in lime sauce are exceptional. Rice is served from a huge silver tureen. Everything here is made from scratch. *471 Eglinton Ave. W, tel. 416/484–0895. Reservations advised. Dress: casual but neat. MC, V. Closed Sun.*

Vegetarian

$ Chinese Vegetarian House. The owner of this sparkling-clean restaurant is well versed in vege-trivia and the delights of dim sum. He's fashioned a vegetarian menu to suit downtown Kensington Market's melting pot neighborhood, including pressed wheat gluten that tastes like barbecued pork, wonton soup afloat with plump dumplings, an eight-vegetable stir-fry with organic brown rice, and bean curd rolls on a sizzling plate. *39 Baldwin St., tel. 416/599–6855. Reservations accepted. Dress: casual. No credit cards. Closed Sat. and Sun. lunch, Mon.*

$ **Renaissance Café.** The good vegetarian food here comes from influences around the globe: Mexican nachos, Lebanese *baba ghanouj* (garlicy eggplant purée), Italian pesto pizza and lasagna, Indonesian rice and stir-fries, Greek *spanakopita* (spinach pie), West Indian roti (vegetable filled pastries), and soup of the day with an all-you-can-eat salad bar. A seat by the window in this quaint corner café gives you a good view of the busy passing parade. *509 Bloor St. W, tel. 416/968–6639. Reservations accepted. Dress: casual. AE, MC, V.*

6 Lodging

Places to stay in this cosmopolitan city range, as one might expect, from luxurious hotels to budget motels to a handful of bed-and-breakfasts in private homes.

Prices are cut nearly in half over weekends and during special times of the year (many Toronto hotels drop their rates a full 50% in January and February).

If you are traveling with children or are planning to do a good deal of sightseeing, you should consider staying in the downtown area (south of Bloor St., east of Bathurst St., west of Jarvis St.). This is where you will find Harbourfront Centre, the CN Tower, Eaton Centre, the Toronto Islands, SkyDome, Chinatown, and most of the finest shopping and restaurants. If you are staying only a day or two, and are mainly interested in visiting the zoo, the Ontario Science Centre, and Canada's Wonderland, then look into some of the places listed below as Off the Beaten Track or along the airport strip.

Accommodation Toronto (tel. 905/629–3800), a service of the Hotel Association of Toronto, is an excellent source for finding the room and price you want. Don't forget to ask about family deals and special packages.

Do remember that the Canadian dollar has recently taken a real dive, meaning that a C$200-room in Toronto costs less than US$140. Furthermore, if appropriate, you may wish to ask "What is your corporate rate?" when you call; it is often a fraction of the "rack rate." And be sure to get a confirmation number on your reservation; even get it faxed to you. This may avoid awkward errors, and a potentially sleepless night.

Highly recommended properties in each category are indicated with a star ★.

Category	Cost*
$$$$	over $200
$$$	$150–$199
$$	$100–$149
$	under $100

All prices are for a standard double room, excluding GST (Goods and Services Tax).

Downtown

$$$$ **Four Seasons Toronto.** It's hard to imagine a lovelier or more exclu-
★ sive hotel than the Four Seasons, which is usually rated among the top two dozen hotels in the world and one of the top three in North America. The location is one of the most ideal in the city: on the edge of Yorkville, a few meters from the Royal Ontario Museum. The 380 units are tastefully appointed. Maids come twice a day, and there are comfortable bathrobes, oversize towels, fresh flowers, and a fine indoor/outdoor pool. Even the special family rates, however, will not drop the cost much below $200 a night. Yet, during such slow months as January through March, sometimes into April, rooms on weekends have been offered for less than $150 (per person), and even in high season, weekend specials can drop the price to around $170 per night, over a hundred dollars less than normal. Ask for upper rooms with views facing downtown and the lake. The Studio Café

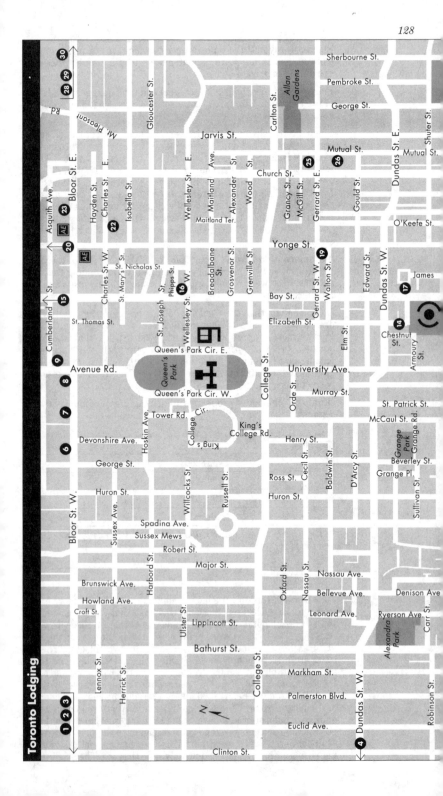

129

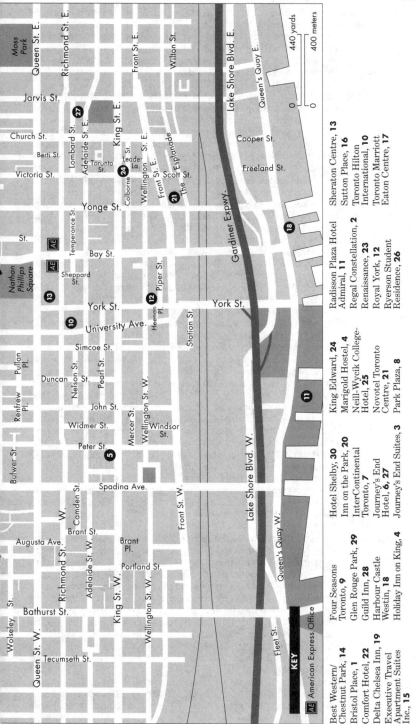

Best Western/
Chestnut Park, **14**
Bristol Place, **1**
Comfort Hotel, **22**
Delta Chelsea Inn, **19**
Executive Travel
Apartment Suites
Inc., **15**

Four Seasons
Toronto, **9**
Glen Rouge Park, **29**
Guild Inn, **28**
Harbour Castle
Westin, **18**
Holiday Inn on King, **4**

Hotel Shelby, **30**
Inn on the Park, **20**
InterContinental
Toronto, **7**
Journey's End
Hotel, **6, 27**
Journey's End Suites, **3**

King Edward, **24**
Marigold Hostel, **4**
Neill-Wycik College-
Hotel, **25**
Novotel Toronto
Centre, **21**
Park Plaza, **8**

Radisson Plaza Hotel
Admiral, **11**
Regal Constellation, **2**
Renaissance, **23**
Royal York, **12**
Ryerson Student
Residence, **26**

Sheraton Centre, **13**
Sutton Place, **16**
Toronto Hilton
International, **10**
Toronto Marriott
Eaton Centre, **17**

is one of the best business breakfast, lunch, or dinner spots in town. Other restaurants include the Lobby Bar, La Serre, and Truffles, the acclaimed formal dining room. It's not by chance that this gorgeous hotel continues to be the *only* one in the city that keeps receiving the greatly coveted American Automobile Association's Five Diamond Award. *21 Avenue Rd., M5R 2G1, a block north of Bloor St., tel. 416/964–0411 or 800/332–3442. AE, DC, MC, V.*

$$$$ **King Edward Hotel.** After too many years of neglect, this Edwardian classic was finally purchased and thoroughly renovated by a group of local investors. Some of the restorations were less than sensitive; the kitschy platform with pergola in Chiaro's, the formal dining room, desecrates one of Toronto's great interiors. Still, it's a treat having this splendid structure restored to its pink marble grandeur, and, under the British Trusthouse Forte group, again attracting the well-heeled clientele it so manifestly deserves. What other hotel gives you not only bathrobes and hairdryers, but even umbrellas? There's a nonsmoker's floor, and family and weekend rates are available. Facilities include a health club. The 315-room King Edward also has Cafe Victoria (open all day), the Consort Bar, and the Lobby Lounge for afternoon tea on weekends. *37 King St. E, M5C 1E9, tel. 416/863–9700 or 800/225–5843. AE, DC, MC, V.*

$$$$ **Park Plaza Hotel.** It may lack a pool, but it has one of the best locations in the city: a short distance from the Royal Ontario Museum, Queen's Park, and Yorkville (one of the city's great shopping areas). In 1990, the first phase of its massive renovation was completed in the South Tower, which has the great views of downtown Toronto. The newer North Tower is also open. The ground floor now consists of upscale retail shops, while the 64 guest rooms (of which 20 are suites) are done in the finest residential/traditional, yet updated style: cornice moldings in the rooms; peachy pink with white trim wood; antique vanity tables. The Roof Restaurant was once described by novelist Mordecai Richler as "the only civilized place in Toronto." For a business breakfast or lunch, you cannot do better than the very comfortable Prince Arthur Room. Additional facilities include a 550-seat ballroom, a business center, a palm court, and a restaurant in the lobby, all designed by Zeidler Roberts Partnership, the same architects who were responsible for the Eaton Centre and Ontario Place. This is très New York Park Avenue. Moderately priced weekend packages are sometimes available. Be sure to check out the hotel's "Baseball Packages" (including two quality seats at a Blue Jays game, one night's accommodation, Continental breakfast for two, free parking, and access to *Miss Saigon* theater tickets). *4 Avenue Rd., M5R 2E8, at corner of Bloor St. W, tel. 416/924–5471 or 800/268–4927. AE, DC, MC, V.*

$$$$ **Radisson Plaza Hotel Admiral.** This small, intimate hotel is exquisitely situated on the edge of Lake Ontario, overlooking Harbourfront Centre. It has only 157 rooms and 17 handsomely furnished suites, as well as a main dining room, the Gallery Café, and a bar. The lacquered wood shines and the polished brass gleams in the stunning lobby. The Promenade Deck on the fifth level, surrounding the outdoor heated swimming pool, allows for fabulous views of the bustling harbor. There's frequent courtesy shuttle bus service for the downtown area. Weekend rates can be as low as $160, which includes free parking and breakfast for one, but this hotel will usually run closer to $200 for a double. *249 Queen's Quay W, M5J 2N5, tel. 416/203–3333. AE, D, DC, MC, V.*

$$$$ **Renaissance.** This relatively small, modern, 256-room hotel is one that Torontonians tend to forget. It's part of the Hudson Bay complex, near the busy intersection of Yonge and Bloor streets. Facilities include a pool and a sauna, a restaurant, and a lounge (which is being renovated). Weekend rates at this Ramada hotel can be as low as $140 a night. *90 Bloor St. E, M4W 1A7, tel. 416/961–8000 or 800/ 323–7500. AE, D, DC, MC, V.*

$$$$ Sutton Place Hotel. This 33-story tower with 280 rooms, located close to the various ministries of the Ontario provincial government, is a favorite of lobbyists, lawyers, and the like. Service is more personal than you would think, because many of the floors have luxury apartments, not hotel rooms. Being next to Wellesley Street means that it's within walking distance of Queen's Park, the Royal Ontario Museum, and many other midtown attractions. Facilities include a pool, health club, 24-hour room service, special floors for nonsmokers, and a stunning restaurant Sanssouci, serving three meals. Family and weekend rates are available. This hotel is now owned by the blue-chip Meridien SA hotel management group, and it's still a handsome place to stay. Indeed, its desire to woo business travelers, and shun its long-time celebrity image, means lower prices much of the time. *955 Bay St., M5S 2A2, tel. 416/924–9221. AE, DC, MC, V.*

$$$ Best Western/Chestnut Park Hotel. One of the newest—and big-
★ gest—additions to Toronto's hotel scene, this handsome 16-floor hotel with glass-enclosed atrium lobby could hardly be more convenient: just steps behind City Hall and a few short blocks from Eaton Centre. The 522 guest rooms, which include 21 for the disabled, are all well decorated, with finely crafted furniture and desks; many have queen- and king-size beds. The Tapestry restaurant is open from 6 AM until 1 AM. Recreational facilities include a large heated indoor pool, sauna, Jacuzzi, health club and gymnasium, and a children's creative center. In addition, the Chestnut Hill is now connected by a walkway from the mezzanine level to a Museum of Textiles, where some 15,000 textiles from around the world are displayed—the only museum of its kind in Canada. Like the Sutton Place and seven other Toronto area hotels that were pushed to the brink of bankruptcy (if not over) in the early 1990s, the Chestnut Park has recently changed ownership—but this has not changed its marvelous location, right on the edge of one of the most dynamic, exciting Chinatowns outside of mainland China. *108 Chestnut St., M5G 1R3, just north of Nathan Phillips Sq., tel. 416/977–5000. AE, D, DC, MC, V.*

$$$ Delta Chelsea Inn. The 977 rooms on the south side of Gerrard Street began as a budget hotel. Prices have crept up, but they're still reasonable by downtown standards. The Chelsea is much favored by tour operators, and the elevators, which were meant to serve the apartment building this was originally intended to be, can be hard to catch when all the buses are leaving at once. On the positive side, the hotel has a creative, supervised day-care service for children ages 3–8, open from 9:30 AM to 10 PM. Facilities include a pool and sauna, and two restaurants (The Market Garden and The Wittles). Since 1992, the hotel has had 1,600 rooms, with weekend specials for under C$125. Ask for the southeast and southwest rooms in the south wing, overlooking downtown and the lake; many rooms are for the disabled. *33 Gerrard St., M5G 1Z5, at the corner of Yonge St., tel. 416/595–1975 or 800/268–1133. AE, D, DC, MC, V.*

$$$ Harbour Castle Westin. This was a Hilton International hotel until 1987, when Westin and Hilton suddenly switched ownership of their major downtown Toronto hotels. A favorite of conventioners, it's located just steps from Harbourfront Centre and the Toronto Island ferry. It's a bit inconvenient to the city's amenities except for those directly on the lakeshore, but it enjoys the best views of any hotel in the city. There's a shuttle bus service to downtown business and shopping, and the swimming pool, squash courts, and health club are among the best in town. Recently, the hotel became connected to the city's mass-transit system by the LRT (light rail transit) out of

Union Station, linking it to Harbourfront, Chinatown, and everywhere else in this dynamic city. The Regatta restaurant is open all day; the revolving Lighthouse restaurant, perched atop the 37th floor, is open for lunch and dinner. And what a view! Its 900 rooms are well appointed and tastefully modern, and the frequent family and weekend rates help bring its regular price down by as much as a third. All rooms have a lake view, but you may wish to ask for a corner one, which also looks up to the glittering bank and office towers just to the north. The North Tower was recently entirely renovated. *1 Harbour Sq., M5J 1A6, tel. 416/869–1600 or 800/228–3000. AE, DC, MC, V.*

$$$ **InterContinental Toronto.** This handsome high rise, part of the respected international chain, is just a half-block west of the major intersection of Bloor Street, Avenue Road, and University Avenue, making it a two-minute walk to the Royal Ontario Museum and the Yorkville shopping area. With 213 rooms (including a dozen suites), a fully equipped fitness center with indoor swimming pool and sauna, and two restaurants (The Signatures and The Harmony Lounge), it's a welcome addition to this prime area. The rooms are spacious and well appointed; the service—especially the superb Executive Business Centre and secretarial service—is topnotch. *220 Bloor St. W, M5S 1T8, tel. 416/960–5200. AE, DC, MC, V.*

$$$ **Novotel Toronto Centre.** This once moderately priced hotel—part of a popular French chain—opened in December 1987. There are 266 modest, modern rooms on nine floors in the heart of downtown, in walking distance of Harbourfront and the CN Tower. Facilities include an indoor pool, whirlpool, exercise room, and sauna. The Café Nicole is open all day. *45 The Esplanade, M5E 1W2, tel. 416/367–8900 or 800/221–4542. AE, DC, MC, V.*

$$$ **Royal York.** Although no longer the largest hotel in the British Commonwealth (after decades with this title, the Delta Chelsea Inn, *above*, is now bigger), the Royal York has 1,403 completely renovated rooms, 100 of which are studio suites, and 13 restaurants and lounges; it's certainly still a monster of a place. The service is necessarily impersonal, and there's always a convention of some sort going on. Still, it's venerable, comfortable, close to the financial core of the city, and rarely booked solid. The hotel's $100-million renovation was completed just in time to celebrate its 65th birthday in June 1994. The refurbishment won first-place honors in the Best Historic Preservation category at the Annual Design Ovation Awards held in Dallas; the hotel had the inspiration to remove dull wood panels and veneer to expose the original block travertine walls and columns—which actually date back to the hotel's 1929 opening. The new health club and skylit lap pool feature rich marblework and a stunning hand-painted trompe l'oeil wall mural. *100 Front St. W, M5J 1E3, tel. 416/368–2511 or 800/828–7447. AE, D, DC, MC, V.*

$$$ **Sheraton Centre.** This 1,430-room conventioneer's tower is located across from the New City Hall, just a block from Eaton Centre. In 1992, $47 million had been spent on renovations, with completely refurbished guest rooms and bathrooms, six new floors in the exclusive Sheraton Towers, and 15 new automated check-in and cashier stations. The below-ground level is part of Toronto's labyrinth of shop-lined corridors, and there are more shops on the ground floor and second floor. The restaurants' reach seems to exceed their grasp, but the Long Bar, overlooking Nathan Phillips Square, is a great place to meet friends for a drink. All views are marvelous; to the south is the CN Tower and SkyDome; to the north, both city halls. Weekday specials can drop to under $140, even less in winter. Facilities include a huge indoor/outdoor pool, hot tub, sauna, and

workout room. *123 Queen St. W, M5H 2M9, tel. 416/361–1000 or 800/ 325–3535. AE, DC, MC, V.*

$$$ Toronto Hilton International. Now that the Toronto Hilton has been massively renovated—especially from the 15th floor and above— everything looks appealingly fresh and comfortable. The hallways in the hotel are now brighter—the wallpaper is a pleasant peach with flecks of black—and light fixtures are far more abundant. The 600 refurbished rooms are now done up in light shades of pastel, with attractive duvets on every bed. The Hilton's nearness to the financial district, New City Hall, the CN Tower, and more makes it a convenient base for most visitors. The indoor/outdoor pool is modest, but the view of the city from the glass-enclosed elevators is a thrill. The Garden Court restaurant in the lobby is open all day; Trader Vic's, on the Convention Level, is open for lunch and dinner. There are family plans and weekend rates, as always, and children can stay free. Although on the top end of the expensive ($$$) scale, specials throughout the week can drop the price of a single or a double to the $125 range. *145 Richmond St. W and University Ave., M5H 3M6, tel. 416/869–3456. AE, DC, MC, V.*

$$$ Toronto Marriott Eaton Centre. As you can tell by its name, the world-famous Marriott chain finally has a solid sibling in this city— and what a location! It is actually connected to the beautiful Eaton Centre (which is, after all, Toronto's number one attraction), and within easy walking distance of SkyDome, the Metro Toronto Convention Centre, and the theater and financial districts. The hotel has 459 pretty guest rooms, all decorated in shades of dusty rose and gray. The bedrooms are actually larger than most you will find in Toronto, and each is equipped with irons and ironing boards, as well as hair dryers in all bathrooms. There are two dozen roomy suites, as well. The hotel plans to be connected underground to the basketball stadium for Toronto's new N.B.A. team, the Raptors, sometime in 1996. The indoor rooftop swimming pool provides a fabulous view of the city. The lobby has two lovely lounges: one, fittingly, is called the Lobby Lounge, painted the same pleasant dusty rose of the rooms; the other, Character's, has lots of pool tables and a dozen televisions. The Toronto Marriott's two restaurants include the Parkside, offering casual, "all-American" fare on the main floor of its open-air atrium; and J.W.'s, a more formal, upscale eatery, with international cuisine and an eye-catching open-air kitchen on one side of the room, where you can watch the cook at work. J.W.'s is a beautiful and surprisingly intimate place, with only a few dozen seats. *525 Bay St., between Dundas and Queen, M5G 2L2, tel. 416/ 597–9200 or 800/228–9290. AE, DC, MC, V.*

$$ Comfort Hotel. Once called the Brownstone, this intimate hotel— 110 units in all—still retains some of the charm of a private club. You could not be closer to the center of town and still get a quiet night's sleep. Ask for one of the recently renovated rooms; there is no additional charge for children under 14. Pralines restaurant is open all day for meals and snacks. During the summer of 1994, there were double rooms for less than $100; in winter, prices can drop another 25%. Some packages include Continental breakfast. *15 Charles St. E, M4Y 1S1, tel. 416/924–7381 or 800/263–8967. AE, DC, MC, V.*

$$ Holiday Inn on King. In the heart of the fashion district, the Holiday Inn is just three blocks north of the Metro Toronto Convention Centre, SkyDome, and the CN Tower. Although the structure is 20 floors high, half of that is office space; the hotel takes up the 9th–20th floors only. Two restaurants—one of them Japanese—and a deli provide for the 426 rooms. The swimming pool is tiny, but the fitness center is good, and one can request views of either Lake Ontario, the downtown skyline, or SkyDome. Executive suites have whirlpool bathtubs. Being a Holiday Inn, there are no surprises. *370 King St. W, M5V 1J9, tel. 416/599–4000. AE, D, DC, MC, V.*

$ Hotel Shelby. Is it possible to stay in a charming, attractive hotel in downtown Toronto, just minutes from Yorkville, the Eaton Centre, the ROM, the CN Tower, SkyDome, Chinatown, and more, at 1960 rates? Well, in a city where multimillion-dollar mansions stand proudly (and safely!) within yards of the heart of downtown, the answer is a most satisfying "yes." Hotel Shelby is actually a Victorian building from the 1880s, located just a block south of Bloor and only a few blocks east of Yonge. It offers free (if limited) parking, 67 rooms (49 of which have private baths), several Victorian suites (complete with working fireplaces), access to a major, quality health club just a few feet away, and even a complimentary Continental breakfast. What an irresistible place—with student, senior citizen, and weekly rates, and prices often less than $60–$75 per night. *592 Sherbourne St., M4X 1L4, tel. 416/921–3142 or 800/387–4788. MC, V.*

$ Journey's End Hotel. The 196 rooms are clean and spartan in this 16-story chain hotel located in the downtown core area, a 10-minute walk from Eaton Centre. There are no pools, saunas, or convention rooms, but prices (less than $125 a night for doubles, and about $75 during winter weekends in 1994) are reasonable. And business-people might be charmed by its offering of free phone calls and less than $50 for a 9–4 "Traveler's Day," which includes free papers and coffee. The Lombard Street location has The Vogue Bistro, and the Bloor Street hotel has Obie's, a fast-food eatery open from 7 AM until 1 AM. *111 Lombard St., M5C 2T9, and 280 Bloor St. W, M5S 1V8, tel. 800/668–4200. AE, DC, MC, V.*

$ Neill-Wycik College-Hotel. This is an attractive alternative for young people or families on a tight budget. From early May through late August, the college residence becomes Toronto's best hotel value. The 265 rooms are private, but guests must share facilities with five or six other hotel guests. A cafeteria serves breakfast 6:30–11:30. There's a great view of the city from the cedar roof deck. Prices have edged up to the high $30s for a single, mid-40s for a small double, and close to $50 for a couple/family, but that's still pretty astonishing. *96 Gerrard St. E, M5B 1G7, tel. 416/977–2320. MC, V.*

$ Ryerson Student Residence. Short-term lodging is available in the heart of downtown at Ryerson—formerly a polytechnical institute and now a university—from early May to late August every summer. True, the 555 rooms are all singles, sharing bath facilities, but there are kitchenettes, laundry facilities, and TV lounges on every floor; each room has a phone. No children under 12 (or pets of any age) are allowed, but for prices ranging from about $25 per night and $125 weekly for students (and about $35/$200 for nonstudents), can you do better anywhere else? You're close to Maple Leaf Gardens and Eaton Centre. *160 Mutual St., M5B 2M2, tel. 416/979–5284. MC, V.*

$ Toronto Bed & Breakfast. More than two dozen private homes are affiliated with this service, most of them scattered across metropolitan Toronto. Singles range from the low $40s to the low $60s; doubles from the low $50s to the mid-$80s. *Tel. 416/961–3676.*

Off the Beaten Track

$$$$ Inn on the Park. This is another classy member of the Four Seasons chain. It is located across the street from the Ontario Science Centre, just off Don Valley Parkway, only a 10-minute drive from downtown Toronto. The only resort in the city, it offers 600 acres of parkland, miles of cross-country ski trails, swimming, biking, jogging, and access to tennis, racquetball, squash, and horseback riding. Children ages 5–12 can disappear all day into a supervised program, complete with swimming, arts and crafts, and other activities. Its two restaurants are the formal Seasons, for lunch and dinner, as well as a lavish Sunday brunch, and the family-style Harvest Room, open daily 6:30 AM–nearly midnight. There are 568 modern rooms and 11 suites. The more expensive rooms are in the 22-story tower, where you should ask for south views, toward downtown and the lake. But the smaller back rooms in the main building (sans vue) can cost as little as $80–$90 for winter weekends and about $100 for the rest of the year. Indeed, throughout all of 1994, every Friday, Saturday, and Sunday had rates from $85 per night, single or double occupancy. "Spring Break" packages in early 1994 offered lodging, full breakfast for two, a complimentary "Innkidz" program (face painting, a hotel tour, even cookie decorating), free parking, use of the hotel health club, cross-country skiing, and a major discount off family admission to the fabulous Ontario Science Centre—a short walk away—for only $99 per night. *1100 Eglinton Ave. E, M3C 1H8, tel. 416/444–2561 or 800/332–3442. AE, DC, MC, V.*

$$ **Guild Inn.** Modern units are built around a 1930s country inn on some 90 acres of forest, gardens, and woodland trails, a 20- to 30-minute drive from downtown Toronto. Facilities include a heated outdoor pool, a tennis court, and dining room. Guests have a choice of 13 traditional rooms in the original building or 67 modern rooms in the newer wing. Weekend rates can be less than $75 for one night, about $100 for two, and $150 for three—extraordinary for a gorgeous and unique resort. *201 Guildwood Pkwy., Scarborough M1E 1P6, tel. 416/261–3331. AE, MC, V.*

$ **Marigold Hostel.** This charming little place is a tiny hotel with dormitory accommodation for both sexes near the Dundas West subway station and beautiful High Park, in western Toronto. You can stay here for little more than $20; the hostel has eight rooms with shared bathrooms, while two rooms have private baths and cost up to $50 a night. There's no curfew or check-out time. You have access to coin lockers and free parking. Coffee and donuts are also free in the morning. Sure, this hostel is for students and backpackers, but at these prices, it could be a lifesaver. *2011 Dundas St. W, M6R 1W7, tel. 416/536–8824 (only after 7 PM).*

The Airport Strip

Few hotels along the airport strip offer anything more than your standard, no-surprises rooms and meals. Most have pools, pay TV, and weekend rates, and their prices vary greatly.

$$$ **Bristol Place.** This has long been considered the ritziest of all the hotels along the airport strip, and, thanks to a $2 million face-lift in 1987, it is more attractive than ever. All 287 bedrooms and suites have been redone. Bedrooms have mahogany armoires, tables, desks, and minibars. Zachary's, the main dining room, is open for lunch and dinner, and Le Café is open every day from 7 AM until midnight. Call its special airport bus from the arrival level when you have your bags; it's only two minutes away. And, for an airport hotel, it's fairly quiet; rooms that face east are the quietest of all. Rates verge on the very expensive, but weekend specials (which run a generous Thursday, Friday, Saturday, and Sunday) in the $100 range are available all year-round. *950 Dixon Rd., M9W 5N4, next to airport, tel. 416/675–9444. Facilities: indoor and outdoor pools, saunas, health club with exercise equipment, children's play area. AE, DC, MC, V.*

$$-$$$ **Regal Constellation.** Now part of the Regal chain out of Hong Kong, the former Constellation continues to be one of the bright lights at the airport, and one of its classiest members, with 900 rooms. There is a stunning, seven-story, glass-enclosed lobby; a fully equipped health club, including saunas and a delightful indoor/outdoor swimming pool; quality dining; and very impressive service. The south wing has minisuites, all of them larger than the other rooms. The Burgundy, the main dining room, is open for lunch and dinner, and the Atrium Restaurant is open daily from 5 AM until midnight. One nice touch: By law, airplanes cannot fly on the north side of Dixon, making this a very quiet hotel. Don't miss the weekend rates of about $100, which actually includes a $20 breakfast for one, for free! *900 Dixon Rd., M9W 1J7, tel. 416/675-1500. AE, DC, MC, V.*

$ **Journey's End Suites.** This is one of the most successful budget motel/hotel chains in Canada, and its new-suites concept near the airport is an irresistible combination: king-size beds, living areas, a large table and even four chairs for business meetings. There's no pool or any health club access, but there's a restaurant, and a courtesy bus runs to/from the airport every half hour. And, like its downtown hotel, J.E.S. provides free papers, free local phone calls, and a Traveler's Day Rate in the area of $60, for a 9–4 day, a superb deal, especially for executives on a budget. *262 Carlingview Dr., Etobicoke, Ont., M9W 5G1, tel. 416/674-8442; 800/668-4200. 258 suites. AE, DC, MC, V.*

Executive Apartments

$$-$$$ **Executive Travel Apartment Suites Inc.** Since 1977 this concern (formerly ETA Suites) has been supplying corporate clients with short-term rates (as little as one night, cheaper by the week or month) for nicely appointed apartment suites in many cities across North America and Europe. It has 10 town houses in Burlington, a half-hour drive southwest of Toronto (on the way to Buffalo), an additional 18 in nearby Oakville, dozens near the corner of Bay and Bloor streets, and two dozen more in such fine neighborhoods as Rosedale, Forest Hill, and the Annex. These quality mini-apartments have fully equipped kitchens and vastly greater space and privacy than conventional hotel rooms. They might be particularly attractive to business travelers who are in the city for several days or even weeks, and who find most hotel rooms claustrophobic. Sample prices from 1994: A one-bedroom executive suite at the corner of Bay and Bloor—just one block from Yorkville and the Royal Ontario Museum—costs only $99 per night for one to six nights, and $80 per night for one month or more. Similar prices exist at other downtown locations, and in Mississauga, not far from the Toronto airport. This is one good idea for lengthy stays. *40 St. Mary St., M4Y 2S8, tel. 416/923-3000. All suites. AE, D, MC, V.*

Family Farms

It's daring and different, but families with children might find it exciting to stay on a farm, not far from the city of Toronto. Including bed and breakfast, rates range from as low as $35 to $100 per person per night, with a weekly average of only $200 per person, which is extraordinary. And we're not talking about sleeping in barns. Some locations actually have riding stables and Jacuzzis! For information, Canadians can call 519/846-9788 and leave a message; Americans can call or write to **Ontario Farm and Country Accommodations** (R.R. 2, Alma, Ontario N0B 1A0). Include a large, stamped, self-addressed envelope. Stick on around 90¢ in U.S. stamps, and don't

American Express offers Travelers Cheques built for two.

Cheques *for Two*℠ from American Express are the Travelers Cheques that allow either of you to use them because both of you have signed them. And only one of you needs to be present to purchase them.

Cheques *for Two* are accepted anywhere regular American Express Travelers Cheques are, which is just about everywhere. So stop by your bank, AAA* or any American Express Travel Service Office and ask for Cheques *for Two*.

AMERICAN EXPRESS **Travelers Cheques** ®

Pack light.
Take the one number you need for any kind of call, anywhere you travel.

Checking in with your family back home? Calling for a tow truck? When you're on the road, the phone you use might not accept your calling card. Or you might get overcharged by an unknown telephone company. Here's the solution: dial 1 800 CALL ATT.[sm] You'll get flawless AT&T service, competitive calling card prices, and the lowest prices for collect calls from any phone, anywhere. Travel light. Just bring along this one simple number: 1 800 CALL ATT.

worry, the group takes return envelopes to the States to mail to you. In winter, U.S. travelers need to call and leave their name and address.

Camping

This is a very citified area; the only location offering tent and trailer camping within metropolitan Toronto is **Glen Rouge Park,** 25 acres in the city's northeast end. Its attractions include nature trails, horseback riding, and proximity to the city's fabulous zoo. For a list of licensed private campgrounds and trailer parks, write to Travel Information, Ministry of Industry and Tourism, 3rd Floor, Hearst Block, Queen's Park, Toronto M7A 2E5. A list of provincial parks and recreation and conservation areas is available from Provincial Parks Information, Whitney Block, Queen's Park, Toronto M7A 1W3.

7 The Arts and Nightlife

The Arts

Toronto is the capital of the lively arts in Canada. True, Winnipeg has a very fine ballet, and Montreal's orchestra is superb. But in nearly every aspect of music, opera, dance, and theater, Toronto is truly the New York City of the North.

It was not always this way; before 1950—four decades ago—Toronto had no opera company, no ballet, and very little theater worthy of the title "professional." Then came the Massey Report on the Arts, one of those government-sponsored studies that usually helps put sensitive subjects on the back burner for several more years, but in this case, all Heaven broke loose: Money began to come from a variety of government grants; two prominent Canadian millionaires passed to their reward, and their death taxes were put toward the creation of a Canada Council, which doled out more money; the Canadian Opera Company, CBC television, and the National Ballet of Canada were born; and a number of little theaters began to pop up, culminating in an artistic explosion throughout the 1970s, in every aspect of the arts.

The reasons for this explosion were many: massive immigration from more culturally nourished countries of Eastern and Central Europe, as well as from England; a growing sense of independence from the mother country; a recognition that if Canada was not to develop its own arts, then the damned Yankees would do it for them; and, in general, a growing civic and cultural maturity.

Some of Toronto's impressive growth in the lively arts was sheer chance; after all, who can explain the miracle of pianist Glenn Gould's birth in this city, or the fact that ballet master Baryshnikov decided to defect here and later came often to teach and dance with the National Ballet of Canada?

But it would not be fair to pass it off as simply as that. Toronto was like an awkward, gawky teenager for many decades, it's true, but there were always a number of cultural events happening; the city did not suddenly give birth to art overnight, like Athena bursting out, fully clothed and mature, from the head of Zeus.

The best places to get information on cultural events are in the Thursday editions of the *Toronto Star* (its "What's On" section is superlative); the Saturday (weekend) *Globe and Mail* (whose entertainment section is the most critically solid); the free, weekly *Now* and *eye* newspapers, as well as *Toronto Life*. To obtain half-price tickets on the day of a performance, don't forget the **Five Star Tickets booth,** located in the Royal Ontario Museum lobby during the winter and, at other times, at the corner of Yonge Street and Dundas Street, outside the Eaton Centre. The museum booth is open daily noon–6, and Tuesday and Thursday to 7; the Yonge and Dundas booth is open—in good weather—Monday–Saturday, noon–7:30, and Sunday, 11–3. Tickets are sold for cash only, all sales are final, and a small service charge is added to the price of each ticket. The booth outside the Eaton Centre also gives out piles of superb brochures and pamphlets on the city.

Concert Halls and Theaters

The **Roy Thomson Hall** (just below the CN Tower) has become since 1982 the most important concert hall in Toronto.

It was to have been named the New Massey Hall, since it was replacing the much-loved original, which had served Toronto since 1894. But then the family of billionaire newspaper magnate Lord Thomson of Fleet gave the largest single donation ($4.5 million of its $43 million cost) and gave his name to the hall instead. Critics were silenced by the beauty of the hall's design and the sensitivity of its acoustics. It is the home today of the Toronto Symphony and the Toronto Mendelssohn Choir, one of the world's finest choral groups. It also hosts orchestras from around the world and popular entertainers from Liza Minnelli to Anne Murray. *60 Simcoe St., at corner of King Street W, a block west of University Ave., tel. 416/593–4828. Tickets $20–$65 (best seats rows H and J in orchestra and row L upstairs). Rush seats (about $15) sold day of performance, beginning two hours before show time. Daily tours, highlighting the acoustic and architectural features of the stunning structure, take place Mon.–Sat. 12:30 PM (cost: $3). Call to confirm; tours subject to cancellation (tel. 416/593–4822, ext. 363).*

Massey Hall has always been cramped and dingy, but its near-perfect acoustics and its handsome, U-shape tiers sloping down to the stage have made it a happy place to hear the Toronto Symphony, or almost anyone else in the world of music, for nearly a century. The nearly 2,800 seats are not terribly comfortable, and a small number are blocked by pillars that hold up the ancient structure, but it remains a venerable place to catch the greats and near-greats of the music world. *178 Victoria St. at Shuster St., just a block north of Queen St. and a few feet east of Eaton Centre; tel. 416/593–4828. Best seats are rows G–M, center, and in balcony, rows 32–50.*

The Edward Johnson Building, in the Bloor Street/University Avenue area, houses the **MacMillan Theatre,** and it is an important place to hear avant-garde artists and the stars of the future. Because it's run by the faculty of music of the University of Toronto, the academic year also brings serious jazz trios and baroque chamber works—at little or no cost. The U of T newspaper, *The Varsity*, found all around the campus, often lists concerts planned for this special place. *Behind McLaughlin Planetarium, just south of Royal Ontario Museum subway exit, tel. 416/978–3744.*

The **O'Keefe Centre** has become the home of the Canadian Opera Company and the National Ballet of Canada. It is also home to visiting comedians, pre-Broadway musicals, rock stars, and almost anyone else who can fill it. When it was built in 1960, its 3,167 seats made it the largest concert hall on the continent. The acoustics leave much to be desired, and its cavernous nature makes almost anything but the most lavish opera or musical seem dwarfed, but you will still feel as if you were attending a cultural event. The city owns the building now and offers half-price seats to students and senior citizens for many of its shows. *1 Front St. E, a block east of Union Station, tel. 416/872–2262. Tickets $25–$60. Try for seats close to A47–48; avoid very front rows, such as AA, BB, etc.*

About 50 yards east of the O'Keefe is the **St. Lawrence Centre for the Arts.** Since 1970, it has been presenting everything from live theater to string quartets and forums on city issues. The main hall, the luxuriously appointed **Bluma Appel Theatre,** hosts the often brilliant productions of the **Canadian Stage Company.** Classical and contemporary plays are often on a level with the best of Broadway and London's West End. *Front St. at the corner of Scott St., a block east of Yonge St., two blocks from Union Station, tel. 416/366–7723. Tickets $20–$50. Try for rows E–N, seats 1–10.*

The other important theater in the city is the **Royal Alexandra,** which has been the place to be seen in Toronto since its opening in 1907. The plush red seats, gold brocade, and baroque swirls and curlicues all make theater-going a refined experience. It's astonishing to recall that all this magnificence was about to be torn down in the 1960s but was rescued by none other than "Honest Ed" Mirvish of discount-store fame. He not only restored the theater to its former glory but also made it profitable. At press time (June 1994), a superb production of the "new Gershwin" musical, *Crazy for You,* was delighting audiences. *260 King St. W, a few blocks west of University Ave., two blocks southwest of CN Tower, tel. 416/872–3333. Tickets $35–$75. Student tickets can be obtained for less than $20. Avoid rows A and B; try for rows C–L center. For musicals, try first rows of first balcony.*

Since the summer of 1989, the gigantic **SkyDome** has been opening its doors (and roof, in good weather). Although its expressed purpose is for baseball and football, its 70,000 seats are often used for concerts—more than likely rock. *Located on the south side of Front St., just west of CN Tower, tel. 416/341–3663.*

One of the most exciting newer theaters in town is the **Pantages,** a 1920 vaudeville theater, which was turned into a complex of half a dozen movie theaters. In 1988-89, the Cineplex/Odeon people poured some $18 million into refurbishing the theater as a majestic work of art. In the fall of 1989, a Canadian company of *The Phantom of the Opera* opened, and the show seems destined to run right through the 1990s. Tickets can be ordered through Ticketmaster. Tickets are $56, $67, $78, and $91, and most audiences seem to believe that only the most expensive seats have decent sightlines and are worth the money. The Lloyd Webber score is only so-so, and the book is unimpressive, in spite of its worldwide success. Still, the production is first-class, with a wonderful set, fabulous costumes, and superior singing. And the theater itself is one of the most beautiful in the world. *263 Yonge St., just a half-block south of Dundas St., across from Eaton Centre, tel. 416/872–2222. Performances Wed.–Sat. 8 PM; Wed., Thurs., and Sat. 2 PM, Sun. 3 PM. Student tickets between $46–70, Wed. matinee only.*

Only Toronto (and the Mirvishes!) would actually build an entirely new (and exquisite) theater in order to house an overrated musical, *Miss Saigon.* But it did, and thank heavens they did. The **Princess of Wales** is in great shape and is (almost) worth the $25–$91 prices. *300 King St. W, just west of University and down the block from the Royal Alexandra, tel. 416/872–1212. Performances Tues.–Sat. 8 PM; Wed., Sat., and Sun. 2 PM.*

Another spectacular new theater complex is the **North York Performing Arts Centre,** where a striking new production of the Kern/ Hammerstein musical classic *Show Boat* will probably play a long time. This complex is conveniently located about 5 miles due north of Bloor. *5040 Yonge St., just above the 401, tel. 416/872–2222. Performances Tues.–Sat. 7:30 PM; Wed. and Sat. 2 PM; Sun. 3 PM. Tickets $50–$90.*

The New Yorker, an older, modest theater, is home to a long-running musical, *Forever Plaid.* This low-priced, disarming delight features popular songs from the 1950s. *651 Yonge St., just below Bloor, tel. 416/872–1111. Performances Tues.–Fri. 8 PM; Sat. 7 and 9:45 PM; Wed. 2 PM; Sun. 3 PM. Tickets $30–$50.*

The other major concert/theater halls in the Toronto area are in **Stratford** and **Niagara-on-the-Lake** (*see* Chapter 8).

Classical Concerts

The Toronto Symphony, now over seven decades old, is not about to retire. Since 1922, with conductors of the quality of Seiji Ozawa, Walter Susskind, Sir Thomas Beecham, and Andrew Davis, it has achieved world acclaim. Its musical director since 1994 has been the young and impressive Jukka-Pekka Saraste, who should do wonders in rejuvenating an already world-class orchestra. When the TS is home, it presents about three concerts weekly from September to May in Roy Thomson Hall and a miniseason each summer at Ontario Place. *60 Simcoe St., on King St., just west of University Ave., tel. 416/593–4828. Tickets $20–$50.*

The **Toronto Mendelssohn Choir** often guests with the Toronto Symphony. This 180-singer group, going since 1894, has been applauded worldwide, and its *Messiah* is handeled well every Christmas (no, we couldn't resist that). You may be impressed to know that some of the heartbreaking and beautiful choral music heard in the Academy Award–winning film *Schindler's List* was sung by this choir. *For program information, tel. 416/598–0422; for tickets, Roy Thomson Hall, tel. 416/593–4828.*

The **Elmer Isler Singers,** a fine group of nearly two dozen members, has also performed around the globe, and is a respected Toronto choir. *Tel. 416/482–1664.*

The **Orford String Quartet,** another world-class musical group, is based in Toronto at the Edward Johnson Building. *Tel. 416/978–3744.*

Tafelmusik ("table music") is a local orchestra that goes for baroque music on original instruments. *St. Paul Centre at Trinity Church, 427 Bloor St. W, near Spadina Ave. subway stop, tel. 416/964–6337.*

Music at Sharon is a marvelous concert series that takes place on weekends every July in the Sharon Temple, located in a small town about a 45-minute drive north of downtown Toronto. The old temple has wonderful acoustics. For over a decade, concerts have ranged from flute offerings and humor in music to Haydn afternoons (and evenings). *Sharon is 4 km north of Newmarket, which is just above Hwy. 9, after taking Don Valley Parkway/Hwy. 404 north from 401. Tel. 905/478–2431, or write to Music at Sharon, Box 331, Sharon, Ont. L0G 1V0.*

Pop and Rock Concerts

Most major international recording companies have offices in Toronto, so it's not by chance that the city is a regular stop for top musical performers of today, including Frank Sinatra, Billy Joel, Whitney Houston, Sting, Michael Jackson, and Bruce Springsteen. Tickets ($15–$40) can usually be booked through **Ticketmaster** (tel. 416/872–1111).

Major venues include the **SkyDome,** just west of the CN Tower, on Front Street, tel. 416/963–3513; **Maple Leaf Gardens,** 60 Carlton Street, a block east of Yonge Street and the College Street subway stop, tel. 416/977–1641; the **O'Keefe Centre,** Yonge and Front streets, tel. 416/872–2262; and **Exhibition Stadium,** at the CNE grounds, tel. 416/393–6000.

Ontario Place (tel. 416/965–7711) has pop, rock, and jazz concerts throughout its summer season at extremely modest prices. This is one of the loveliest and least expensive places to see and hear a concert in all of Toronto.

Kingswood Music Theatre, next to Canada's Wonderland, also has important rock and pop concerts during the warmer months. *Located along Hwy. 400, 10 min north of Hwy. 401, tel. 416/832–8131. Admission usually about $10 above cost of entry to Canada's Wonderland.*

Opera

Since its founding in 1950, the **Canadian Opera Company** has grown into the largest producer of opera in Canada and the fifth largest company on the continent. From the most popular operas, such as *Carmen* and *Madama Butterfly*, usually performed in the original language, to more modern or rare works, such as *Jenufa*, and the erotic success of 1988, *Lady Macbeth of Mtsensk*, the COC has proven trustworthy and often daring.

Each year, at Toronto's O'Keefe Centre, more than 150,000 people attend its season of seven operas, which have included such memorable productions as Canada's first presentation of Benjamin Britten's *Death in Venice*, the North American premiere of Tchaikovsky's *Joan of Arc*, and the continent's second presentation of the complete three-act *Lulu* by Alban Berg.

Like all important companies, the COC often hosts world-class performers such as Joan Sutherland, Grace Bumbry, Martina Arroyo, Marilyn Horne, and Canada's own Louis Quilico and Maureen Forrester. The company also pioneered the use of surtitles, which allow the audience to follow the libretto in English in a capsulized translation. The COC also performs mini-operas in a tent during the summer, down at Harbourfront, on the shores of Lake Ontario. *Tel. 416/363–8231 or 416/393–7469.*

Dance

The Bolshoi is two centuries old; the **National Ballet of Canada** can trace itself all the way back to November 12, 1951, when it made its official debut on the cramped stage of the old Eaton Auditorium on College Street. In less than four decades, the company has done some extraordinary things and reaped some revered awards, with such principal dancers as Karen Kain, Frank Augustyn, Kevin Pugh, and Owen Montague all wowing the Russians at the Moscow competitions. Today, Canada's premier dance company has 70 dancers; it is the third largest troupe in North America and the fifth largest in the world. *Performances Nov., Feb., and May at O'Keefe Centre, at corner of Front and Yonge Sts.; in summer at Ontario Pl. Office, tel. 416/362–1041, 416/872–1111, or 416/872–2277; O'Keefe Centre, 416/872–2262. Tickets $15–$75. Student and senior citizen standby tickets at about $15 are sometimes available the day of performance.*

Toronto Dance Theatre, its roots in the Martha Graham tradition, is the oldest contemporary dance company in the city. Since its beginnings in the 1960s, it has created close to 100 works, over a third using original scores commissioned from Canadian composers. It tours Canada and has played major festivals in England, Europe, and the United States. After a decade of steady success, it purchased a beautiful renovated church, St. Enoch's, built in 1891, and a neighboring hall in the heart of Cabbagetown. They serve as home for its school and over three dozen full-time students. *Most perfor-*

mances are in the Premiere Dance Theatre, at Harbourfront Centre, 235 Queen's Quay W, tel. 416/869–8444.

Dancemakers is another important Toronto modern-dance company, drawing on everyone from Martha Graham to Jose Limon and Merce Cunningham. It performs at both the Premiere Dance Theatre and Solar Stage (First Canadian Pl., on King St. near Bay St., tel. 416/ 368–5135 or 416/535–8880).

Theater

There are over four dozen performing spaces in Toronto; we will mention only a handful of the most prominent.

The **Royal Alexandra,** the **O'Keefe,** the **St. Lawrence Centre,** the **Princess of Wales,** and the **North York Performing Arts Centre** are noted in the Concert Halls and Theaters section, above.

Bathurst Street Theatre, almost at the corner of Bathurst and Bloor streets (another unfashionable address), is a church converted to theater space, but the gods have remained. The premises are used by dance groups and many of the more interesting theater groups in the city. The pews aren't terribly comfortable, but now they don't stop in the middle of the plays and pass the hat. *736 Bathurst St., just south of Honest Ed's, and around the corner from Mirvish Village, tel. 416/535–0591.*

The **Elgin** and **Winter Garden Theaters** are two of the newest/oldest jewels in the crown of the Toronto arts scene. Both are old vaudeville places, stacked upon one another (The Elgin, downstairs, has about 1,500 seats, and is more suited for musicals; the Winter Garden, upstairs, is some 500 seats smaller, and more intimate; both are stunningly attractive.) Recently renovated, they have been used for jazz festivals, locally produced musicals *(The Wizard of Oz)*, and—a pleasant example—British actor/director Kenneth Branagh's Renaissance Theatre Company's productions of *King Lear* and *A Midsummer Night's Dream. 189 Yonge St., just north of Queen St., tel. 416/872–5555.*

Factory Theatre is another major alternate theater devoted to original and experimental work. *125 Bathurst St., at Adelaide St. W, tel. 416/864–9971.*

Hart House Theatre is smack in the middle of the University of Toronto campus and is the main theater space of the U of T. Amateur, student, and occasional professional productions have been presented here for a half century, many of them controversial (and uncommercial). *Just off Queen's Park Crescent W, about one block west of Parliament buildings, and a few blocks south of Royal Ontario Museum, tel. 416/978–8668.*

Second City, the Toronto version of the famous Chicago company, is the place where the inspired SCTV series had its genesis. Its revues tend to be the brightest, most reliable comedy in town. *The Old Firehall Theatre, 110 Lombard St., downtown, just east of Yonge St, tel. 416/863–1162.*

The **Tarragon Theatre,** located in an unpleasant area of railroad tracks and old factories, is the natural habitat for indigenous Canadian theater. Almost anything worthwhile in this country's drama first saw the light of day here. *30 Bridgman Ave., 1 block east of Bathurst St. and north of Dupont St., tel. 416/531–1827.*

Le Théâtre Français de Toronto, until recently known as Le Théâtre du P'tit Bonheur, has been providing French-language drama of high quality for many years. Its repertoire has ranged from classical to contemporary, from both France and French Canada. It has a marvelous location at Harbourfront, next door to the stunning Queen's Quay Terminal. In 1988, the theater performed a bilingual play, so English-speaking theatergoers could follow along. *The Du-Maurier Centre, 231 Queen's Quay W, tel. 416/534–6604.*

Théâtre Passe Muraille, in the unfashionable area of Bathurst and Queen streets, has long been the home of fine collaborative theater—Canadian, good, innovative. *16 Ryerson Ave., running north from Queen St. W, 1 block east of Bathurst St., tel. 416/363–2416.*

Toronto Free Theatre, although no longer free (and recently joining forces with the major Canadian Stage Company, which operates out of the St. Lawrence Centre), remains freewheeling and fascinating. This space has seen most of Canada's finest performers and playwrights showing their wares. *26 Berkeley St., just south of Front St. and 1 block west of Parliament St., tel. 416/368–2856.*

Toronto Workshop, one of the city's more beloved (and convenient) theater spaces, now serves as the home for **Buddies in Bad Times,** an important and often impressive theater company that presents poetic, musical, and usually gay-related productions. Those theater goers interested in the state of gay arts in the city should not miss this place. *12 Alexander St., 1 block north of College/Carlton, a few steps east of Yonge St., tel. 416/863–9455.*

The **Young People's Theatre** is the only theater center in the country devoted solely to children. But unlike purveyors of much of traditional children's fare, this place does not condescend or compromise its dramatic integrity. *165 Front St. E, near Sherbourne St., 8 blocks east of Yonge St. Take Yonge St. subway to King St. and then King St. streetcar east, and walk down 1 block. Tel. 416/864–9732.*

Two of the most entertaining presentations of the past few years are free and take place in two major parks each July and early August: Skylight Theatre and Dream in High Park, the latter named after its original production of Shakespeare's *A Midsummer Night's Dream.*

At its own amphitheater, the first-rate **Skylight Theatre** has presented such productions as *The Little Prince, Frankenstein,* and *Twelfth Night,* and some of them have surpassed presentations at Stratford. *Earl Bales Park, take Bloor St. subway to Bathurst St., then Bathurst St. bus about a mile north of Hwy. 401. You enter park at Bainbridge Ave., a few blocks south of Sheppard Ave. W. Tel. 416/781–4846. Admission free.*

Dream in High Park, now more than a half-dozen years old, presents quality productions of Shakespeare (and occasionally a musical) each July in the heart of Toronto's most glorious area, High Park. The open-air productions are usually a knockout. *Bloor and Keele Sts., tel. 416/368–2856. Take Bloor St. subway to High Park stop, then walk south into park.*

Dinner Theater There are many local productions of Broadway musicals and comedies presented in Toronto's numerous dinner theaters. These include **Harper's Restaurant and Dinner Theatre** (26 Lombard St., downtown, tel. 416/863–6223) and **Limelight Supper Club** (2026 Yonge St., just below Eglinton Ave., tel. 416/482–5200). This city just doesn't stop.

Mysteriously Yours . . . should be of special interest to murder-mystery buffs. On Thursday, Friday, and Saturday evenings, a "despicable crime" is perpetrated at the Royal York Hotel. The mystery begins to unravel just after dinner, which begins at 6:30; it's usually solved miraculously and wittily around 9:30 or 10. The complete dinner and mystery game costs between $55 and $60, which includes all taxes and gratuities. If you wish to enjoy the mystery only, without the food, you can do so on Thursday and Friday for about $20; on Saturday for about $30. Call Brian Caws at 416/486–7469 or 800/668–3323.

Film

Every September since 1976, Toronto had been holding a world-class film festival, called—with no great modesty—**The Festival of Festivals.** In late 1993, it changed its name to the slightly more modest **Toronto International Film Festival** (tel. 416/967–7371). Whether retrospectives consist of the films of Marguerite Duras, Jean-Luc Godard, and Max Ophuls, or tributes to the careers of Martin Scorsese, Robert Duvall, and John Schlesinger, this is the time for lovers of film.

Toronto is one of the film capitals of the world, and you can often catch a movie here that is not showing anywhere else—or even available on video. The Cineplex concept, which now has over 1,500 screens across North America, was created in Toronto; the multiscreened one in Eaton Centre was its genesis. Foreigners will be either delighted or disappointed to discover that Toronto is still subject to the strange machinations of a provincial—in more ways than one—censor board, and therefore has no friendly neighborhood porno movies.

Carlton Cinemas (20 Carlton St., just steps east of College St. subway, tel. 416/296–3456) part of the Cineplex chain, shows rare, important films from around the world in nearly a dozen screening rooms.

Fox Beaches (2236 Queen St. E, tel. 416/691–7330) is an old-style movie house that will flood anyone over 40 with warm nostalgia.

Ontario Film Theatre is in the Ontario Science Centre (770 Don Mills Rd., near Eglinton Ave. E, tel. 416/429–4100). A provincially funded film house, it is much admired for its foreign art films and retrospectives.

Reg Hartt Presents is one of the more delightful traditions of underground film in the city. For many years now, Hartt has thrilled and amazed film lovers with his highly eclectic, often grotesque minifestivals, shown at various locations around the city. Now he has his own place, **Cineforum,** (463 Bathurst St., tel. 416/777–2022), a small house near downtown. This movie maniac shows such films as *The History of Animation* and *The Uncensored History of Warner Brothers Looney Tunes & Merrie Melodies.* ("Warning: Many of these cartoons are sexist, racist, and as violent as a two-by-four in the face!" read his ads.) Tickets cost $8–$20; sometimes a special film and lecture are offered together.

Other places in Toronto with regular showings of important films and film series—often free or close to it—include the **Art Gallery of Ontario** (317 Dundas St. W, tel. 416/977–0414); **Harbourfront Centre** (235 Queen's Quay W, tel. 416/973–4000); the **Metro Toronto Reference Library** (789 Yonge St., tel. 416/393–7141); **Innis Film Society** of the University of Toronto (2 Sussex Ave., tel. 416/588–8940);

Cinesphere, at Ontario Place (955 Lakeshore Blvd. W, tel. 416/965–7711); and the **Royal Ontario Museum** (100 Queen's Park Crescent, at Bloor St. and University Ave., tel. 416/586–5549).

Nightlife

Jazz Clubs

In spite of the sad passing of the wonderful **Café des Copains,** a whole slew of new places have opened up across Toronto, providing superior jazz and happy audiences once again.

Chick 'n Deli has long been one of the great jazz places in Toronto. A casual atmosphere prevails, and the lack of a dress code helps with the neighborhood-bar ambience. There's a dance floor and dark wood everywhere, giving it a pub-like feel. It's also famous for wings and live music; the former half-price, Mon.–Tues. until 9, the latter playing at 9 PM most nights, and 7:30 on Sunday. Check out the occasional earlier jazz shows, and the Sunday brunch—all you can eat for around $10. You can always count on a fine jam session between 5 and 8 PM on Sunday. *744 Mount Pleasant Rd., near Eglinton Ave., tel. 416/489–3363 or 416/489–7931.*

A few blocks east of the Eaton Centre is **George's Spaghetti House,** the oldest continuously running jazz club in the city. The music starts at 8:30 PM, with the world-famous Moe Koffman (of Swinging Shepherd Blues fame) performing one week each month. (For Moe, and on weekends, you'll need reservations.) George's has a modest cover charge and a decent Italian menu. *290 Dundas St. E, corner of Sherbourne St., tel. 416/923–9887. Closed Sun.*

Mezzeta is not strictly a jazz club, but where else can you get regular fixes of that glorious, Jewish-oriented music from Eastern Europe known as Klezmer? Check this one out for an often enriching musical experience. *681 St. Clair W, west of Bathurst St., tel. 416/658–5687.*

Top O' The Senator is this city's first club exclusively for jazz, and, sitting right atop the Senator diner, the room has the atmosphere of a between-the-wars jazz lounge. With its long wooden bar and dark-blue, towering ceilings, this is one fabulous 125-seat place. *249 Victoria St., tel. 416/364–7517.*

Other clubs have jazz periodically; you may wish to visit **Jambalaya** (501 Yonge St., tel. 416/922–5262), a fine little place right in the heart of the city, near Bloor and Yonge; or **The Old Nick** (123 Danforth Ave., the eastern continuation of Bloor St., just 2 mi east of Yonge, tel. 416/461–5546).

Rock

Upstairs, above the Spadina Hotel, along an unfashionable strip of King Street, is the very popular **Cabana Room.** Paneling recalling the rec room of your youth is combined with crazy red wallpaper—all the better to watch some of the local talent. There's no food, the cover charge varies, and long hair and jeans are worn by all. Everything goes here, from garage bands to country and folk groups. It's an endless party every night but Sunday, from 8 PM on. *460 King St. W, tel. 416/368–0729.*

Along Bloor Street West is **Clinton's Tavern,** which has been described as "the city's best taproom with a stage view." There's only a tiny dance floor, but this is where the brilliant Cowboy Junkies have put on shows. The logs on the walls may be fake, but not the great rock. *693 Bloor St. W, tel. 416/535-1429.*

Not far away is **Cameron Public House,** a small, eclectic kind of place. The music here alternates from jazz to hard rock to new wave; "alternative music," they proudly call it. Because it's close to the Ontario College of Art, the Cameron gets a creative crowd, with many regulars. The suburbanite scene gets heavy on weekends, as do the crowds. *408 Queen St. W, tel. 416/364-0811.*

For dozens of years, the **El Macambo** was one of the most glorious, trustworthy places for classic rock and roll; indeed, the Rolling Stones would even come here to jam after their million-dollar concerts at Maple Leaf Gardens. It was recently resurrected, after a few years in the dark. Here, just on the edge of Chinatown and only blocks from the heart of the University of Toronto, you can hear everything from punk-rock bands to rocking country acts. It has two levels, with an enormous capacity of close to 700. The downstairs is more a rock bar; the upstairs tends to be rented out for such things as African Night and other diverse entertainments. *464 Spadina Ave., near College St., tel. 416/928-3566.*

Pop rock reigns at the famous **Horseshoe Tavern,** also along the Queen Street strip. Good bands perform here, six days a week, with no food but lots of booze and a cover charge. It's a real tavern, with a pool table, lots of flannel-shirt types, mostly blue collar. Rock memorabilia lines the walls, and far more men than women line the bar. On weeknights, the ages range from 25 to 40; on weekends, it's younger. For over four decades, the Horseshoe was known across the city as the tavern with entertainment, especially country music. (Charlie Pride, Tex Ritter, Hank Williams, Loretta Lynn all played here.) There's lots of country-style dancing, but also live roots, blues, and rockabilly: "Conway Twitty meets Chuck Berry," according to one critic. *370 Queen St. W, corner of Spadina Ave., tel. 416/598-4753. Closed Sun.*

A major showcase for more daring arts in Toronto has long been **The Rivoli,** along the Queen Street "mall." A place for new, local artists not yet established enough to have their own gallery showings, the back room functions as a club, with theater happenings, "new music" (progressive rock and jazz), comedy troupes providing very funny improvisations twice a month, and more. Try to catch the "Poetry Sweatshop" every fourth Wednesday, in which local, nonliterary personalities judge various poets. Dinner for two, without alcohol, runs about $25. *332 Queen St. W, just west of University Ave., tel. 416/596-1908. No dress code. Cover charge $5-$10. Closed Sun.*

Sneaky Dee's is a very popular rock space, not far from the "neon palms" of El Macambo (*see above*). In its upstairs space, you can hear and enjoy rock music, funk, and various other kinds of live bands. *431 College St., near Bathurst, tel. 416/368-5090.*

The Ultrasound Showbar is that rarest of things, an actual showcase room for bands and even songwriters. The intimate space is long, narrow, and dark, dark, dark. The cover is usually under $10, and the more-often-than-not capacity crowd of 100 cannot help but enjoy itself. After all, its booker advertises: "Local, original talent, must be good, no bloody rubbish." *269 Queen St. W, along the famous strip, just west of University, tel. 416/593-0540.*

Rhythm and Blues

Albert's Hall has been called one of the top 25 bars in all of North America, in spite of its shabby decor. It features top blues bands. The crowd's older and more laid-back than downstairs, in the Brunswick, but it's still noisy and friendly—and *loud. 481 Bloor St. W, near Spadina Ave., tel. 416/964-2242. Cover charge on weekends; closed Sun.*

Black Swan was an old-time bar for three quarters of a century; today, its 120 customers nightly watch, listen and tap toes to wonderful, live rhythm and blues. Located out in the east end—where Bloor Street turns magically into "The Danforth," on the other side of the Don Valley Parkway—this spot will zap classic R&B lovers back into the 1960s. *154 Danforth Ave., tel. 416/469-0537.*

Chicago's, along the delightful Queen Street West strip, heading west from University Avenue, is a real charmer. Downstairs is a cowboyish bar and good hamburgers; upstairs is where you can see and hear the blues stars of tomorrow, and the day after. Dig the red neon sign in the shape of a beer cap. *335 Queen St. W, tel. 416/598-3301.*

Free Times Cafe is a relatively small space, where you'll find blues and folk singers, along with New Age, jazz, fusion, and other musical forms. A lot of acoustic performers love to put on quality shows here, especially singers/songwriters. To see the next stars of Mariposa and other festivals, this is the place to come. *320 College St., near Bathurst, tel. 416/967-1078.*

Surrounded by Chinese eateries and discount stores, the old, raunchy **Grossman's Tavern** has the best Saturday afternoons in the city. As one writer has noted, "long established, but never entirely reputable, Grossman's is perhaps a little too elemental for more refined tastes, but it's hard to imagine a more apt home for the blues." *379 Spadina Ave., tel. 416/977-7000.*

The Rex Hotel, along the Queen Street strip, is a long established hotel in an area that used to be the really seedy part of town. Now, the hotel can get jammed full with young men and women who want to enjoy blues, jazz, and jams almost every night. *194 Queen St. W, tel. 416/598-2475.*

Reggae and Caribbean

BamBoo serves reasonably priced Thai/Caribbean food. At this crazy old building, a one-time commercial laundry hidden behind the popular Queen Street strip, you can find everything from reggae to calypso, Caribbean to African, and even jazz. The sightlines can be terrible, and it's no place for a quiet conversation, but it's still wildly popular: great eating and great music. *312 Queen St. W, tel. 416/593-5771.*

Bars

There is something to be said for the province's liquor laws. Having a legal drinking age of 19 and a police force that regularly stops cars (whether driven suspiciously or not—something unconstitutional in the United States) to check the driver's sobriety with a Breathalyzer has cut down on drunken driving considerably. All the police have to discover is a greater amount than .08% of alcohol in the blood level of a driver and it's jail.

For a European atmosphere and a friendly, relaxed place to meet people, one of the most popular bars is **The Amsterdam.** It was recently voted "the most crowded bar," and although its busiest night is Thursday, it's jammed every business day at 5. Expect a 20- to 60-minute wait Thursday–Saturday evenings. The clientele is Bay Street—up-and-coming stockbrokers and business types. On weekends, suburbanites come out, and the population turns younger. The fixed menu is low ($10–$15), and reservations are a must. The extensive beer list includes three homemade brews. *133 John St., near University Ave. and Queen St., tel. 416/595–8201. No cover.*

In the middle of the ever-popular Yorkville area is the **Bellair Cafe,** *the* meeting place in Toronto. The outdoor patios are lovely in the summer, and the upstairs lounge has been converted to the Club Bellair, an ever-so-trendy, glitzy dancing spot, with a DJ spinning the top 40. The dress code is "upscale casual to evening attire." It's a moneyed crowd, ages 25–55 and *très* sophisticated; if you wear gray, you might vanish into the ultramodern surroundings. Some live bands perform here, too. *100 Cumberland St., tel. 416/964–2222. No cover.*

Bemelmans is all chandeliers, mirrors, marble, wood, and great beauty. The patio is lovely, but the real action is the crowded bar, where performers and artists pour in after their shows. (It doesn't hurt to have a 3 AM closing time, a rarity in this once staunchly WASP city.) And just a few hundred feet away from the heart of the city, Bloor and Yonge streets. *83 Bloor St. W, tel. 416/960–0306.*

In the unfashionable Bathurst Street/Spadina Avenue area is the ever-popular **Brunswick House,** where "Rocking Irene" has been singing for centuries. Doctors and lawyers keep coming back to visit their old favorite watering hole, to hear the same songstress of their university days. (It's near the University of Toronto.) Irene's repertoire is of the "Roll Out the Barrel" variety, and everyone sings and drinks along. It's loud, raucous, and fun. *481 Bloor St. W, tel. 416/964–2242. No cover.*

The **Hard Rock Cafe,** and its very classy, wildly popular younger sibling, **Hard Rock SkyDome** (guess where!), both feature rock bands. Rock-and-roll memorabilia decorate the walls. These are busy hangouts where young people go to see and be seen. Most are in their early twenties; those who are in their thirties obviously want to hang out with 20-year-olds. *Hard Rock Cafe: 283 Yonge St., across from the Eaton Centre, north of Queen, tel. 416/362–3636. Hard Rock SkyDome: Gate 1, 277 Front St. W, tel. 416/341–2388.*

One of the most crowded singles' bars in Toronto is **Hemingway's,** also conveniently located in the Yorkville area. Three-quarters are regulars, middle- to upper-class professionals, and not as pretentious as the bar's name. The atmosphere is sort of homey here, and it's less tense than at other Yorkville hangouts. The stand-up bar has a nice and easy atmosphere, and the decor is not glitzy, but literary, with a green interior, comfortable high-back chairs, mirrors, artsy posters, and real, live books lining one wall. As of 1991, this has also become a home to pop, MOR (middle-of-the-road), and blues, with nightly entertainment. Sunday evenings, R&B predominates. And there are even Australian and New Zealand theme nights! Dress is casual—just as Ernest would have wanted. *142 Cumberland St., near Avenue Rd. and Bloor St., tel. 416/968–2828. No cover.*

Kremlin is one of the city's major gay bars–cum–dance clubs, just on the edge of one of the largest gay communities in North America. There are gay and lesbian nights, but on many other nights, there's disco for all, and straights are welcome, free to visit, drink, and dance. *504 Jarvis St., tel. 416/462–7540.*

Remy's seems to top the list of places for successful people to go in the early 1990s: Being right next door to the elegant Four Seasons Hotel means that Jane Fonda and nearly everyone else filming in Toronto seems to end up here. It's very elegant, so if you see casually attired men at the bar, you can be sure they can afford to look scruffy. The decor is European-inspired, all brass and shiny. There's an outdoor patio, three bars, and a restaurant where two can eat from the Italian menu for $50, including wine. *115 Yorkville Ave., near Avenue Rd., tel. 416/968–9429.*

Comedy Clubs

Second City, just east of the heart of downtown, has been providing some of the best comedy in Toronto—and North America—since its owner Andrew Alexander bought the rights to the name from its Chicago godfather, Bernie Sahlins, for one dollar. Interestingly, Alexander recently bought the original company and has since opened other clubs in London, Ontario, and Los Angeles—Canadian imperialism in action. This converted fire hall has given much to the world, through both *Saturday Night Live* and the inspired *SCTV* series. Among those who have cut their teeth on the Toronto stage are Dan Aykroyd, Martin Short, Andrea Martin, Catherine O'Hara, and the late John Candy and Gilda Radner. Shows can be seen alone or as part of a dinner-theater package. Try to catch the free improvisations, Monday–Thursday at 10:30 PM, when the troupe works out new material for future shows. *110 Lombard St., corner of Jarvis St., just a few blocks northeast of Front and Yonge Sts., tel. 416/863–1111.*

Yuk-Yuk's Komedy Kabaret has always been the major place for comedy in Toronto. This is where the zany comedian Howie Mandel and the inspired impressionist Jim Carrey got their start, and where such comic luminaries as George Carlin, Rodney Dangerfield, Robin Williams, and Mort Sahl have presented their best routines. The original downtown locale on Bay Street has closed, but the other venues continue to thrive. At Yonge Street and Eglinton Avenue, new talent pipes up on Tuesdays. A dinner-show package can run $25 and up per person. *2335 Yonge St., just above Eglinton Ave.; and 5165 Dixie, just above Eglinton; tel. 416/967–6425. No dress code. Cover charge: $5–$10, occasionally more for a huge name act.*

Dancing

Berlin quickly became one of the most popular spots in Toronto, within a year of its opening in early 1987. There's no dress code, but people dress up for this upscale, European-styled multilevel club. There is a Continental menu for dining and a seven-piece band for jazz, pop, Latin, salsa, and R&B. The crowd is 25–35 years old, and very rich, and the club radiates a feeling of exclusivity. A classy cross between the BamBoo and the Imperial Room, Berlin is one very hot/cool place. *2335 Yonge St., north of Eglinton Ave., tel. 416/489–7777. Open Tues.–Sat., to 2 or 3 AM on weekends. Cover: $8–$15.*

DJs play '60s music (downstairs) and '90s music (upstairs) in a four-story century-old fun house named **Big Bop.** Drinks Wednesday nights cost $2.50; Thursday nights are Ladies' Nights, with no cover for women. The decor is early bizarre and late weird; you walk in and feel as though you've already had two drinks. In rebellion against the New York School of Glitzy, there is no chrome or mirrors—just a deliberate effort to be campy, vibrant, and unpretentious. The clientele is 18–25 years old. It's a true meat market, but it doesn't pretend to be otherwise. Capacity is 800, and jeans are de rigueur. Many international stars walk in, but the owner insists that it's no big deal. (No big deal? Jack Nicholson. William Hurt. Matt Dillon.) One DJ is a grad of the Wolfman Jack School of Strangeness. You can see why the kids love it here. You'll encounter alternative rock, dance music, and disco, depending on which floor you're on, and which night it is. *651 Queen St. W, tel. 416/366–6699. Open weekends to 3 AM.*

It's out in the northeast, in the town of Markham, but the **Cotton Club** has become one of the dancing hot spots of Toronto. Here one encounters alternative and underground dance music, with DJs keeping the crowds up and moving every night of the week except Monday. "Coffee House Sunday" has live jams; cover charge on weekends is in the modest $5 range. *7750 Markham Rd., tel. 416/471–4314.*

Right on the edge of the University of Toronto campus is the double-trouble combination of **The Dance Cave,** with wild, live rock groups and dancing (open till 3 AM Fri. and Sat.), and the equally popular **Lee's Palace** downstairs, where rock-and-roll and blues are delivered by local talent. There, jams last from 8 PM on, with varying (low) cover. And dig that crazy, wild decor! *529 Bloor St. W, tel. 416/532–7632; 532–7983.*

Earl's Tin Palace has been described as the star attraction of the Yonge/Eglinton/Mt. Pleasant singles scene, and it does its job well: The fashionable, affluent people have made this place their home, and many arrive in groups. The decor is stunning: a big, airy tin palace with elaborate props, such as stuffed birds. The restaurant has real cuisine, not just fries. (Dinner and drinks for two, $60.) The clientele dresses very well, with men even in (gasp) suits. The 35–40 crowd is better represented here than in most other clubs. *150 Eglinton Ave. E, not far from Yonge St., tel. 416/487–9281. No cover.*

Hard Rock Cafe and **Hard Rock SkyDome** (*see* Bars, *above*).

Klub Max is just steps from the monstrous SkyDome, as you can tell by its address on Blue Jays Way. It's an enormous dance club, with three floors of dance parties going on. There are alternative and industrial nights (the latter, means techno-pop, heavy-something sounds). If Batman had turned his cave into a dance club, it might resemble this club—one giant, eerie maze. *106 Blue Jays Way, tel. 416/597–1567.*

Back on Yorkville Avenue is **P.W.D. Dinkel's,** which has been attracting the trendies of the area for many years. The age range is 20–40, and regulars make up much of the crowd. The ratio of men to women is 50/50; the two stand-up bars are where the action is. A black-and-white–tile dance floor has the usual mirrored ball and flashing disco lights nearby. Live bands play Top-40–style, yet original, music. There's finger food and dinner at about $50 for two, with wine. *88 Yorkville Ave., tel. 416/923–9689. Open Mon.–Sun. to 2 AM. Cover charge: about $10 on weekends.*

Pete & Martys is an up-tempo rock-and-roll alternative, a DJ-and-dancing spot, often with pool tables and dining. Of the 13 members of this chain, five are in the Toronto area. All offer dancing on weekends—except the Eaton Centre location. *York Corporate Centre, 125 York Blvd., Richmond Hill, tel. 416/881–0151; 160 Eglinton*

Ave. E, tel. 416/482-4084; 777 Bay St. at College Park, tel. 416/596-6955; Eaton Centre, tel. 416/593-4660; 14 Duncan St., near King St. and Spadina Ave., tel. 416/971-9708.

RPM, down at Harbourfront, is a psychedelic dance palace with light shows, go-go girls, and more. (Time warp, anyone?) There's a new streetcar service from Union Station for the young (19–25), blue-collarish, meat-market crowd. Lots of funk and pop tunes to dance to, and it's very *loud.* On Sunday, there's no alcohol, and it becomes an all-ages dance party. Wednesday is Student Night, with free admission and a complimentary buffet. Thursdays are now retro-disco nights. Upstairs, there's a nice quiet bar with lovely views of Lake Ontario. *132 Queen's Quay E, tel. 416/869-1462. Cover charge.*

A bar/club called **StiLife** recently opened downtown and is very popular. It caters to an older (25–35) crowd and to rapidly aging 40-year-olds. The decor is metallic and modular, with all the furnishings custom-made. The art is aided by sophisticated lighting. No jeans or sneakers. A DJ provides dancing music, and the clientele is Yorkville-ish, with many clothing designers, people who own other restaurants, etc. Check out the bathrooms—you'll find out why. *217 Richmond St. W, tel. 416/593-6116. Closed Sun. Cover charge: $10–$20.*

The most exciting 1950s-type place is **Studebaker's,** in the University Avenue/King Street area. It's bright and colorful, with memorabilia, a jukebox, and a DJ. During the week, it attracts a business crowd, with far more males than females. On weekends, a younger, suburban crowd gathers after 8 or 9; expect a 30-minute wait. No T-shirts. Celebs spotted here include actor Steve Guttenberg, Darryl Hall (the rock star), and G. W. Bailey (of "M*A*S*H"). *150 Pearl St., tel. 416/591-7960.*

Rockit has been described as "the mainstream dance crowd's terrestrial equivalent to rock 'n roll heaven." The pizza is dynamite, the wood-and-brass bar is gorgeous, and upstairs are the college kids in uniform (cool ties and designer jeans), dancing away to the Big Hits. Dancing to DJs on Thursday, Friday, and Saturday nights; Monday nights feature live jazz. *120 Church St., just east of Yonge, tel. 416/947-9555.*

Whiskey Saigon, no relation to the mega-buck musical, *Miss Saigon,* is one of the most popular new clubs of the '90s. It has three gigantic floors, with DJs, laser shows, and everything from rock to funk. This is a great (and very attractive) alternative for the hip crowd. *250 Richmond St. W, near University, tel. 416/593-4646.*

Lounges

Up on the 51st floor of the ManuLife Centre, **The Aquarius Lounge** is the highest piano lounge in the city, even before you take your first, expensive drink. The busy time in the summer is Thursday–Saturday after 8:30 PM, but there's a high turnover, so the wait is never too long. In the winter, the lines begin as early as 8 PM. This is not a place to meet people, and it is not trendy in the way that most bars in the Yorkville area are. But its romantic atmosphere makes this a marvelous place for a date. No shorts, but jeans are allowed. *55 Bloor St. W, at Bay St., tel. 416/967-5225.*

In the classy Four Seasons Hotel is **La Serre,** which looks like a library in a mansion: plush and green, with lots of brass and dark wood. It has a stand-up piano bar and a pianist worth standing for.

Drinks, coffees, and teas are all expensive, but what can you expect in one of the costliest hotels in the country? Weekdays attract a business crowd, weekends bring out the couples. *Avenue Rd. and Yorkville Ave., tel. 416/964–0411.*

For countless years, the Brownstone Hotel had a wonderful little bar in it called Notes, where one could be guaranteed some lovely, often moving piano solos. Recently, the hotel changed to **Comfort Hotel,** and Notes turned into **Louis Janetta's Place,** but the live piano, thank heavens, remains. The pink-and-beige tones have given way to greenish ones, but the lighting remains dim, so it's still a good, quiet place to get to know someone. Dinner is reasonable, with pasta less than $10 a person, and chicken not that much more. You can always find a fine pianist to get you in the mood, every Monday through Saturday evening. *15 Charles St. E, near Bloor and Yonge, tel. 416/921–0003.*

The **Park Plaza Roof Lounge** has been used as a setting in the writings of such Canadian literary luminaries as Margaret Atwood and Mordecai Richler. The decor used to be plush, in an older European style, with chandelier, marble tables, and waiters in red jackets. It remains an important hangout for the upper-middle class, businesspeople, professionals, and, *bien sûr,* literary types. Since 1990, it has been redone, but it's still gorgeous and tasteful. *In Park Plaza Hotel, Avenue Rd. and Bloor St., tel. 416/924–5471.*

You can't get much handier to downtown Toronto than **The Silver Rail,** standing proudly opposite the Eaton Centre. Let's face it: they no longer put up taverns with 18-foot ceilings and giant mirrors. Welcome to 1947—when this place was built. *225 Yonge St., tel. 416/368–8697.*

At the corner of King and Bathurst streets sits the nearly 150-year-old **Wheat Sheaf Tavern.** You can't get more run-down than this, in spite of its recent face-lift. But if you're in a run-down, century-old mood, it's good, solid fun. *667 King St. W, tel. 416/364–3996.*

Pubs

The best pub in town is **The Madison,** right next door to Ecology House, on the edge of the U of T campus. It has the atmosphere of an English pub, with lots of brass, burlap lampshades, solid oak bars, ceiling fans, exposed brick, and dart boards. Most important, it offers 16 brands of beer on tap, as well as a large selection of imported draft. It serves finger food, and its chicken wings, prepared literally from scratch, are famous. There is nightly piano entertainment at the second-floor bar; the bar in the basement has a fireplace and is dark and cozy. The clientele consists of students, yuppies, and a strong British/Scottish/Irish contingent. The patios are lovely in the summer. *14 Madison Ave., 1 block east of Spadina Ave., just steps north of Bloor St., tel. 416/927–1722.*

On the edge of Cabbagetown, less than a mile east of the downtown core, is the **Queen's Head Pub.** Very quaint and typically English, it has a good lineup of imported beer and may remind you of the attic on an antique farm: fireplace, oodles of oak, and mahogany. Flowers on the wallpaper, pâté sandwiches on the plate, chandeliers on the ceiling, beer in the belly. And tiny Union Jacks all over the dart boards. It's attached to a pleasant restaurant—Pimblett's. *263 Gerrard St. E, west of Parliament St., tel. 416/929–9525.*

The Unicorn, in the very hot area of Yonge/Eglinton/Mt. Pleasant, has a friendly, young (20–25) crowd. The atmosphere is very British, with a 6-foot TV screen. It has a nice, homey atmosphere that is missing from too many singles bars. Indeed, that often-unpleasant pressure just doesn't exist here; you can talk to other people without feeling as though you're about to be picked up. On one side, there's a seating area for quiet conversation; on the other, a wine bar and dart board. Both snack food and complete dinners are served. Live guitar or piano Wednesday–Monday nights. *175 Eglinton Ave. E, a few blocks east of Yonge St., tel. 416/482–0115.*

8 Excursions

Stratford, Ontario

Ever since July 1953, when one of the world's greatest actors, Alec Guinness, joined with probably the world's greatest Shakespearean director, Tyrone Guthrie, beneath a hot, stuffy tent in a backward little town about 90 minutes from Toronto, the Stratford Festival has been one of the most successful, most widely admired theaters of its kind in the world.

The origins of the town of Stratford are modest. After the War of 1812, the British government granted a million acres of land along Lake Huron to the Canada Company, headed by a Scottish business-man. When the surveyors came to a marshy creek surrounded by a thick forest, they named it "Little Thames" and noted that it might make "a good mill-site." It was later christened Stratford, which purportedly means a narrow crossing. The year was 1832, 121 years before the concept of a theater festival would take flight and change Canadian culture forever.

For many years Stratford was considered a backwoods hamlet. Although it had the highest elevation of any town in Ontario—1,150 feet above sea level—it was too swampy to grow anything. In 1871, "Muddy Stratford" was made a division point for a major railway, attracting both industry and population. Though the river was renamed Avon, it was a stump-filled, filthy disaster, bordered by a livery stable, a junkyard, and the city dump.

Then came the first of two saviors of the city, both of them (undoubting) Thomases. In 1904, an insurance broker named Tom Orr transformed Stratford's riverfront into a park. He also built a formal English garden, where every flower mentioned in the plays of Shakespeare—monkshood to sneeze worse, bee balm to bachelor's button—blooms grandly to this day. When Tyrone Guthrie compared an aerial photograph of Stratford's park with a photo of the park in Stratford-upon-Avon, England, he was stunned to find the two nearly identical.

Then came Tom Patterson, a fourth-generation Stratfordian born in 1920, who looked around; saw that the town wards and schools had names like Hamlet, Falstaff, and Romeo; and felt that some kind of drama festival might save his community from becoming a ghost town. (The diesel was coming in, and all the steam-engine repair shops that had kept Stratford alive for generations were soon to close down.)

The story of how he began in 1952 with $125 (a "generous" grant from the Stratford City Council), tracked down the directorial genius Tyrone Guthrie and the inspired stage and screen star Alec Guinness, obtained the services of the brilliant stage designer Tanya Moiseiwitsch, and somehow pasted together a world-class theater festival in a little over one year is almost unbelievable. It is told in its entirety in Patterson's memoirs, *First Stage—The Making of the Stratford Festival*.

The festival is now moving into middle age and it has had its ups and downs. Soon after it opened and wowed critics from around the world with its professionalism, costumes, and daring thrust stage, the air was filled with superlatives that had not been heard in Canada since the Great Blondin walked across Niagara Falls on a tightrope.

The early years also brought giants of world theater to the tiny town of some 20,000: James Mason, Siobhan McKenna, Alan Bates, Christopher Plummer, Jason Robards, Jr., and Maggie Smith. But the years also saw an unevenness in productions, a dreadful tendency to go for flash and glitter over substance, and a focus on costumes and furniture rather than on the ability to speak Shakespeare's words with clarity and intelligence. Many never lost faith in the festival; others, such as Canada's greatest critic, the late Nathan Cohen of the *Toronto Star*, once bemoaned that "Stratford has become Canada's most sacred cow."

Sacred or not, Stratford's offerings are still among the best of their kind in the world, with at least a handful of productions every year that put most other summer arts festivals to shame. The secret, of course, is to try to catch the reviews of the plays, which have their debuts in May, June, July, and August in the festival's three theaters, and then book as early as you can. *(The New York Times* always runs major write-ups, as do newspapers and magazines in many American and Canadian cities.)

In recent years, the famous thrust stage at the Festival Theatre witnessed *Hamlet, Cyrano de Bergerac, Long Day's Journey into Night, Guys and Dolls,* and *Carousel.* Be warned that due to the great fidelity of the stage to its Shakespearean original, it is imperative to have seats that are fairly central in the audience; otherwise, words and even whole speeches can be lost.

There is also a traditional proscenium stage, the **Avon,** where *All's Well That Ends Well, Our Town, Twelfth Night,* and the musical *Irma La Douce* have recently been presented. Connoisseurs of more daring theater—as well as the budget-conscious—should not miss **The Tom Patterson Theatre** (formerly **The Third Stage),** a more recent space that presents plays in the round and in experimental modes. In the last few years, *Twelfth Night* and *King Lear* were seen here. This is often the most exciting place to see plays, so don't panic if you can't get seats at the two larger theaters.

Arriving and Departing

By Car "Who's going to drive from Toronto to Stratford to see Shakespeare?" was almost a mantra in the early 1950s, when the festival was struggling to get off the ground; you don't hear it much anymore. The town is only about 90 miles southwest of Toronto, and it takes but 1½ hours to drive there. Take Highway 401 west to interchange 35, then 90 north on Highway 8 and west again on the combined Highways 7/8.

By Train This is probably the most pleasurable way to go, especially in the fall, when the leaves are doing their quick-change act. **Via Rail** (tel. 416/366–8411 or 800/561–3949) leaves Union Station at least two times a day during Stratford's high season. The trip takes about two hours. **Amtrak** (tel. 800/872–7245) service from Chicago to Toronto stops in Stratford.

By Bus Two buses leave the Dundas and Bay streets terminal each day, beginning as early as 9:30 AM. The trip can take up to three hours, though, and stops at places you never knew existed. Tel. 416/393–7911.

Guided Tours

Stratford Tours Inc. arranges a variety of tours, including dining and theater. *Box 45, Stratford, N5A 6S8, tel. 519/271–8181.*

The Avon Historical Society conducts charming one-hour tours of the city, July 1–Labor Day, daily except Sunday at 9:30 AM. Meet at the tourist information booth at Lakeside Drive and Ontario Street. *Tel. 519/271–5140.*

Exploring

The Gallery Stratford has regular exhibits of local and Inuit art, as well as design sketches and costumes of the present year's productions. *54 Romeo St., just northeast of Festival Theatre, tel. 519/271–5271. Admission: $3.50 adults, $2.50 senior citizens and students during festival's run, free at other times. Open June–Labor Day, Tues.–Sun. 9 AM–6 PM; Labor Day–Oct., Tues.–Sun. 10 AM–5 PM; Nov.–May, Tues.–Fri. and Sun. 1–5, Sat. 10–5.*

There are many tasteful shops in the downtown area, including antiques stores, arts and crafts studios, galleries, and new and rare bookshops.

The Stratford Festival For tickets and information, phone from Toronto, tel. 416/363–4471; from Detroit, 313/964–4668; from elsewhere 519/273–1600. Or write the Festival Theatre, Stratford, N5A 6V2.

The **Festival Theatre** (55 Queen St.) and the **Avon Theatre** (99 Downie St.) are open from early May to early November. They have evening performances Tuesday–Saturday, with matinees Wednesday, Saturday, and Sunday. Tickets are $30–$50; musicals cost 10%–15% more. Rush seats are as little as one half the cost. The **Tom Patterson Theatre** (Lakeshore Drive) has a shorter season, from late May to early September. Prices here are only a few dollars less.

Don't forget that **rush seats** are always available on the day of a performance, either at the **Five Star Tickets booth** in Toronto or at the various box offices, beginning at 9 AM. Tickets can also be ordered by telephone after 10 AM, but they are usually in the lowest price category.

Since the early 1990s, other money-saving options have been available. "Family Experience" allows a discount for young people who are accompanied by an adult. So, if one regularly priced adult ticket is purchased in any seating category, you are entitled to buy up to two young people's tickets at less than $20 for each guest 18 years of age or younger. Ask for this discount when you purchase your seat. (This is not applicable for any Saturday performances, whether matinee or evening.)

There are also "2 for 1" Tuesdays and Thursdays at the Avon Theatre; Seniors' Preview Bonus seats for about $20—a savings of over 50% on regular prices—and student tickets for about $20 each, available throughout the 1995 season, with a student I.D. card.

Wheelchair seating and a mobility bus are available if requested in advance (tel. 519/271–4000). A Phonic Ear F.M. Transmitting System for the hearing impaired is available at the two larger theaters at a nominal fee; book when ordering your tickets.

Meet the Festival is a series of informal discussions with members of the company. *Kiwanis Centre, next to Tom Patterson Theatre. Admission free; no reservations required. July–Aug., Wed. and Fri. 9:30 AM–10:30 AM.*

Thirty-minute **post-performance discussions** take place at the Festival Theatre Tuesday and Thursday nights, late June to early September. *Meet at Aisle 2, Orchestra Level, after the performance. Admission free; no reservations required.*

Backstage tours are offered Sunday morning from mid-June to mid-November. Tours depart from the Festival Theatre every 15 minutes from 9 to 10:30 AM. Admission: $5 adults, $3 students and senior citizens. Book in advance through the Festival Box Office, although some tickets are usually available at the door.

Dining

Reviews by
Sara Waxman

The Stratford Festival. To go or not to go? That is the question. We came, we saw, we enjoyed. That is the answer. But there's more to Stratford than its theatrical performances. The creation of the Stratford Chef's School a decade ago, with 100% employment for its yearly graduating class, has made an enormous difference in the quality of restaurant dining in the area. Though there is a something-for-everyone range of eateries in this small town, they all have one act in common: They'll get you to the show on time.

"All the world's a stage," said William Shakespeare. And during the festival, from early May to mid-November, even the restaurants get into the act with culinary tableaux.

Highly recommended restaurants are indicated by a star ★.

Category	Cost*
$$$$	over $40
$$$	$30–$40
$$	$20–$30
$	under $20

per person for a three-course meal, excluding drinks, service, and sales tax

$$$$
★
The Church Restaurant. Constructed in 1873 as a Congregational church, this building—once dark and a little intimidating—has been lightened and brightened. White cloths gleam in the afternoon light that pours through the stained-glass windows, and greenery thrives. If your plan is to run in for a quick bite, you're in the wrong pew. Fixed price or à la carte, the meals here are production numbers, and the menu alone takes time going through. Tea-smoked salmon comes with sea scallops and shrimp; warm salad of spiced veal sweetbreads is lively with a cherry-tomato compote. The roast Ontario lamb with garlic custard and eggplant flan is outstanding. *70 Brunswick St., tel. 519/273–3424. Reservations accepted. Dress: casual but neat. AE, DC, MC, V. June–Nov.: lunch Wed. and Sat., brunch Sun., dinner daily, closed Mon.; closed Dec.–May.*

$$$$
★
The Old Prune. The setting is a converted Victorian house with a number of charming dining rooms all furnished with period pieces, and a glass-enclosed conservatory surrounded by a tidy sunken garden. The kitchen coaxes fresh local ingredients into innovative dishes: smoked rainbow trout with apple radish and curry oil; coiled vegetable lasagna with roasted tomato sauce; or with a nod to the East, chicken seasoned with coriander and cumin. Desserts are baked fresh for each meal and come straight from the oven. *151 Albert St., tel. 519/271–5052. Reservations advised. Dress: casual but neat. AE, MC, V. Closed Nov.–Apr., Mon., Tues. lunch.*

$$$$
Rundles Restaurant. The look here is upmarket cafeteria, with modern, hard-edge decor and furnishings, such as arborite tables, paper napkins, and artistic sheet metal birds that hang from the ceiling. The food and service, however, is somewhat pretentious and self-conscious, emphasizing haute French nouvelle cuisine. Expect a tiny gastronomic dinner at astronomic prices. An appetizer, for ex-

ample, is a few pretty slices of rabbit sausage with a splash of beetroot oil and a tiny salad of organic greens with a sliced, cured breast of duck. A smallish piece of Atlantic salmon is crusted with sliced potatoes, while lobster and sea-scallop ragout trembles with freshness in a sweet pepper and basil sauce. The summer berry desserts are delicious. *9 Cobourg St., tel. 519/271–6442. Reservations advised. Dress: casual but neat. AE, DC, MC, V. Closed Nov.–Apr.; Mon., Tues., Thurs., Fri. lunch.*

$$ **The Belfry at the Church Restaurant.** The upstairs level of the
★ Church Restaurant uses the same excellent kitchen, but you'll find a more casual ambience here and some lighter dishes. Typical dishes may include crab cakes with a zippy tequila and orange salsa; appetizer-size pasta with olive oil herbs and garlic; and medallions of Perth country pork, partnered with black linguini that is sauced with caper–flecked goat cheese cream. Forget your vows of prudence and go for the raspberry crème brûlée with orange. *70 Brunswick St., tel. 519/273–3424. Reservations accepted. Dress: casual. AE, DC, MC, V. Closed Sun. lunch and Mon. May.–Oct.; Sun. and Mon. Nov.–Dec.*

$$ **Movable Feast.** You can enjoy a special picnic prepared by the chefs of
★ the green room (where the actors eat) at the Festival Theatre. Dine on the banks of the Avon or the Festival Theatre terraces. The Molière picnic consists of marinated goat cheese, salad niçoise, and pudding, while the Cyrano includes fresh asparagus vinaigrette, grilled chicken breast with Thai rice-noodle salad, and lemon cheesecake. You can order your picnics in advance up to 8 PM the day before a performance from May 31 to October 2. *Festival Theatre, 55 Queen St., tel. 800/567–1600. Reservations required. Dress: casual. AE, MC, V.*

$ **Anna Banana's Cheesecakes and Cones.** The beautiful garden patio is a fine place to indulge in frozen yogurt, ice cream, cheesecakes, muffins, and a gourmet barbecue with four different kinds of natural 100% all-beef hot dogs. Nothing costs over $5. *39 George St., tel. 519/272–0065. No reservations accepted. Dress: casual. No credit cards. Closed mid-Oct.–Mar.*

$ **Bentley's Inn.** At this long and narrow British-style pub that is part
★ of an inn, the well-stocked bar divides the room into two equal halves. It seems there's an unspoken tradition here: The actors have claimed one side, and the locals the other. Darts are played here, seriously, and getting a bull's-eye is the norm. The menu consists of pub fare such as good fish and chips, grilled steak and fries, and steak and mushroom pie. The ultimate club sandwich on homemade multigrain bread hits the spot for lunch or dinner, while the sturdy dessert of fruit crumble and ice cream is big enough for two. The regulars say they come for the imported, domestic, and microdraft beers—the easygoing ambience and camaraderie are added bonuses. *99 Ontario St., tel. 519/271–1121. Reservations advised. Dress: casual. AE, MC, V.*

Lodging

Because Stratford is not a hotel city, visitors with the most savvy like to stay at bed-and-breakfasts. Write to **Tourism/Stratford** (City of Stratford, Box 818, 88 Wellington St., Stratford N5A 6W1, tel. 519/271–5140, fax 519/274–5041) for the superb *Visitors' Guide: Festive Stratford*, which should be out in early February. Highly recommended hotels are indicated with a star ★.

Category	Cost*
$$$$	over $100
$$$	$75–$100
$$	$50–$75
$	under $50

All prices are for a standard double room, excluding GST (Goods and Services Tax).

$$$ **Festival Inn.** An old-English atmosphere has survived modernization and the installation of Jacuzzi water beds in some rooms here; located on the eastern outskirts of town, it's just a brief ride to the theater. *1144 Ontario St., Box 811, Stratford N5A 6W1, tel. 519/273–1150. 151 rooms with bath. Facilities: restaurant, coffee shop, baby-sitting services, tennis, indoor pool, whirlpool, golf nearby. AE, MC, V.*

$$$ **Queen's Inn.** Built in 1914 to replace an earlier inn that was destroyed by fire, this 30-room inn has been gutted and turned into an elegant, if still quite small, hotel. The walls are a pleasant two-tone gray and white; the large, curved windows and bright, floral chintz sofas will charm any visitor. The dining room can be quite inventive, and next door stands a "brewpub," where homemade beer is sold only on the premises. *161 Ontario St., Stratford N5A 3H3, tel. 519/271–1400. 30 rooms with bath. Facility: lounge. AE, MC, V.*

$$$ **Stone Maiden Inn.** This is a beautiful and exotic place near the city
★ center, furnished with antiques and Anglo-Indian arts from the British Raj period. Rooms vary from deluxe with whirlpool to smaller, less expensive rooms. Rates include full English breakfast. *123 Church St., Stratford N5A 2R3, tel. 519/271–7129. 14 rooms with bath. Facilities: guest lounge, outdoor area. No credit cards.*

$$–$$$ **23 Albert Place.** This late-19th-century hotel was completely redecorated several years ago. It is conveniently located in the heart of the downtown shopping area, just a few hundred yards from the Avon Theatre. Suites and minisuites are available, and pets are allowed. *23 Albert St., Stratford N5A 3K2, tel. 519/273–5800. 34 rooms with bath. Facilities: coffee shop, restaurant, baby-sitting services, golf nearby. AE, MC, V.*

$$ **Majer's Motel.** A good distance from the highway, this motel sits on landscaped grounds. No pets. *Hwys. 7 and 8, about a mile east of the city, Stratford RR4, N5A 6S5, tel. 519/271–2010. 31 rooms (some small) with bath. Facilities: coffee shop, outdoor pool, golf nearby. MC, V.*

$$ **Swan Motel.** This motel is in a quiet country setting on generous grounds, just 2 miles south of the Avon Theatre. *959 Downie St. S, RR2, Stratford N5A 6S3, tel. 519/271–6376. 24 rooms with bath. Facilities: outdoor pool, golf nearby. MC, V.*

$ **Stratford General Hospital Residence.** Students, or those traveling on a very tight budget, pay less than $25 a night for a single room. It's modern, bright, serviceable. *Housekeeping Supervisor, Stratford General Hospital Residence, 130 Youngs St., Stratford N5A 1J7, tel. 519/271–5084 or 271–2120, ext. 586. Facilities: access to lounges, kitchenettes, laundry facilities, and parking. No credit cards.*

Niagara Falls, Ontario

Cynics have had their field day with Niagara Falls, calling it everything from "water on the rocks" to "the second major disappointment of American married life" (Oscar Wilde).

Others have been more positive. Missionary and explorer Louis Hennepin, whose books were widely read across Europe, first described the falls in 1678 as "an incredible Cataract or Waterfall which has no equal." Nearly two centuries later, novelist Charles Dickens wrote, "I seemed to be lifted from the earth and to be looking into Heaven. Niagara was at once stamped upon my heart, an image of beauty, to remain there changeless and indelible."

Writer Henry James recorded in 1883 how one stands there "gazing your fill at the most beautiful object in the world." And a half-century later, British author Vita Sackville-West wrote to Sir Harold Nicolson, "Niagara is really some waterfall! It falls over like a great noisy beard made of cotton-wool, veiled by spray and spanned by rainbows. The rainbows are the most unexpected part of it. They stand across like bridges between America and Canada, and are reproduced in sections along the boiling foam. The spray rises to the height of a skyscraper, shot by sudden iridescence high up in the air."

Understandably, all these rave reviews began to bring out the professional daredevils, as well as the self-destructive amateurs. In 1859, the great French tightrope walker Blondin walked across the Niagara Gorge, from the American to the Canadian side, on a 3-inch-thick rope. On his shoulders was his (reluctant, terrified) manager; on both shores stood some 100,000 spectators. "Thank God it is over!" exclaimed the future King Edward VII of England, after the completion of the walk. "Please never attempt it again."

But sadly, others did. From the early 18th century, dozens went over in boats, rubber balls, and those famous barrels. Not a single one survived, until schoolteacher Annie Taylor did in 1901. Emerging from her barrel, she asked the touching question, "Did I go over the Falls yet?" The endless stunts were finally outlawed in 1912, but not before the province of Ontario created the first provincial park in all of Canada—Queen Victoria Park—in 1887.

The Falls alone—with a combined flow of close to 800,000 gallons per second—are obviously worth the 75-minute drive from Toronto, the 30-minute drive from Buffalo, New York, or whatever time it takes to come from anywhere else. It is, after all, the greatest waterfall in the world, by volume.

Over 10,000 years ago—long before the first "My Parents Visited Niagara Falls and All They Got Me Was This Lousy T-Shirt" T-shirts—the glaciers receded, diverting the waters of Lake Erie northward into Lake Ontario. (Before that time, they had drained south; such are the fickle ways of nature.)

There has been considerable erosion since that time: More than 7 miles in all, as the soft shale and sandstone of the escarpment have been washed away. Wisely, there have been major water diversions for a generating station (in 1954) and other machinations (1954–1963), which have spread the flow more evenly over the entire crestline of the Horseshoe Falls. The erosion is now down to as little as one foot every decade, so you needn't rush your visit.

There's some interesting history to the rest of the area, as well. The War of 1812 had settlers on both sides of the river killing one another, with the greatest battle taking place in Niagara Falls itself, at Lundy's Lane (today, the name of a major street, with a Historical Museum on the site of the battle). Soon after, at the Treaty of Ghent, two modest cities of the same name arose on each side of the river—one in the United States, the other in Canada.

Only some 70,000 people actually live in Niagara Falls, Ontario, and when one considers that close to 15 million visitors come and see the Falls every year, you can get an idea of just how central tourism is to the area. Central? Try its very raison d'être.

It's true: Niagara Falls has something for everyone. For the children, there's Marineland, water slides, wax museums, haunted houses, and more. For newlyweds, there's a Honeymoon Certificate, and free admission for the bride to everything from the giant Imax Theatre to the Elvis Presley Museum.

Sure, many of the motels and attractions are corny, even tacky, but that's really part of the charm. Three towers present their awesome views of the Falls—the **Skylon,** the **Minolta,** and the **Kodak.** The Minolta Tower has a hands-on display of high-tech camera equipment, an aquarium, and a Reptile World display. The Kodak Tower is located in **Maple Leaf Village,** which has over 80 shops, the Elvis Presley Museum, and the world's second largest ferris wheel. **Clifton Hill,** known for its rather wide selection of museums (Tussaud's Wax Museum, the Houdini Hall of Fame, Ripley's Believe It or Not, the Criminal Hall of Fame, and the Haunted House), that you somehow managed to survive without experiencing until now, had over $1.5 million worth of improvements during 1987, including a widening of sidewalks and planting of trees. A "People Mover" system has recently been introduced, so visitors can leave their cars a good distance away and ride the system all day for a single, nominal fee.

And don't allow a winter visit to the area to put you off. **The Festival of Lights** runs from late December into mid-February. The festival is a real stunner. There are 70 trees illuminated with 34,000 lights in the parklands near the Rainbow Bridge every night from 5:30 to 10:30, plus animated tableaux of various Canadian scenes, and even a Father Frost who welcomes visitors to the Magic of Winter theme park on Buchanan Avenue in Murray Hill. *Tel. 905/374–1616; in U.S., tel. 800/461–5373. Falls illuminated nightly Nov.–Feb. 7–9:30; Mar. 7–10; Apr. 8:30–11; May–Aug. approximately 9–midnight; Sept.–Oct. approximately 8–11.*

Important Addresses and Numbers

Tourist Information
Contact the **Niagara Falls, Canada Visitor and Convention Bureau** (4673 Ontario Ave., Niagara Falls L2E 3R1, tel. 905/356–6061).

There is also an **Information Center** at the corner of Highway 420 and Stanley Avenue. You'll see the big TRAVEL ONTARIO sign shortly after you leave Queen Elizabeth Way, heading east into Niagara Falls.

Arriving and Departing

By Plane
The closest airport to Niagara Falls is **Buffalo International Airport. Niagara Scenic Bus Lines** (tel. 716/648–1500) operates a shuttle service from the airport to both the American and Canadian Niagara Falls. Fares are about $10 one-way.

By Car Niagara Falls is about 80 miles southwest of Toronto, less than a 90-minute drive. Take the Gardiner Expressway west from downtown, which quickly turns into Queen Elizabeth Way (QEW), heading south around Lake Ontario. Exit at Highway 420, which runs straight into the downtown area.

By Train **Via Rail** (tel. 416/366-8411; in Niagara Falls 716/357-1644) runs three trains a day from Toronto.

By Bus **Gray Coach** (tel. 416/393-7911) has three buses leaving the Bay and Dundas streets terminal every morning, and then one each hour from 10 AM to 7 PM. The trip takes about two hours and costs about $40 round-trip.

Guided Tours

Double Deck Tours are exactly that: A double-decker bus tours the Falls and environs. During the high season, the buses operate every 30 minutes from 9:30 AM, stopping at many of the major points of interest. Although the complete tour lasts 90 minutes, you may get off at any stop and grab another bus later in the day. *Tel. 905/374-7423. Cost: approximately $17 adults, $9 children 6–12. A more complete tour lasting 5 hours costs twice as much. Meet at the Maid of the Mist bldg.; no reservations required.*

The following all have air-conditioned limos: **Embassy Limousine Service** (6276 Main St., tel. 905/374-8401); **Honeymoon Tours** (4943 Clifton Hill St., tel. 905/295-3034); **Niagara Scenic Drive** (5876 Victoria Ave., tel. 905/374-7511).

Niagara Helicopters (Victoria Ave. at River Rd., tel. 905/357-5672) let you see the Falls at an unforgettable angle. Yes, major credit cards are accepted, so you won't feel the cost for weeks. *Departures Mar.–Nov., 9 AM–sunset.*

Winery Tours takes you on a 90-minute walk through the vineyards, followed by a wine tasting. The tours are free, but the bottles at the recently expanded retail wine shop are most decidedly not. *4887 Dorchester Rd., off Hwy. 420, tel. 905/357– 2400. Tours May–Oct., Mon.–Sat. 10:30 AM, 2 PM, and 3:30 PM; Nov.–Apr., 2 PM only. Sun. year-round 2 and 3:30 PM.*

Exploring

Numbers in the margin correspond to points of interest on the Niagara Falls, Ontario, map.

The city of Niagara Falls, Ontario, is quite easy to picture: To the west, running north–south (and eventually east, around Lake Ontario and up to Toronto), is Queen Elizabeth Way. To the east is the Niagara River and the glorious Falls. One of the best ways to get a sense of the layout is to go up the **Skylon Tower.** It's not cheap, but the view is breathtaking. Next to the tower is the **IMAX Theater,** with its giant screen.

Clifton Hill, right near the Falls, and northeast of the Skylon Tower, is the place where most bus and boat tours begin and where many of the better attractions are located: The Oakes Garden Theater; Louis Tussaud's Waxworks; the Rainbow Carillon Tower; the Niagara Falls Museum (which is less vulgar than most); and the Daredevil Hall of Fame. In the same area is **Maple Leaf Village,** with dozens of shops, eateries, and fun-fun-fun, sell-sell-sell. (The word "souvenir" comes from the French, meaning "remember." The big question is,

"Do I *really* want to remember my trip to Niagara Falls with this ugly beer glass that has a giant, drenched gorge etched into its side?")

To the north, past Robert Street, is where the Via Rail trains pull in. Here is where you go for the Spanish Aerocar, the helicopter tours, and the Great Gorge Adventure; for the latter attraction, you take an elevator down to the river's edge and walk along a boardwalk beside whirlpool rapids.

Just west of the Skylon and the Falls is **Lundy's Lane,** where the rows of motels and hotels look like a Monopoly board run wild. Nearby is the fine **Lundy's Lane Historical Museum.** To the south and east of the Falls is **Marineland.** Along the river is the very beautiful **Queen Victoria Park,** which also has an attractive greenhouse and even a modest-size golf course.

From early May to mid-October, you can purchase the **Explorer's Passport** (tel. 905/357–9340), a money-saving deal that includes admission to three major attractions: Table Rock Scenic Tunnels, Great Gorge Adventure, and Niagara Spanish Aerocar—plus the right to use all-day buses around the area. Cost is about $17 for adults, $9 for children 6–12; children under 6 free. Naturally, full exchange is paid on all U.S. currency.

❶ *Maid of the Mist* boats are surely an unforgettable experience; they sail right to the foot of the Falls, and you'll be thankful for the raincoats they give out and for the exciting trip itself. *Boats leave from foot of Clifton Hill St. Tel. 905/358–5781. Cost: approximately $10 adults, $6 children 6–12. Daily mid-May–late-Oct. Late June through Labor Day, trips leave as often as every 15 minutes, 9:45–7:45; off-season boats leave every 30 minutes 9:45 –5:45 on weekends, 4:45 weekdays.*

❷ At **Table Rock Scenic Tunnels,** you don a weatherproof coat and boots, and an elevator takes you down to a fish-eye view of the Canadian Horseshoe Falls and the Niagara River and a walk through three tunnels cut into the rock. *Tours begin at Table Rock House, in Queen Victoria Park. Tel. 905/354–1551. Cost: approximately $6 adults, $5 senior citizens, $3 children 6–12. Open mid-June–Labor Day 9 AM–11 PM; 9–5 rest of year. Closed Christmas.*

❸ **Skylon** overlooks the Falls and is more than just a tower; there are amusements for children, entertainment, and shops. Rising 775 feet above the Falls, it does, indeed, have the best view of both the great Niagara and the entire city. There is also an indoor/outdoor observation deck and a revolving dining room. *Tel. 905/356–2651. Cost: approximately $7 adults, $6 senior citizens, $4 children under 13. Open 8:30 AM–1 AM. Go when Falls are illuminated, especially during Winter Festival of Lights.*

❹ The **Niagara Spanish Aerocar** (the Whirlpool Aerocar) is a cable car that carries you high over the Niagara Gorge—and back, one hopes—on a 1,650-foot-long cable. Far, far below are the river and Whirlpool Basin. *Located on River Rd., about 2 mi north of falls, tel. 905/354–5711. Cost: approximately $5 adults, $3 children 6–12. Ride runs June 1–Labor Day, 9–9; and from then until mid-Oct. when weather permits.*

❺ **Marineland** is, after the Falls themselves, the highest-quality attraction in the area. The 4,000-seat aqua theater has the world's largest troupe of performing sea lions and dolphins, as well as two killer whales, Kandu and Nootka. The "Hot Air Fantasy" consists of

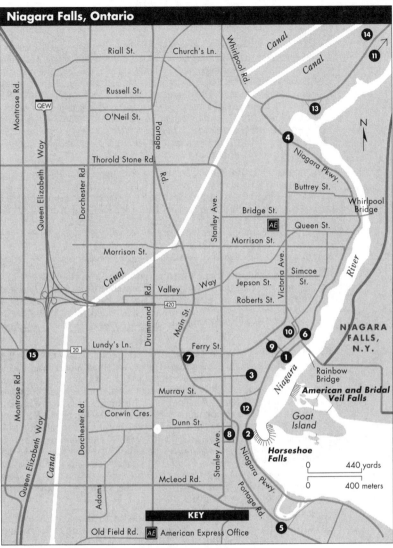

Niagara Falls, Ontario

various animated, singing characters suspended in balloons above the aquarium. The children will be ecstatic (and so will the adults).

There are rides for all ages as well, including the world's largest steel roller coaster, spread over one mile of track and traveling through 1,000 feet of tunnels, double spirals, and giant loops. The Game Farm is also a delight, with its herd of buffalo, sloth of bears, and over 400 deer to be pet and fed. *Located 1 mi south of Falls; follow Marineland signs along parkway by Falls, or exit QEW at McLeod Rd. (Exit 27) and follow signs. Tel. 905/356–9565. Admission: approximately $21 adults, $16 senior citizens and children 4–9. In winter, prices fall to less than half, because rides are closed. Open summers 9–6, off-season 10–4:30.*

6 **Niagara Falls Museum,** at the Rainbow Bridge, includes everything from shlock to quality. Here you'll find the Daredevil Hall of Fame, dinosaurs, and a solid collection of Egyptian mummies dating from before the Exodus from Egypt. There are also Indian artifacts and zoological and geological exhibits. *5651 River Rd., tel. 905/356–2151. Admission: approximately $6.50 adults, $4.50 students and senior citizens, $3.50 children 5–10. Open June–early Oct. 8:30 AM–midnight; other months, weekdays 10–5, weekends 11–5.*

7 **Lundy's Lane Historical Museum,** dating to 1874, is on the site of a savage battle in the War of 1812. There are displays of the lives of settlers of that era, as well as military artifacts. *5810 Perry St., a little over 1 mi west of Falls, on Hwy. 420, tel. 905/358–5082. Admission: about $2. Open May–Nov., 9–4; other months, weekdays noon–4.*

8 The **Minolta Tower-Centre** has its own attractions, beyond its rising some 665 feet above the gorge. There's an indoor observation deck and three more open ones overlooking the Falls, and the aquarium and reptile exhibit will ease the pains of children who might be denied a day at Marineland. There's an Incline Railway that will take you to and from the brink of the Falls, and its Top of the Rainbow dining rooms have won at least four restaurant awards during this decade. *6732 Oakes Dr., tel. 905/356–1501. Admission to exhibits or tower: approximately $6 adults, $4 senior citizens and children 5–18. Combination tickets: $7 adults, $6 senior citizens and children. Tower open summers 9 AM–midnight, other times: 10–10. Aquarium and reptile exhibit open May–Nov., and cost approximately $5 adults, $4 students and senior citizens.*

9 Children, and adults with great patience, will get a kick out of **Clifton Hill** (tel. 905/356–2299), where you can visit the Movieland Wax Museum, The Haunted House, The House of Frankenstein, The Funhouse, The Guinness Museum of World Records, Louis Tussaud's Waxworks, Ripley's Believe It or Not Museum, and the Super Star Recording Studio, where you can make a tape/video of your fabulous voice/face. This is tourism at its most touristy.

10 **Maple Leaf Village** is a 350-foot observation tower with rides, games, shops, shows, and one of the largest Ferris wheels in captivity. This is where you'll find—if you dare—the That's Incredible Museum and The Elvis Presley Museum. *Clifton Hill and Falls Ave., at Canadian terminus of Rainbow Bridge, tel. 905/374–4444. Prices vary for various rides; admission to village itself is free. Attractions are open mid-June–Labor Day 10 AM–midnight. Tower open year-round.*

11 The **Floral Clock** is less than 6 miles north of the Falls, along River Road. Nearly 20,000 plants that bloom from earliest spring to late autumn make up one of the world's biggest, bloomin' clocks. Chimes ring every quarter-hour, and it actually keeps the right time. *Admission free.*

⑫ **Queen Victoria Park** (tel. 905/356–4699) runs along the Niagara River for 24 miles. The Niagara Parks Greenhouse has four major horticultural displays each year, and there is an outdoor fragrance garden for the visually handicapped.

About 4 miles due north of the Falls, along the Niagara Parkway,
⑬ you can visit the **Niagara Glen Nature Area,** another free and most attractive attraction. You can actually work your way down to the gorge, observing the plant life. And just a bit north, along the park-
⑭ way, is the **Niagara Parks School of Horticulture,** with 100 acres of free exhibits. *Tel. 905/356–8554.*

⑮ **Whitewater** is a water park with everything from minislides and minipools to five giant slides and a wave pool. *7430 Lundy's La. at QEW, tel. 905/357–3380. Open mid-May–mid-Sept. Special rates after 6 PM.*

Dining

Reviews by Allan Gould

We hope you came here for the Miracle of Nature, not for any taste-bud magic. What Niagara Falls offers is mainly fast foods, faster foods, and fastest foods, with a handful of modest exceptions. You'll find all your old family friends—the King (of the Burger), the Baron (of Beef), Harry (of Char Broil fame), the Colonel (still frying that greasy, finger-lickin' chicken), and Mr. Ronald McDonald, whom we sense needs no introduction whatsoever. Still, there are respectable restaurants at rather moderate prices, considering what a tourist mecca this place is.

At the restaurants listed below, expect to pay $15–$25 for a three-course meal, excluding drinks, service, and sales tax.

$$ Capri Restaurant. One of the better Italian restaurants in the area, this place offers ethnic dishes as well as steak and seafood. Its most popular dish is a huge Maritime Platter, piled high with lobster, shrimp, scallops, salmon, and more, at about $60 for two. There are three rooms, and the owner has won the "Restaurateur of the Year Award" several times. *5438 Ferry St. (Hwy. 20), about ½ mi from Falls, tel. 905/354–7519. Reservations not necessary. Dress: casual. AE, DC, MC, V.*

$$ Hungarian Village Restaurant. Family-owned for a half-century, it offers classic Eastern European dishes, as well as traditional Hungarian specialties—and a "famous Gypsy trio from Budapest" entertains in the evenings. There are three rooms, one of them more elegant and formal than the others. *5329 Ferry St. (Hwy. 20), tel. 905/356–2429. Reservations recommended for weekends. Dress: casual. AE, DC, MC, V.*

$$ The Minolta Tower Dining Room. This is on the top of you know what, and the food—veal Oskar and other meaty dishes—is trustworthy. The 26th-floor dining room is in pink and burgundy; the 27th-floor dining room is a more formal white and navy blue. *6732 Oakes Dr., tel. 905/356–1501. Reservations recommended. Dress: casual. AE, DC, MC, V.*

$$ Reese's Country Inn. A real cut above the other restaurants in the area, it is a bit off the beaten track. It offers international cuisine in a country setting, complete with an open patio, fresh flowers, fireplace, and greenhouse. The most popular meal is rack of lamb. *3799 Montrose Rd. (Exit 32B from the QEW, then west about ½ mi on*

Thorold Stone Rd., and north on Montrose Rd.), tel. 905/357–5640. Reservations requested. Jacket and tie recommended. AE, MC, V. Sunday brunches and dinner; closed Mon.

$$ Rolf's Continental Dining. The French and German menu features rabbit, fillet of lamb, Dover sole, and Chateaubriand. Meals are served in three small rooms in an old house, with candlelight, fresh flowers, and sparkling china. The full-course "early dinner," served between 5 and 6 PM, costs around $15 a person. *3840 Main St., tel. 905/295–3472. Reservations recommended. Dress: casual but neat. MC, V. No lunch; closed Mon.*

$$ Table Rock Restaurant. Standard American and Canadian fare is served in the pink-and-green dining room. As they love to advertise: "If you were any closer, you'd go over the Falls." It's true. *Located just above Scenic Tunnels, tel. 905/354–3631. Reservations advised. Dress: casual. AE, MC, V.*

$$ Victoria Park Restaurant. Like the Table Rock, it is run by Niagara Parks. Located directly opposite the American Falls, and all done in yellows and earth tones, the eatery offers breakfast, lunch, and dinner on a patio overlooking the crashing waters. It is known for its fresh salmon, prime ribs, and generally good dining—but the view is the best of all. *Corner of River Rd. and Murray St., tel. 905/356–2217. Reservations not necessary. Dress: casual. AE, MC, V.*

Lodging

There are so many hotels and motels in the area that you can take your pick from almost any price range, services, or facilities. Heart-shaped bathtubs, waterbeds, heated pools, Jacuzzis, baby-sitting services—the choice is yours. Prices fall by as much as 50% between mid-September and mid-May, and less expensive packages for families, honeymooners, and others are usually available.

Category	Cost*
$$$$	over $100
$$$	$75–$100
$$	$50–$75
$	under $50

All prices are for a standard double room, excluding GST (Goods and Services Tax).

$$$$ Michael's Inn. Located by Rainbow Bridge, there's a view of the Falls from several balconies. *5599 River Rd., Niagara Falls L2E 3H3, tel. 905/354–2727. 130 rooms with bath. Facilities: wading pool, heated indoor pool, sauna, whirlpool, waterbeds, theme rooms, restaurant, baby-sitting services, golf and tennis nearby, tours. AE, DC, MC, V.*

$$$$ Old Stone Inn. Its charm comes from the renovated mill at its heart. Many suites have fireplaces. There is no charge for children under 14. *5425 Robinson St., Niagara Falls L2G 7L6 (by Skylon Tower), tel. 905/357–1234. 114 rooms with bath. Facilities: restaurant, baby-sitting services, outdoor pool, whirlpool. AE, MC, V.*

$$$ Lincoln Motor Inn. A pleasant landscaped courtyard gives this motor inn an intimate feeling. The Falls are within walking distance. Connecting family suites sleep up to a dozen. *6417 Main St., Niagara Falls L2G 5Y3, tel. 905/356–1748. 57 rooms with bath. Facilities: extra-large heated pool, 102-degree outdoor whirlpool spa, restaurant, baby-sitting services, beach, golf nearby. AE, MC, V.*

$$$ **Quality Inn Fallsway.** Located very near the Falls, the inn is on nicely landscaped grounds complete with patio. Pets are allowed. *4946 Clifton Hill, Box 60, Niagara Falls L2E 6S8, tel. 905/358–3601. 265 rooms with bath. Facilities: indoor and outdoor pool, lounge, restaurant, baby-sitting services, golf nearby, whirlpool. AE, MC, V.*

$$ **Canuck Motel.** Located a few blocks from the Falls, this motel has fancy tubs, waterbeds, and yet retains a family atmosphere. Housekeeping units are available. It was recently remodeled and enlarged. *5334 Kitchener St., Niagara Falls L2G 1B5, tel. 905/ 358–8221. 79 rooms with bath. Facilities: heated outdoor pool, baby-sitting services, golf nearby. AE, MC, V.*

$$ **Vacation Inn.** Only two blocks from the Minolta Tower, this hotel offers easy access to the bus terminal and highways. Some rooms have waterbeds. *6519 Stanley Ave., Niagara Falls L2G 7L2, tel. 905/ 356–1722. 95 rooms with bath, some family-size. Facilities: heated outdoor pool, restaurant. AE, MC, V.*

$ **Alpine Motel.** This is a disarmingly small place, set back from the road. Rooms have refrigerators, and housekeeping units are available. *7742 Lundy's La., Niagara Falls L2H 1H3, tel. 905/356–7016. 10 rooms with bath. Facilities: heated outdoor pool, patio, golf nearby. MC, V.*

B&Bs Contact the **Niagara Region Bed & Breakfast Service** (2631 Dorchester Rd., Niagara Falls L2J 2Y9, tel. 905/358–8988).

Niagara-on-the-Lake

Since 1962, Niagara-on-the-Lake has been considered the southern outpost of fine summer theater in Ontario—the Shaw Festival. But offering far more than Stratford, its older theatrical sister to the north, this city is a jewel of Canadian history, architectural marvels, remarkable beauty, and, of course, quality theater. Though the town of 14,000 is worth a visit at any time of the year, its most attractive period is from late April to mid-October, when both the Shaw Festival and the flowers are in full bloom.

Being located where the Niagara River enters Lake Ontario has both its advantages and disadvantages. Because of its ideal placement, it was settled by Loyalists to the British Crown, who found a haven here when most other Americans opted for independence. Soon after, it was made the capital of Upper Canada by John Graves Simcoe. When the provincial parliament was later moved to York—today's Toronto—it changed its name from Newark to Niagara. But that, too, was wisely changed since it was continually confused with a more spectacular town of the same name, just 12 miles to the south.

The downside of its location came in the War of 1812 when the Americans came calling, but not as tourists. They captured nearby Fort George in 1813, occupied the town itself that summer, and burned it to the ground that December. The fort is now open for touring mid-May to October. Like so many other heritage sites in Ontario, it is staffed by people in period uniform, who conduct tours and reenact 19th-century infantry and artillery drills.

Some of Niagara-on-the-Lake's best days were in the 1850s, when it was connected to Toronto by steamer and to Buffalo, New York, by train. But that era soon passed with the opening of the Welland Canal and the transfer of the county seat to St. Catharines. It remained a sleepy town until the last quarter-century, when the plays of George Bernard Shaw and his contemporaries began to be performed in the Court House. Today, Niagara-on-the-Lake is one of the best-preserved 19th-century towns on the continent, with many neoclassical and Georgian homes still standing proudly—and lived in, too.

The three theaters used by the Shaw Festival do indeed present quality performances—the 10 productions in the summer of 1994 ranged from epics to murder mysteries, musicals to comedies, even lunchtime theater—but what's also special is the abundance of orchards and flower gardens, sailboats, and the utterly charming town of Niagara-on-the-Lake.

Important Addresses and Numbers

Festival schedules, lists of hotels and restaurants, and a Historic Guide are available from The Festival (Box 774, Niagara-on-the-Lake, Ont. L0S 1J0, tel. 905/468–2153 or from Toronto 361–1544. Also contact the Chamber of Commerce, 153 King St., Box 1043, L0S 1J0, tel. 905/468–4263).

Arriving and Departing

By Car Take the QEW south and west, around the lake, to St. Catharines. At the first exit past the Garden City Skyway, drive back north 4 kilometers (2.5 miles) to Highway 55, then turn right for 11 kilometers (7 miles). It's a 90-minute drive.

By Bus Most buses require a change in St. Catharines, which can be a drag. Call **Gray Coach** in Toronto, tel. 416/393–7911.

From Niagara Falls When you recall that Niagara-on-the-Lake is but 45 minutes from Buffalo, and less than 20 minutes from Niagara Falls, you may be wise to consider hooking your trip to this sparkling town with a visit to the Falls. Contact **Blue Bird Buses** (tel. 905/356–5462).

By Limo from the Airports **Laskey's Airport Transportation Service of St. Catharines** (tel. 905/685–8404 or 800/263–3636) offers door-to-door ground transportation to and from the Toronto and Buffalo airports, and from Niagara-on-the-Lake.

Guided Tours

The **Niagara Foundation** visits local homes and gardens every spring. Phone the Chamber of Commerce (tel. 905/468–4263).

Hillebrand Estates Winery (Hwy. 55, Niagara Stone Rd., tel. 905/468–7123) offers free tours, followed by a free sampling of their award-winning products.

A much larger, more established firm is **Inniskillin Wine,** which offers tours and has numerous displays that illustrate the wine-making procedure inside a 19th-century barn. *Off Niagara River Pkwy., just south of town, tel. 905/468–3554. Tours June–Oct., daily 10:30 AM and 2:30 PM; Nov.–May, weekends only, 2:30.*

Exploring

This is a very small town that can easily be explored on foot. Queen Street is the core of the commercial portion of this thriving miniopolis. Walking east along that single street, with Lake Ontario to your north, you encounter many pleasures.

At **209 Queen Street** is the handsome Richardson-Kiely House, built around 1832 for a member of Parliament, with later additions at the turn of the century. At **187 Queen Street** is an 1822 house, with later Greek Revival improvements. **165 Queen Street** is an 1820 beauty, once lived in by a veteran of the Battle of Lundy's Lane, which took place in Niagara Falls in 1814. **157 Queen Street,** built in 1823, is still occupied by descendants of the Rogers-Harrison family, prominent since the early 19th century in church and town affairs. **McClelland's West End Store** (106 Queen St.) has been in business on this same site since the War of 1812, and with good reason: Its local jams and cheeses are top-notch. The huge "T" sign means "provisioner."

Across the street, but facing Victoria Street, is **Grace United Church,** built as recently as 1852. (It began as a congregation of "Free" Presbyterians, who later sold it to the Methodists.) Also at the corner of Queen and Victoria streets is the **Royal George Theater,** one of the three showcases of the Shaw Festival.

Still going east, you will come across the **Court House,** on the next block, which, until 1969, served as the municipal offices of the town of Niagara; it recently underwent an award-winning restoration. It is another of the three theaters of the Shaw Festival.

Across the street (5 Queen St.) is the **Niagara Apothecary,** built in 1820 and moved here in 1866. The oldest continuing pharmacy in Upper Canada, it was restored in 1971. Note the exquisite walnut fixtures, crystal pieces, and rare collection of apothecary glasses. *Admission free. Open mid-May–Labor Day, daily noon–6.*

Behind the Apothecary is the **Masonic Hall,** also known as the Old Stone Barracks. It went up in 1816, possibly from the rubble of the town after the War of 1812. It still houses the first Masonic Lodge in Upper Canada, and some experts believe that the first meeting of the first Parliament of Upper Canada took place on this site in 1792, when it was used as a church as well.

Continue along Queen Street to Davy Street, and turn right (south) for two blocks. At 43 Castlereagh Street is the **Niagara Historical Society Museum,** one of the oldest and most complete museums of its kind in Ontario, with an extensive collection relating to the often colorful history of the Niagara Peninsula from the earliest Indian times through the 19th century. *Tel. 905/468–3912. Admission: approximately $3.50 adults, $1.50 students, 75¢ children under 12. Open May–Oct., daily 10–5; Jan.–Feb., weekends only, 1–5; March, April, Nov., and Dec., daily 1–5.*

Two blocks east, and a few steps north, is the handsome **Shaw Festival Theatre.** Just beyond it, on a wide stretch of parkland, is **Fort George National Historic Park.** Built in the 1790s to replace Fort Niagara, it was lost to the Yankees during the war of 1812. It was recaptured after the burning of the town in 1813, and largely survived the war, only to fall into ruins by the 1830s. It was reconstructed a century later, and visitors can explore the officers' quarters, barracks rooms of the common soldiers, the kitchen, and more. *Tel. 905/ 468–4257. Admission: $2.50 adults, $1.50 senior citizens and children 5–16, $6 families. Open mid-May–late June, 9–5; July 1–Labor Day, 10–6; Labor Day–Nov., 10–5.*

The Shaw Festival. The festival began modestly back in the early 1960s with a single play and an unpromising premise: To perform the plays of George Bernard Shaw and his contemporaries. Fortunately, Shaw lived into his 90s, and his contemporaries included nearly everyone of note for nearly a century.

The Shaw season now runs from April into October and includes close to a dozen plays.

Box office tel. 905/468–2172 or from Toronto 416/361–1544; from the U.S. and Canada 800/267–4759 to order tickets with credit cards; fax in your order to 905/468–3804. Tickets in Festival Theatre run from about $30 to $50 (depending on if it is a weekday or weekend); in Court House and Royal George, from $20 to $50. Lunchtime Theatre, usually a minor one-act play, costs as little as $10. Half-price tickets available at Five Star Ticket Booth, near Eaton Centre in Toronto, and there are always half-price Rush Seats available on day of performance, on sale at Festival Theatre Box Office. There are performances in all 3 theaters Tues.–Sun. evenings, and matinees occasionally on Wed., Fri., Sat., and Sun.

Dining

Reviews by
Allan Gould

The food in Niagara-on-the-Lake is not at the level of the finest dining in Toronto, or even of Stratford. But meals are usually decent, and served in romantic, century-old surroundings.

Category	Cost*
$$$	over $25
$$	$15–$25

* *per person for a three-course meal, excluding drinks, service, and sales tax*

$$$ **The Luis House—Bella's Great Food.** This family-owned restaurant features seafood and prime ribs. The ambience is homey. *245 King St., tel. 905/468–4038. Reservations recommended. Dress: casual. AE, MC, V.*

$$$ **The Oban Inn.** Just after Christmas 1992, this charming 1824 inn burned to the ground. Thankfully, less than one year later, it reopened—at the cost of $21 million, plus another half-million for furniture and equipment. Once again, this is an elegant country lodging where you can lunch on the patio and enjoy a superior view of the lake. The fare is standard—steak, beef, duck, and lobster—with a solid Sunday brunch. The fresh poached salmon is popular in the summer. The fresh-cut flowers are from the inn's own gardens. *160 Front St., tel. 905/468–2165. Reservations required. Dress: casual. AE, DC, MC, V.*

$$$ **The Prince of Wales Hotel.** Continental cuisine is served in a handsome Victorian setting. Lamb, fresh Atlantic salmon, and pickerel are the summer specialties. The luncheon buffet and Sunday brunches offer good value. *6 Picton St., tel. 905/468–3246. Reservations required. Dress: casual. AE, MC, V.*

$$ **Angel Inn.** This is an English dining pub, located in the oldest operating inn in town. Specialties are steak, duck, and seafood, with an emphasis on the latter. Lots of antiques make this a handsome place to dine. *224 Regent St., tel. 905/468–3411. Reservations recommended. Dress: casual. AE, MC, V.*

$$ **Buttery Theatre Restaurant.** Meals are served on a cozy terrace. On Friday and Saturday, there's a 2½-hour feast, "Henry VIII," that will have you looking like him when you finish. *19 Queen St., tel. 905/468–2564. Reservations recommended. Dress: casual, but jacket appropriate at dinner. AE, MC, V.*

Lodging

There are few accommodations in Niagara-on-the-Lake, but the ones that are here have unusual charm.

Category	Cost*
$$$	over $140
$$	$80–$140
$	under $80

*All prices are for a standard double room, excluding GST (Goods and Services Tax).

$$$ **Pillar & Post Inn.** This hotel, six long blocks from the heart of town, was built early in the century and restored in 1970. Most rooms have wood-burning fireplaces, hand-crafted pine furniture, and patchwork quilts. Wake up to free coffee and a newspaper. *48 John St., Box 1011, Niagara-on-the-Lake LOS 1J0, tel. 905/468–2123. 91 rooms with bath. Facilities: restaurant, baby-sitting services, hair dryers in rooms, outdoor pool, sauna, whirlpool, tennis, golf nearby. AE, MC, V.*

$$$ **Prince of Wales Hotel.** First built in 1864, this charming Victorian hotel is in the heart of town and has been tastefully restored. Deluxe and superior rooms are worth the extra price. The Prince of Wales Court, adjacent to the main hotel, has many larger, newer rooms at higher prices. *6 Picton St., Niagara-on-the-Lake LOS 1J0, tel. 905/468–3246 or from Toronto 800/263–2452. 104 rooms with bath, some with fireplaces; housekeeping units available. Facilities: restaurant, lounge, coffee shop, heated indoor pool, saunas, whirlpool, health club, tennis courts, baby-sitting services, massage, golf nearby. AE, MC, V.*

$$$ **Queen's Landing.** The Inn at Niagara-on-the-Lake is a remarkable new addition to an old town that has had no new places in many a year. Somehow, the owners—affiliated with the Pillar & Post— have obtained antique furnishings, and given most rooms fireplaces, and even canopy beds (and whirlpool baths, just like Granny used to have). The views are a knockout, since it is located right across from the historic Fort Niagara, at the mouth of the Niagara River. And, unlike the other century-old country inns of this lovely town, Queen's Landing has a superb indoor swimming pool, lap pool, and a fully equipped exercise room. It's a most welcome new/old inn. *Byron St., Box 1180, LOS 1J0, tel. 905/468–2195; from Toronto direct, 847–7666. 137 rooms with bath. Facilities: restaurant, lounge, heated indoor pool, sauna, whirlpool, lap pool, weight room, golf nearby.*

$$–$$$ **The Angel Inn.** Each room has antiques and beds with canopies. Built in 1823, this English-style inn even claims to have a resident ghost. *224 Regent St., Niagara-on-the-Lake LOS 1J0, tel. 905/468–3411. 5 rooms with bath. Facilities: restaurant, English tavern, golf nearby. AE, MC, V.*

$$–$$$ **Moffat Inn.** This is a charmer, with individually appointed rooms, some with original 1835 fireplaces, outdoor patios, brass beds, and wicker furniture. Enjoy breakfast fritters on the outdoor patio. *60 Picton St., Niagara-on-the-Lake LOS 1J0, tel. 905/468–4116. 22 rooms with bath. Facilities: restaurant, baby-sitting services, golf nearby. AE, MC, V.*

$$–$$$ **The Oban Inn.** Built about 1824 for a sea captain from Oban, Scotland, it was restored in 1963 and then rebuilt entirely in 1993, after a fire. The charming inn, centrally located, has broad verandas and beautifully manicured gardens. The attractive rooms have lovely floral wallpaper and Victorian-style furniture, with gas fireplaces in four rooms that overlook a lake. Readers will enjoy the guest library. Pets are allowed. *160 Front St., Box 94, Niagara-on-the-Lake LOS 1J0, tel. 905/468–2165. 21 rooms with bath; housekeeping units*

and rooms with fireplaces available. Facilities: restaurant, pub, patio bar, baby-sitting services, golf nearby. AE, MC, V.

$ **Royal Anchorage.** On the river, this is a clean and spartan place with only 21 rooms. But what other hotel/motel in this lovely town has prices starting at less than $75 a room? *186 Ricardo St., Niagara-on-the-Lake L0S 1J0, tel. 905/468–2141. AE, MC, V.*

Bed-and-Breakfasts

Contact the **Niagara-on-the-Lake Bed & Breakfast Association** (153 King St., Box 1043, L0S 1J0, tel. 905/468–4263). The more than 60 lovely homes range in price from $60 per night up to double that.

And bear in mind: If you call the Shaw Festival (*see* Exploring, *above*) and ask for their exquisite guidebook, you'll find over a half-dozen pages filled with bed-and-breakfasts, each described in charming detail. For those of you who are on a strict budget, but are determined to see and experience *both* the delightful town of Niagara-on-the-Lake and the noisy, vulgar Niagara Falls, remember that they are less than 20 minutes drive from each other. Consider staying in the Falls area at a low-priced motel, and then drive up to Niagara-on-the-Lake for an overdose of loveliness and quality theater.

Index